Daily Reading Comprehension

GRADE 7

Editorial Development: Renee Biermann
Bonnie Brook
Communications
James Spears
Kathleen Wendell
Copy Editing: Lauric Westrich
Art Direction: Cheryl Puckett
Cover Design: Cheryl Puckett
Illustration: Greg Harris
Design/Production: Carolina Caird
Yuki Meyer

EMC 3457

Evan-Moor®
EDUCATIONAL PUBLISHERS
Helping Children Learn since 1979

Visit
teaching-standards.com
to view a correlation
of this book.
This is a free service.

*Correlated to State and
Common Core State Standards*

**Congratulations on your purchase of some of the
finest teaching materials in the world.**

*Photocopying the pages in this book
is permitted for <u>single-classroom use only</u>.
Making photocopies for additional classes
or schools is prohibited.*

For information about other Evan-Moor products, call 1-800-777-4362,
fax 1-800-777-4332, or visit our Web site, www.evan-moor.com.
Entire contents © 2013 EVAN-MOOR CORP.
18 Lower Ragsdale Drive, Monterey, CA 93940-5746. Printed in USA.

CPSIA: Printed by McNaughton & Gunn, Saline, MI USA. [10/2012]

Contents

Daily Reading Comprehension • EMC 3457 • © Evan-Moor Corp.

How to Use *Daily Reading Comprehension*

Daily Reading Comprehension provides a unique integration of instruction and practice in both comprehension strategies and comprehension skills.

Strategies—such as visualizing or asking questions—are general, metacognitive techniques that a reader uses to better understand and engage with the text. **Skills**—such as finding a main idea or identifying a sequence of events—focus on particular text elements that aid comprehension. See page 6 for a complete list of strategies and skills covered in *Daily Reading Comprehension.*

The first six weeks of *Daily Reading Comprehension* introduce students to comprehension strategies they will apply throughout the year. Weeks 7–30 focus on specific skill instruction and practice. All 30 weeks follow the same five-day format, making the teaching and learning process simpler. Follow these steps to conduct the weekly lessons and activities:

STEP 1   The weekly teacher page states the strategy or skills that students will focus on during that week and provides a brief definition of the strategy or the skills. Read the definition(s) aloud to students each day before they complete the activities, or prompt students to define the skills themselves. You may also wish to reproduce the comprehension skill definitions on page 8 as a poster for your classroom.

STEP 2   The teacher page provides an instructional path for conducting each day's lesson and activities. Use the tips and suggestions in each day's lesson to present the strategy and skills and to introduce the passage.

STEP 3   Each student page begins with directions for reading the passage. These directions also serve as a way to establish a purpose for reading. Help students see the connection between setting a purpose for reading and improving comprehension.

STEP 4   Because much of reading comprehension stems from a reader's background knowledge about a subject, take a moment to discuss the topic with students before they read the passage. Introduce unfamiliar phrases or concepts, and encourage students to ask questions about the topic.

STEP 5   After students have read a passage, two comprehension activities give them an opportunity to practice the strategies and skills. In weeks 1–6, the first activity is an open-ended writing or partner activity that encourages students to reflect on the reading process, applying the weekly strategy. The second activity provides four multiple-choice items that help students practice the week's skills in a test-taking format.

         In weeks 7–30, students complete the multiple-choice skill activity before completing the strategy activity. The teacher page for these weeks offers suggestions for teaching the skills and gives tips for reminding students of the strategies. Throughout the week, use the student record sheet on page 9 to track student progress and to note which skills or strategies a student may need additional practice with. Weekly skills are explained at the top of each teacher page.

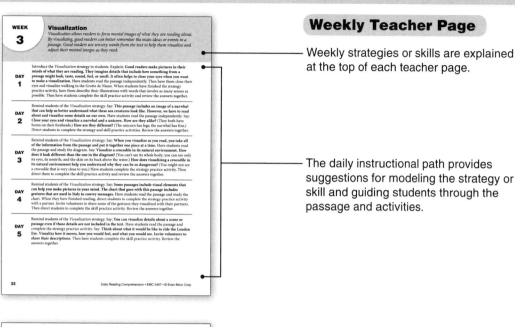

Weekly Teacher Page

Weekly strategies or skills are explained at the top of each teacher page.

The daily instructional path provides suggestions for modeling the strategy or skill and guiding students through the passage and activities.

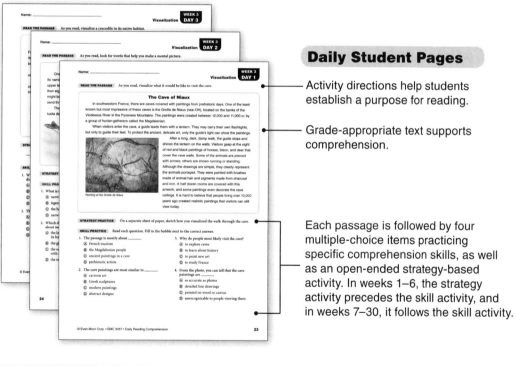

Daily Student Pages

Activity directions help students establish a purpose for reading.

Grade-appropriate text supports comprehension.

Each passage is followed by four multiple-choice items practicing specific comprehension skills, as well as an open-ended strategy-based activity. In weeks 1–6, the strategy activity precedes the skill activity, and in weeks 7–30, it follows the skill activity.

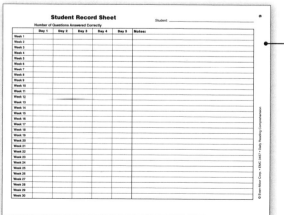

Student Record Sheet

The record sheet allows you to record students' progress and identify areas in which individuals need improvement.

Comprehension Strategies and Skills

In *Daily Reading Comprehension,* students learn and practice the following commonly tested comprehension strategies and skills, all proven to increase students' ability to read and understand a wide range of text types. You may also wish to post or distribute copies of page 8, which provides a student-friendly list of skills and helpful questions that students can ask themselves as they read.

Strategies

Monitor Comprehension
Students learn to pay attention to their own reading process and notice when they are losing focus or when comprehension is breaking down. They can then employ another strategy to help them overcome their difficulty.

Make Connections
Students make connections to the text to aid their comprehension. Connections can be made to personal experiences or to things the students have seen or read.

Visualization
Students make mental images of what they are reading. They learn to look for vivid language, including concrete nouns, active verbs, and strong adjectives.

Organization
Students learn to find the organizational pattern of a text. This allows them to anticipate what they are reading and helps them focus on the author's central message or important ideas.

Determine Important Information
Students learn to categorize information based on whether or not it supports an author's central message or is important for a specific purpose.

Ask Questions
Students learn to ask questions before reading to set a purpose for reading, during reading to identify when their comprehension breaks down, and after reading as a way to check their understanding of a passage.

Skills

Main Idea and Details
Students identify what a passage is mostly about and find important details that support the main idea.

Sequence
Students look for the order in which things happen or identify the steps in a process.

(Skills, continued)

Cause and Effect
Students identify what happens (effect) and why it happens (cause).

Evaluate Evidence
Students study an author's claims and the evidence that the author gives to support those claims.

Compare and Contrast
Students note how two or more people or things are alike and different.

Make Inferences
Students use their background knowledge and clues from the text to infer information.

Prediction
Students use their background knowledge and clues from the text to figure out what will happen next.

Character and Setting
Students identify who or what a story is about and where and when the story takes place.

Theme
Students look for the moral or lesson in a fiction story or an author's view about the world in nonfiction.

Author's Purpose
Students determine why an author wrote a passage and whether the purpose is to entertain, to inform, to persuade, or to teach.

Nonfiction Text Features
Students study features that are not part of the main body of text, including subheadings, captions, entry words, and titles.

Visual Information
Students study pictures, charts, graphs, and other forms of visual information.

     Daily Reading Comprehension • EMC 3457 • © Evan-Moor Corp.

Scope and Sequence

Scope and Sequence chart showing skill coverage across 30 weeks.

Comprehension Strategies

Week 30	Week 29	Week 28	Week 27	Week 26	Week 25	Week 24	Week 23	Week 22	Week 21	Week 20	Week 19	Week 18	Week 17	Week 16	Week 15	Week 14	Week 13	Week 12	Week 11	Week 10	Week 9	Week 8	Week 7	Week 6	Week 5	Week 4	Week 3	Week 2	Week 1	Skill
		•			•			•			•			•	•		•			•			•						•	Monitor Comprehension
	•		•		•				•				•		•				•		•							•		Make Connections
		•			•			•			•			•			•			•			•				•			Visualization
•			•			•			•			•						•			•					•				Organization
•				•		•				•		•				•		•				•			•					Determine Important Information
	•			•			•			•				•		•			•			•		•						Ask Questions

Comprehension Skills

Week 30	Week 29	Week 28	Week 27	Week 26	Week 25	Week 24	Week 23	Week 22	Week 21	Week 20	Week 19	Week 18	Week 17	Week 16	Week 15	Week 14	Week 13	Week 12	Week 11	Week 10	Week 9	Week 8	Week 7	Week 6	Week 5	Week 4	Week 3	Week 2	Week 1	Skill
					•						•						•				•						•		•	Main Idea and Details
					•						•						•					•			•					Sequence
	•						•						•						•						•				•	Cause and Effect
				•						•						•						•			•	•				Evaluate Evidence
			•						•						•						•			•	•					Compare and Contrast
			•						•						•						•							•		Make Inferences
	•						•						•						•										•	Prediction
		•						•						•						•								•		Character and Setting
		•						•						•						•				•				•		Theme
				•						•						•						•		•						Author's Purpose
•						•						•						•							•		•			Nonfiction Text Features
•						•						•						•									•			Visual Information

How to Be a Good Reader

Ask yourself these questions to help you understand what you read:

Main Idea and Details

What is the story mostly about?
What tells me more about the main idea?

Sequence

What happens first, next, and last?
What are the steps to do something?

Cause and Effect

What happens? (the effect)
Why did it happen? (the cause)

Evaluate Evidence

What claims is the author making?
What evidence supports these claims?

Compare and Contrast

How are these people or things the same?
How are these people or things different?

Make Inferences

What clues does the story give?
What do I know already that will help?

Prediction

What clues does the story give?
What do I know already that will help?
What will happen next?

Character and Setting

Who or what is the story about?
Where and when does the story take place?

Theme

What lesson does this story teach?
How does the author feel about this topic?

Author's Purpose

Does the story entertain, inform, or try to persuade me, or does it teach me how to do something?

Nonfiction Text Features

What kind of text am I reading?
What does it tell me?

Visual Information

Is there a picture, chart, or graph?
What does it tell me?

Student Record Sheet

Student: _____

Number of Questions Answered Correctly

	Day 1	Day 2	Day 3	Day 4	Day 5	Notes:
Week 1						
Week 2						
Week 3						
Week 4						
Week 5						
Week 6						
Week 7						
Week 8						
Week 9						
Week 10						
Week 11						
Week 12						
Week 13						
Week 14						
Week 15						
Week 16						
Week 17						
Week 18						
Week 19						
Week 20						
Week 21						
Week 22						
Week 23						
Week 24						
Week 25						
Week 26						
Week 27						
Week 28						
Week 29						
Week 30						

Monitor Comprehension

When students monitor their comprehension, they keep track of how well they understand the material and identify when their understanding breaks down. Related activities include asking questions, taking notes, and paraphrasing what has been read.

DAY 1

Introduce the *Monitor Comprehension* strategy to students, and explain: **Good readers pay attention as they read to ensure understanding. If readers are confused, they can reread, ask questions, make notes, or try to put the information into their own words.** Have students read the passage independently. Model the strategy: **As I was reading, I didn't understand why Tom Sanders decided to jump out of airplanes. I went back and reread his quote about enjoying "the most out of this life." This helped me understand that Sanders finds enjoyment in activities after conquering his fear.** Direct students to complete the strategy practice activity. Then direct students to complete the skill practice activity and review the answers as a group.

DAY 2

Remind students of the *Monitor Comprehension* strategy, and point out the direction line at the top of the page. Explain: **Good readers look for clues that give information about how characters are feeling, about the setting, or about the mood or tone of the story. Which words from the first line of the passage give you clues about Kim?** (shrank, horrified) Have students read the rest of the passage. When they have finished, ask them to circle clue words within the passage that give details about Kim's new house. After students complete the strategy practice activity, have them share their responses. Then direct students to complete the skill practice activity. Review the answers together.

DAY 3

Remind students of the *Monitor Comprehension* strategy. Model using the strategy: **Part of monitoring my comprehension is making sure I understand the information that is being presented. This passage is about lichens. After I read the passage, I can look up images of lichens on the Internet to better understand what I have read.** Tell students they can also use a dictionary, encyclopedia, or thesaurus to aid comprehension. When students have finished reading, direct them to complete the strategy practice activity. Provide access to research tools if needed. Then direct students to complete the skill practice activity and review the answers together.

DAY 4

Remind students of the *Monitor Comprehension* strategy. Read aloud the directions at the top of the page. Remind students to pause briefly when they see a footnote indicator. Explain: **When I see a number, I will pause and read the information that goes with that number at the bottom of the passage. Then I will return to where I left off and keep reading.** After students have finished reading the passage, have them complete the strategy practice activity and share their responses. Then direct students to complete the skill practice activity. Review the answers together.

DAY 5

Remind students of the *Monitor Comprehension* strategy. Then point out the chart, and say: **Sometimes a passage will have a nonfiction text feature, such as a chart, that accompanies it. It's important that we understand both the main passage and the chart.** Have students read the passage and chart independently. When they have finished, direct them to complete the strategy and skill practice activities. Review the answers together.

READ THE PASSAGE   Read slowly. Reread any section you do not understand.

Camera in the Sky

Professional photographers often have to take calculated risks to get the perfect shot. But few photographers are willing to "take the plunge" like Tom Sanders. His enthusiasm and daring have made him one of the world's most legendary skydiving photographers.

From Fearful to Fearless

If you watched Sanders leaping out of a plane today, weighed down with heavy camera equipment, you would never guess that he was once terrified of heights. But that fear is what launched his remarkable career. "I was doing a course in building self-confidence," says Sanders, "and one of the assignments had to involve something you were scared of doing. I was petrified of heights, so my assignment was to jump out of a plane." After about 50 jumps, Sanders did more than conquer his fear; he began to enjoy the thrill of parachuting. Today, Sanders never lets fear prevent him from trying something new. He says he wakes up every morning and asks himself, "How am I going to enjoy the most out of this life?"

Falling Feats

These days, Sanders is comfortable enough to shoot astonishing photographs while dropping thousands of feet in freefall. For one advertisement, he snapped photos of stunt riders driving motorcycles out of an airplane door. For another ad campaign, he photographed a sofa as it plummeted to the ground. He has also recorded enormous group dives in which hundreds of skydivers join hands to create beautiful flower-like formations.

STRATEGY PRACTICE   Was there any part of the passage that you found confusing? How did you figure it out?

_____

_____

SKILL PRACTICE   Read each question. Fill in the bubble next to the correct answer.

1. What is the main idea of the section "From Fearful to Fearless"?
   Ⓐ Professional photographers are fearless.
   Ⓑ Skydiving is extremely dangerous.
   Ⓒ Photographic equipment is very heavy.
   Ⓓ Skydiving helped a man overcome his fear.

2. According to the passage, Sanders will most likely _____.
   Ⓐ keep taking risks to get great photos
   Ⓑ become afraid of heights again in the future
   Ⓒ fly in an airplane to another state
   Ⓓ try to start a new career

3. Sanders first jumped out of an airplane to _____.
   Ⓐ photograph a falling sofa
   Ⓑ show his enthusiasm
   Ⓒ create a flower-like formation
   Ⓓ build his self-confidence

4. What do the headings tell?
   Ⓐ important information about skydiving
   Ⓑ how Sanders became a photographer
   Ⓒ the topic of each section
   Ⓓ the advertising campaigns Sanders photographed

READ THE PASSAGE As you read, look for clues that help you understand what is happening in the story.

The New House

When Kim's mother pulled into the driveway of the spookiest house on the block, Kim shrank in her seat, horrified.

"Mom!" she hissed. "This can't be our new house."

The house was tall and narrow and looked like the creepiest, crawliest, most haunted house in the world. Kim could not imagine anyone wanting to live in this house. She wondered what kind of people lived here before—and why they left. But then again, maybe she didn't want to know the reason.

"The outside needs some work," Mom admitted. "But wait until you see your room."

"Does that mean it has the most spiders, or the fewest?" Kim asked. Still, she had to admit that she was a little curious about her new room. She hopped out of the car and walked quickly to the front door. It was a deep red, and the door handle was made from black wrought iron in the shape of a twisted tree. When Kim touched the handle to open the door, a bright blue spark of electricity zapped her hand.

"Ouch!" Kim shrieked. She kicked the door open the rest of way, and her jaw dropped open. She was looking at the ocean! Instead of a dusty old living room, there was a wide window with a view of an endless stretch of beach, the shimmering blue ocean, and the sun shining brightly. It was beautiful, and Kim felt the thrill of a new adventure.

"Nice, isn't it?" Mom asked, moving past Kim with a box of dishes. "Your swimsuit is in the white suitcase. I'll call you when it's time for dinner."

STRATEGY PRACTICE   List one part of the passage that you did not understand right away. What did you do to better understand that part?

_____

_____

SKILL PRACTICE   Read each question. Fill in the bubble next to the correct answer.

1. Kim was afraid of the new house because it _____.

 Ⓐ had a bedroom for her

 Ⓑ was full of spiders

 Ⓒ looked like it was haunted

 Ⓓ was smaller than their last house

2. Which of these will Kim most likely do next?

 Ⓐ go back to her old home

 Ⓑ unpack the box of dishes

 Ⓒ get ready for dinner

 Ⓓ go swimming in the ocean

3. What caused Kim to change her mind about the new house?

 Ⓐ She liked her new bedroom.

 Ⓑ She found out it was near the beach.

 Ⓒ She got a shock from the doorknob.

 Ⓓ She realized there were no spiders inside.

4. Which of these will Kim probably do in the future?

 Ⓐ discover more surprising things about the house

 Ⓑ become friends with the previous owners

 Ⓒ decide the house is too creepy

 Ⓓ argue with her mom about her room

READ THE PASSAGE   Underline or make notes about words or concepts you do not understand.

The Truth About Lichens

Many lichens look like patches of moldy lettuce stuck to rocks and trees. They can be green, gray, yellow, or even black. They can live in deserts, in tundras, on tops of mountains, and along rocky coastlines. But perhaps the most amazing thing about a lichen is that it is not a single organism but two!

A Lichen Liker

During the 1800s, a Swiss scientist named Dr. Simon Schwendener was interested in how the shapes of plant parts helped the plant thrive. He studied plants in Germany and Switzerland. In 1867, Dr. Schwendener published his idea that lichens were not single organisms but two organisms—fungi and algae—living together. At the time, scientists thought Dr. Schwendener was wrong. They believed it was impossible for two organisms to work together as one unit.

A Dependent Partnership

Dr. Schwendener was right—a lichen is not just one living thing. Every lichen is made up of a fungus that lives with another organism, usually an alga. The alga uses photosynthesis to make food. The fungus retains water for the alga to use. Sometimes the fungus brings in nutrients from the environment where the lichen is growing. This kind of relationship is called "mutualistic symbiosis," which means that the organisms benefit from living together. These organisms have grown so dependent on each other that they cannot survive on their own.

STRATEGY PRACTICE   List one or two words or concepts you found confusing, and explain what you did to figure out the meaning.

_____

_____

SKILL PRACTICE   Read each question. Fill in the bubble next to the correct answer.

1. Dr. Simon Schwendener claimed that lichens _____.

   Ⓐ include more than one living thing

   Ⓑ do not need water to grow

   Ⓒ can survive in deserts

   Ⓓ have interesting plant parts

2. The main idea of the passage is that lichens _____.

   Ⓐ did not exist before 1867

   Ⓑ were discovered by Dr. Schwendener

   Ⓒ are made up of organisms that work together

   Ⓓ depend on photosynthesis and water

3. What led to Dr. Schwendener's discovery?

   Ⓐ the publication of his ideas

   Ⓑ his study of the shapes of plant parts

   Ⓒ the wide range of places lichens live

   Ⓓ what other scientists believed about lichens

4. Algae in lichens help them survive by _____.

   Ⓐ retaining water

   Ⓑ giving them unique shapes

   Ⓒ using photosynthesis to make food

   Ⓓ gathering nutrients from the environment

READ THE PASSAGE   Read slowly. When you see a sentence with a footnote, pause to read the footnote. Then read the sentence again before you continue.

Web Crawlers

If everyone stopped using the Internet for one day, the Internet would still be a pretty busy place. Even when people are not online, automatic programs travel the Internet.

Programs known as web crawlers[1] constantly browse the Internet. They follow coded instructions to gather specific data. These programs scurry invisibly, collecting and sending information 24 hours a day.

What sort of data do web crawlers collect? They report information about how many people are using the Internet and which pages they are visiting. They also make copies of web pages, which are stored and indexed by search engines. The result is faster and more accurate web searches.

Some web crawlers serve a more menacing function. They harvest e-mail addresses for advertisers who send unsolicited e-mail messages known as spam.[2] When your mailbox fills up with spam, chances are good that a web crawler helped put it there.

[1] Web crawlers are sometimes called "spiders" because they "crawl" around the Web.

[2] According to one report, about 183 billion spam messages are sent in a single day, accounting for 88% of all e-mail messages sent.

STRATEGY PRACTICE   How did the footnotes help you understand the passage?

_____

_____

SKILL PRACTICE   Read each question. Fill in the bubble next to the correct answer.

1. The main idea of the passage is that web crawlers automatically _____.
   A collect data by browsing the Internet
   B fill up mailboxes
   C work around the clock
   D copy webpages and store them

2. How do web crawlers benefit Internet users?
   A They count the number of users.
   B They speed up web searches.
   C They are at work all the time.
   D They make webpages more accurate.

3. How can web crawlers contribute to spam?
   A They write unwanted messages.
   B They collect e-mail addresses.
   C They delete genuine e-mail messages.
   D They help advertisers improve websites.

4. According to the passage, it is most likely that web crawlers will _____.
   A damage the Internet one day
   B stop contributing to spam soon
   C replace e-mail in the future
   D continue to be used for many years

READ THE PASSAGE   Read the passage and the chart. Pay attention to how the information in the chart supports the passage.

Let the Buyer Beware

Advertisers have many ways of making products desirable to people. But not all of these techniques are good for customers. When you see an ad for something that seems too good to be true, it just might be. Use the information in this chart to help you understand, and avoid, some of the worst tricks of advertisers.

Technique	How It Works	Example
Bait-and-Switch	A store advertises an item for a very low price. At the store, salespeople persuade customers to buy more expensive products.	When you get to a store, the employees tell you that the advertised TV is out of stock. They offer to sell you a more expensive model instead.
Fine Print Exemptions	Advertisers list low prices but include restrictions in very small print in the ad.	A camera price is very low, but the fine print explains that the price does not include a lens or a case.
Inflated Price Comparisons	A store compares its own sale prices to its "regular" prices that are never actually charged.	A portable music player is advertised as 25% off when the product usually sells for the sale price listed.
Hidden Fees	Ads do not mention fees that must be paid in order to make a product or service usable.	A cellphone ad does not mention the activation fee that must be paid in order to use the phone.

STRATEGY PRACTICE   How did the chart help you understand the author's main point?

_____

_____

SKILL PRACTICE   Read each question. Fill in the bubble next to the correct answer.

1. The advertised price for a bicycle does not include wheels or a seat. Which technique was used?
   Ⓐ bait-and-switch
   Ⓑ fine print exemption
   Ⓒ inflated price comparison
   Ⓓ hidden fee

2. Advertisers most likely use inflated price comparisons to _____.
   Ⓐ make their prices seem like a good value
   Ⓑ make their products seem expensive
   Ⓒ convince customers to buy a different product
   Ⓓ give customers an additional discount

3. The bait-and-switch technique works for some stores because some customers _____.
   Ⓐ do not keep track of prices
   Ⓑ do not mind paying extra fees
   Ⓒ travel to the store to buy something and do not want to waste the trip
   Ⓓ forget to read the fine print before they go to the store

4. What is the main idea of the chart?
   Ⓐ to help advertisers deceive customers
   Ⓑ to describe tricks advertisers use
   Ⓒ to teach people about sale pricing
   Ⓓ to help customers find good deals

Make Connections

This strategy helps students put what they are reading into context by helping them see the connections between the text and themselves, the world around them, and other things they have read or seen.

DAY 1

Introduce the *Make Connections* strategy to students, and explain: **Good readers think about what they are reading and make connections to their own lives, to their communities, to other texts, or to greater issues in the world. To make a connection, ask yourself as you read:** *What does this remind me of?* After students read the passage, read aloud the strategy practice activity directions. Have students share their answers and compare how the leaders they chose are alike and different. Then direct students to complete the skill practice activity. Review the answers together.

DAY 2

Remind students of the *Make Connections* strategy. Say: **When you make a text-to-text connection, you connect what you are reading to other things you have read or seen before.** Have students read the passage independently. Then direct them to complete the strategy practice activity. Ask volunteers to share their responses and discuss the scary stories they have heard before. Then direct students to complete the skill practice activity. Review the answers together.

DAY 3

Remind students of the *Make Connections* strategy. Explain: **You can make text-to-world connections by thinking about how events in a passage might be different if they happened in a different time.** Have students read the passage and direct them to complete the strategy practice activity. Invite volunteers to share how they feel the Great Chicago Fire investigation would be conducted differently today. Then direct students to complete the skill practice activity. Review the answers together.

DAY 4

Remind students of the *Make Connections* strategy. Ask students to list words that describe how they have felt in new situations or around new people. (scared, intimidated, worried, excited) Have students read the passage independently. Ask students to share how they might feel if they were one of the Fugees. Say: **Which part of their experience would be the most difficult for you?** Then have students complete the strategy and skill practice activities. Review the answers together.

DAY 5

Remind students of the *Make Connections* strategy. Ask students to list activities they are involved with, such as band, sports, or choir. Have students share how they feel before performances, games, or special events. Say: **You can make a connection to a character in a story when you think about how he or she feels about what is happening. Compare how the character feels to how you have felt in the past.** Then have students read the passage and compare their own experiences to Marco's. Direct students to complete the strategy and skill practice activities. Review the answers together.

Daily Reading Comprehension • EMC 3457 • © Evan-Moor Corp.

READ THE PASSAGE   As you read, think about other leaders you know about and compare them to Henry VIII.

A Musical King

Henry VIII is best known for being one of England's most powerful kings, for founding the Church of England, and for having had many wives. However, there is another side to this Renaissance king. Like many educated men of his day, Henry VIII had a full education in the fine arts.

Henry VIII learned to write poetry and to dance. He learned to play many instruments, and he played them well. Henry VIII also learned to compose music. He wrote two different musical compositions for Catholic Church ceremonies called "Masses." Though his Masses have not survived the centuries, some of his popular songs have.

For a long time, many people believed that Henry VIII wrote the famous English song "Greensleeves," but there is little evidence to support this claim. On the other hand, Henry VIII apparently did write another song that became popular early in his reign called "Pastime with Good Company." In this song, the lyrics, or words, celebrate the joys of hunting, dancing, and spending time with "good company." In fact, these pastimes, or hobbies, are said to prevent idleness, which some people believe leads to bad actions. This song that became popular throughout Europe during Henry VIII's time is still performed today.

STRATEGY PRACTICE   Describe a leader you know or are familiar with who reminds you of Henry VIII.

_____

_____

SKILL PRACTICE   Read each question. Fill in the bubble next to the correct answer.

1. Because "Pastime with Good Company" is still performed today, you can conclude that _____.
   Ⓐ some people still enjoy the song
   Ⓑ most songs in England were written by kings
   Ⓒ it is a better song than "Greensleeves"
   Ⓓ songs from the past are better than songs today

2. According to the passage, which best describes Henry VIII?
   Ⓐ a talented king with a stern personality
   Ⓑ a powerful ruler with limited skills
   Ⓒ an important king with some creative talents
   Ⓓ a good artist but a bad ruler

3. One theme of "Pastime with Good Company" is that _____.
   Ⓐ dancing is a waste of time
   Ⓑ hunting is the best way to spend time
   Ⓒ keeping busy can keep people out of trouble
   Ⓓ writing music is very important

4. How is Henry VIII best known?
   Ⓐ as a dancer
   Ⓑ as a hunter
   Ⓒ as a songwriter
   Ⓓ as a king

READ THE PASSAGE As you read, think about scary stories you know.

The Frightening Neighborhood House

When Mrs. Delgado asked her daughter Sonia to bring blueberry muffins to a sick neighbor, Sonia said sure. But when Sonia found out who the neighbor was, she was *not* so sure. The neighbor's name was Mrs. Craverham, and kids in the neighborhood said she was the meanest person who ever lived.

Sonia walked up the path to Mrs. Craverham's. She did not like the idea of anyone being sick and alone, but what if the kids were right? A girl in Sonia's science class swore that Mrs. Craverham had poked her with a stick last Halloween. Sometimes there were screams and moans heard coming from inside. And a boy in Sonia's math class said Mrs. Craverham had hung him upside down and painted him yellow when he accidentally kicked a soccer ball onto her lawn. Torn between wanting to help someone in need and not wanting to come home a different color, Sonia decided to be brave.

Finally Sonia knocked on the door. After a few moments, Mrs. Craverham answered the door and asked in a harsh tone, "Who are you? What are you doing here?"

Sonia said timidly, "My mother heard you were ill. She baked you muffins."

Mrs. Craverham relaxed. "My, that's sweet. I'm sorry if I seemed rude, but young people sometimes dare each other to come to my door because they think I'm going to do something to them. As soon as I answer the door, they run off laughing or play a prank on me."

Suddenly, Sonia heard a loud howl. Mrs. Craverham laughed as Sonia jumped. "Oh, that's just Norbert, my parrot. He's watched too many scary movies—like you, I think!"

STRATEGY PRACTICE How is this passage different from other scary stories you have read?

_____

_____

SKILL PRACTICE Read each question. Fill in the bubble next to the correct answer.

1. **Which words best describe Sonia?**
   - Ⓐ bold and silly
   - Ⓑ selfish and cunning
   - Ⓒ kind but scared
   - Ⓓ funny but mean

2. **What is the setting of most of the passage?**
   - Ⓐ science class
   - Ⓑ Sonia's house
   - Ⓒ math class
   - Ⓓ Mrs. Craverham's house

3. **According to the passage, what do you think Mrs. Craverham will do next?**
   - Ⓐ become friends with Sonia
   - Ⓑ paint Sonia yellow
   - Ⓒ ask Sonia to go away
   - Ⓓ scare Sonia's friends

4. **What is the theme of this passage?**
   - Ⓐ Frightening things live in frightening places.
   - Ⓑ People are not always as they seem.
   - Ⓒ What you do to others comes back to you.
   - Ⓓ It is important to keep up appearances.

READ THE PASSAGE Think about how people from today and long ago investigate fires or crimes.

Mrs. O'Leary and Her Cow

The Great Chicago Fire took place in 1871. In a little over a day, approximately 300 people died, and around 90,000 buildings were destroyed before the fire was put out. Although this all took place over a century ago, the story of how the fire started lives on. According to articles written at that time, people claimed that Mrs. Catherine O'Leary saw one of her cows knock over a lamp in her barn on the night the fire began. The blaze started there and went on to consume much of Chicago, though not, interestingly, the cottage where Mrs. O'Leary lived.

Is there any truth to the story? Experts today say that the fire did indeed start close to where Mrs. O'Leary (and her cows) lived. But Mrs. O'Leary always stated that she went to bed early that night and never saw her cow kick over a lantern. Also, the O'Learys rented out the front of their home to people who were entertaining friends that night. Perhaps the renters or guests accidentally started the fire and let the cow take the blame.

Some 40 years later, a reporter for a Chicago newspaper bragged that he and two friends had made up the story about the cow for their own amusement. Other people have also claimed to be the original source of the story. The truth behind the beginning of the Great Chicago Fire may never be known, but Mrs. O'Leary's cow is hard to forget.

STRATEGY PRACTICE How might officials investigate the Great Chicago Fire if it happened today?

_____

_____

SKILL PRACTICE Read each question. Fill in the bubble next to the correct answer.

1. **Based on the passage, which inference can be made about fires?**
   Ⓐ Barn fires are worse than house fires.
   Ⓑ Fires happen often in Chicago.
   Ⓒ Fighting fires was harder in 1871 than now.
   Ⓓ Cattle are responsible for most fires.

2. **Because more than one person took credit for starting the cow story, you can conclude that _____.**
   Ⓐ the story was very famous and popular
   Ⓑ people were ashamed of the story
   Ⓒ Mrs. O'Leary was the real source of the story
   Ⓓ everyone could tell that the story was false

3. **Which theme does the passage communicate?**
   Ⓐ Historical detectives can always uncover the truth.
   Ⓑ Journalists do not write true stories.
   Ⓒ Newspaper stories about fires are important.
   Ⓓ It can be difficult to separate fact from fiction.

4. **If Mrs. O'Leary was indeed in bed at the time of the fire, which words best describe her character?**
   Ⓐ dishonest and sneaky
   Ⓑ honest but unlucky
   Ⓒ cheerful but unreliable
   Ⓓ well-rested and happy

As you read, think about how you feel in new places or around new people.

The Fugees

For the past two decades, thousands of refugees from war-torn countries such as Iraq, Liberia, the Congo, and Afghanistan have made their new home in Clarkston, Georgia. Life for these refugees has not been easy. Many of the young people do not speak English, which makes communication difficult. Some also struggle with education. Their native communities were in hostile disorder, which caused education to be a low priority. These refugees often face academic hurdles, along with teasing from other students about the way they look and speak.

A few years ago, Luma Mufleh, a young Jordanian woman who lived in nearby Atlanta, drove through Clarkston. She saw young people playing soccer barefoot. She decided to form a soccer program to help players like these, who call themselves the "Fugees" (short for "refugees").

Players in the soccer program must agree to Coach Mufleh's strict rules on and off the field, and they must spend some of their time getting tutored by volunteers. To help those learning English, all team members must speak English during practice. The players, many of whom have witnessed the violence of war, also have to figure out how to get along and play well with teammates from other countries.

Coach Mufleh demands a lot from the players, but she has given them a lot in return. Since she started the Fugees program several years ago, she has led teams to win championships; more importantly, her players have gone on to succeed in school and in the workplace. They have found a new family in their teammates and coaches.

STRATEGY PRACTICE   Describe a personal experience with a new situation, similar to something the Fugees experience.

_____

_____

SKILL PRACTICE   Read each question. Fill in the bubble next to the correct answer.

1. **What is the theme of the passage?**
   - Ⓐ Refugees have many problems.
   - Ⓑ Sports programs can help people succeed.
   - Ⓒ Clarkston, Georgia, is a tough city.
   - Ⓓ Cultural differences are impossible to overcome.

2. **Luma Mufleh can best be described as _____.**
   - Ⓐ driven but unfocused
   - Ⓑ passive and gentle
   - Ⓒ tough and aggressive
   - Ⓓ strict but supportive

3. **What does Coach Mufleh's tutoring program tell you about her?**
   - Ⓐ She wants to win at all costs.
   - Ⓑ She likes to be in control.
   - Ⓒ She cares about education.
   - Ⓓ She is most concerned about soccer.

4. **What lesson can you learn from the passage?**
   - Ⓐ Winning championships is more important than school.
   - Ⓑ Working by yourself will help you succeed.
   - Ⓒ One person can make a difference in the world.
   - Ⓓ Hard work and discipline take too much time.

READ THE PASSAGE   Think about a time when you had to do something important.

The Recital

Marco had played piano since he was seven years old. Now, at 13, he was performing in his first recital. Oh, he had had the chance to be in many recitals before, but he was always too nervous. The few times Marco had tried to play in front of people other than his family and his teacher, his hands shook so much he could barely hit the notes.

This time, though, Marco had prepared the pieces so well that he was almost certain he could get through them easily. His teacher, Ms. Marshall, had told him that if he visualized himself playing beautifully in front of a crowd, he would be able to conquer his nerves. Because of his long hours of practice and daily visualizing, Marco was almost looking forward to the big day.

On the morning of the recital, Marco woke with a start. All those people would be watching him, and it was so easy to make mistakes! As he tried to think more positively, he looked out the window and saw snow falling heavily. The trees, cars, and houses were already covered in several inches of snow. Then he heard the phone ring. When he answered, he heard Ms. Marshall say, "Bad news, Marco. I had to postpone the recital because of this awful blizzard!"

STRATEGY PRACTICE   When have you felt like Marco? How did you handle your fear?

_____

_____

SKILL PRACTICE   Read each question. Fill in the bubble next to the correct answer.

1. **Which words best describe Marco?**
   Ⓐ conceited and showy
   Ⓑ hardworking and nervous
   Ⓒ lazy and daydreaming
   Ⓓ carefree and confident

2. **What is the theme of the passage?**
   Ⓐ Practice always pays off in the end.
   Ⓑ Thinking is not as useful as doing.
   Ⓒ Some things are beyond our control.
   Ⓓ You should put off things that you do not like.

3. **Which inference can you make about Ms. Marshall?**
   Ⓐ She cares about Marco and the recital.
   Ⓑ She makes her students nervous.
   Ⓒ She wants people to think she is a good teacher.
   Ⓓ She is relieved that the recital is postponed.

4. **How did Marco probably feel at the end of the passage?**
   Ⓐ He felt foolish for wasting time practicing.
   Ⓑ He was a little disappointed that the recital was postponed.
   Ⓒ He was worried about the blizzard.
   Ⓓ He was relieved that he would never have to perform in a recital.

Visualization

Visualization allows readers to form mental images of what they are reading about. By visualizing, good readers can better remember the main ideas or events in a passage. Good readers use sensory words from the text to help them visualize and adjust their mental images as they read.

DAY 1

Introduce the *Visualization* strategy to students. Explain: **Good readers make pictures in their minds of what they are reading. They imagine details that include how something from a passage might look, taste, sound, feel, or smell. It often helps to close your eyes when you want to make a visualization.** Have students read the passage independently. Then have them close their eyes and visualize walking in the Grotte de Niaux. When students have finished the strategy practice activity, have them describe their illustrations with words that involve as many senses as possible. Then have students complete the skill practice activity and review the answers together.

DAY 2

Remind students of the *Visualization* strategy. Say: **This passage includes an image of a narwhal that can help us better understand what these sea creatures look like. However, we have to read about and visualize some details on our own.** Have students read the passage independently. Say: **Close your eyes and visualize a narwhal and a unicorn. How are they alike?** (They both have horns on their foreheads.) **How are they different?** (The unicorn has legs; the narwhal has fins.) Direct students to complete the strategy and skill practice activities. Review the answers together.

DAY 3

Remind students of the *Visualization* strategy. Say: **When you visualize as you read, you take all of the information from the passage and put it together one piece at a time.** Have students read the passage and study the diagram. Say: **Visualize a crocodile in its natural environment. How does it look different than the one in the diagram?** (You can't see its whole body; you can see only its eyes, its nostrils, and the skin on its back above the water.) **How does visualizing a crocodile in its natural environment help you understand why they can be so dangerous?** (You might not see a crocodile that is very close to you.) Have students complete the strategy practice activity. Then direct them to complete the skill practice activity and review the answers together.

DAY 4

Remind students of the *Visualization* strategy. Say: **Some passages include visual elements that can help you make pictures in your mind. The chart that goes with this passage includes gestures that are used in Italy to convey messages.** Have students read the passage and study the chart. When they have finished reading, direct students to complete the strategy practice activity with a partner. Invite volunteers to share some of the gestures they visualized with their partners. Then direct students to complete the skill practice activity. Review the answers together.

DAY 5

Remind students of the *Visualization* strategy. Say: **You can visualize details about a scene or passage even if those details are not included in the text.** Have students read the passage and complete the strategy practice activity. Say: **Think about what it would be like to ride the London Eye. Visualize how it moves, how you would feel, and what you would see. Invite volunteers to share their descriptions.** Then have students complete the skill practice activity. Review the answers together.

Daily Reading Comprehension • EMC 3457 • © Evan-Moor Corp.

READ THE PASSAGE As you read, visualize what it would be like to visit the cave.

The Cave of Niaux

In southwestern France, there are caves covered with paintings from prehistoric days. One of the least known but most impressive of these caves is the Grotte de Niaux (nee-OH), located on the banks of the Vicdessos River in the Pyrenees Mountains. The paintings were created between 12,000 and 11,000 BC by a group of hunter-gatherers called the Magdalenian.

When visitors enter the cave, a guide leads them with a lantern. They may carry their own flashlights, but only to guide their feet. To protect the ancient, delicate art, only the guide's light can show the paintings.

Painting at the Grotte de Niaux

After a long, dark, damp walk, the guide stops and shines the lantern on the walls. Visitors gasp at the sight of red and black paintings of horses, bison, and deer that cover the cave walls. Some of the animals are pierced with arrows; others are shown running or standing. Although the drawings are simple, they clearly represent the animals portayed. They were painted with brushes made of animal hair and pigments made from charcoal and iron. A half dozen rooms are covered with this artwork, and some paintings even decorate the cave ceilings. It is hard to believe that people living over 10,000 years ago created realistic paintings that visitors can still view today.

STRATEGY PRACTICE On a separate sheet of paper, sketch how you visualized the walk through the cave.

SKILL PRACTICE Read each question. Fill in the bubble next to the correct answer.

1. The passage is mostly about _____.
   - Ⓐ French tourism
   - Ⓑ the Magdalenian people
   - Ⓒ ancient paintings in a cave
   - Ⓓ prehistoric artists

2. The cave paintings are most similar to _____.
   - Ⓐ cartoon art
   - Ⓑ Greek sculptures
   - Ⓒ modern paintings
   - Ⓓ abstract designs

3. Why do people most likely visit the cave?
   - Ⓐ to explore caves
   - Ⓑ to learn about history
   - Ⓒ to paint new art
   - Ⓓ to study France

4. From the photo, you can tell that the cave paintings are _____.
   - Ⓐ as accurate as photos
   - Ⓑ detailed line drawings
   - Ⓒ painted on wood or canvas
   - Ⓓ unrecognizable to people viewing them

READ THE PASSAGE As you read, look for words that help you make a mental picture.

Unicorn of the Sea

One of the strangest-looking sea mammals is the narwhal. It is a type of whale found in Arctic waters. Its name means "corpse whale," probably because its skin is a death-like bluish-gray. All narwhals have two upper teeth. However, one of the male narwhal's teeth grows into a long, spiral tusk that can reach more than eight feet in length. No one knows the exact purpose of the narwhal's tusk. Some scientists think it might be used during courtship. Others believe it amplifies the sonar pulses, or sound waves, that narwhals send through the water.

The narwhal tusk is highly valued. The royal scepter of England is made from a narwhal tusk, and the tusks decorate the royal palaces in Denmark and Japan. Today, many countries limit the number of narwhals that may be hunted. The population is decreasing due to climate change and may soon be threatened.

It is not certain which came first, narwhal sightings or stories about the unicorn, a one-horned, horse-like creature of myth and legend. Certainly, though, narwhal sightings reinforced the idea of the unicorn. It may not be as magical or exotic as the unicorn, but the narwhal is still a unique, fascinating creature of the sea.

STRATEGY PRACTICE Underline words or phrases from the passage that were easy for you to visualize.

SKILL PRACTICE Read each question. Fill in the bubble next to the correct answer.

1. What is the passage mostly about?
   - Ⓐ narwhals and past rulers
   - Ⓑ legends about narwhals
   - Ⓒ the habitat of narwhals
   - Ⓓ narwhals and their tusks

2. Which detail does the illustration give you about narwhals?
   - Ⓐ the length of a narwhal's tusk compared to its body
   - Ⓑ the geographic region where narwhals live
   - Ⓒ the sounds narwhals make to communicate with each other
   - Ⓓ the swimming habits of narwhals

3. The narwhal's tusk is actually a _____.
   - Ⓐ tooth
   - Ⓑ horn
   - Ⓒ nose
   - Ⓓ scepter

4. Royal people probably like to own narwhal tusks because the tusks are _____.
   - Ⓐ legendary
   - Ⓑ inexpensive
   - Ⓒ magical
   - Ⓓ rare

As you read, visualize a crocodile in its native habitat.

A Well-Designed Hunter

Crocodiles have several adaptations that make them excellent predators both in the water and on land. For example, a crocodile's eyes, ears, and nostrils are on the top of its head, allowing it to keep the rest of its body underwater as it sneaks up on its prey. Also, a crocodile can stay underwater for two hours without breathing, which gives it more time to hunt or to hide from danger.

Crocodiles are extremely fast runners and swimmers due to their strong legs and powerful tails. They can easily chase down their prey or escape threats from other animals.

In addition to having great speed, crocodiles have cone-shaped teeth and powerful jaws—perfect for capturing prey and crushing bones. Their digestive systems are able to process every part of their prey, including hides and hooves.

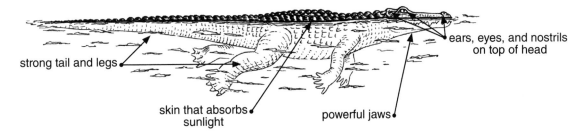

strong tail and legs

ears, eyes, and nostrils on top of head

skin that absorbs sunlight

powerful jaws

STRATEGY PRACTICE Write three nouns (people, places, or things) that were easy for you to visualize.

_____

SKILL PRACTICE Read each question. Fill in the bubble next to the correct answer.

1. Which crocodile feature is pointed out in the diagram but *not* in the passage?
   Ⓐ strong legs
   Ⓑ skin that absorbs sunlight
   Ⓒ powerful jaws
   Ⓓ eyes, ears, and nostrils on top of head

2. The labels in the diagram name _____.
   Ⓐ parts the crocodile uses to swim
   Ⓑ parts that help the crocodile rest
   Ⓒ the crocodile digestive system
   Ⓓ crocodile adaptations

3. The diagram helps you best determine what a crocodile looks like when it is _____.
   Ⓐ resting submerged
   Ⓑ hunting a deer
   Ⓒ eating prey
   Ⓓ escaping danger

4. Crocodiles can crush bones easily using their _____.
   Ⓐ sun-absorbing skin
   Ⓑ long heads
   Ⓒ cone-shaped teeth
   Ⓓ digestive systems

READ THE PASSAGE Think about how you communicate with people you know.

Learning a Foreign "Body Language"

When we think about learning a foreign language, we often focus on how the words from one language translate to another. But have you ever considered how body language translates? Many gestures mean different things in different countries. And many countries have their own gestures that are not used anywhere else. This chart shows some common gestures used in Italy. Do you recognize any of them?

Common Italian Gestures

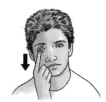

What this gesture means: tricky

Why people use it: to inform a cheater that he or she has been discovered.

In the United States, the expression "I've got my eye on you" has a similar meaning.

What this gesture means: call me

Why people use it: to request a phone call when the person is free.

Both Europeans and Americans claim this as a nearly universal gesture.

What this gesture means: it's good

Why people use it: to let someone know that their food was delicious.

In other countries, a loud belch at the table after a meal is a sign of respect to the chef.

STRATEGY PRACTICE Work with a partner. Take turns talking about friendly gestures you would use if you saw a friend across the room. Visualize the gestures and discuss their meanings.

SKILL PRACTICE Read each question. Fill in the bubble next to the correct answer.

1. What is the title of the chart?
   Ⓐ Common Italian Gestures
   Ⓑ Learning a Foreign "Body Language"
   Ⓒ What this gesture means
   Ⓓ Why people use it

2. If an Italian girl pulls down on her eye, what is she saying?
   Ⓐ "Give me a call when you can."
   Ⓑ "That makes me want to cry."
   Ⓒ "I think you're trying to trick me."
   Ⓓ "I really enjoyed the food."

3. The gestures in the chart that feature arrows are gestures that _____.
   Ⓐ include sound
   Ⓑ use motion
   Ⓒ are about food
   Ⓓ are a sign of praise

4. What is the main idea of the passage?
   Ⓐ It is important to learn new languages.
   Ⓑ Most gestures are the same everywhere.
   Ⓒ All Italian gestures are used in the United States.
   Ⓓ Gestures, like languages, are unique.

READ THE PASSAGE Visualize what it would be like to ride the London Eye.

London Eye

The London Eye, which opened to the public in 2000, is one of the tallest Ferris wheels in the world. The London Eye took seven years to plan and build, and it is an amazing engineering feat.

Dimensions

It rises almost 443 feet (135 meters) above the city and is the fourth-tallest structure in London. Almost five million pounds of concrete hold it in place, and huge cables anchor it to the ground.

The Ride

There are 32 capsules for visitors to ride in, representing London's 32 boroughs. Each capsule has a heating and cooling system to keep riders comfortable. The capsules do not stop moving for people to enter. The wheel moves slowly enough that people can step in and out while the giant wheel rotates. Once you step into your capsule, you are moving at .6 miles per hour (about 1 km per hour). That is about twice as fast as a sprinting tortoise. It takes 30 minutes to go once around.

The View

From the top, if it is a clear day, riders can see as far as 25 miles (about 40 km) in every direction. They can see treetops, parks, and building rooftops, including those of landmarks such as the Big Ben clock tower and the Palace of Westminster. Looking directly down, they see the Thames River with ferryboats and bridges spanning its width.

Popularity

If you take a ride on the London Eye, you will have plenty of company. It holds 800 people per rotation and is London's most popular tourist attraction, with 3.5 million visitors a year.

STRATEGY PRACTICE On a separate sheet of paper, sketch your visualization of the view from the London Eye.

SKILL PRACTICE Read each question. Fill in the bubble next to the correct answer.

1. Another title for this passage could be _____.
   - (A) Designing Ferris Wheels
   - (B) Europe's Giant Ferris Wheel
   - (C) Tourist Attractions in London
   - (D) How the London Eye Was Built

2. How does the London Eye differ from most other Ferris wheels?
   - (A) It is faster.
   - (B) It is older.
   - (C) It is taller.
   - (D) It is lighter.

3. In which section can you find information about the height of the London Eye?
   - (A) Dimensions
   - (B) The Ride
   - (C) The View
   - (D) Popularity

4. Why can visitors see so far from the London Eye?
   - (A) because it takes a long time to go around
   - (B) because there are no tall buildings
   - (C) because the sky is always clear
   - (D) because it is higher than what is around it

Organization

By looking at how a passage or selection is organized, students can better understand the author's intent, as well as predict what information is likely to appear later in the text. Texts are often organized sequentially, around main idea and details, according to cause and effect, or by comparison and contrast.

DAY 1

Introduce the *Organization* strategy to students, and explain: **Authors try to organize their writing in ways that will help readers best understand the information.** Read aloud the title and the headings in the passage. Say: **This author has organized information about diet crazes into different sections. As you read, pay attention to the type of information included under each heading.** Have students read the passage. When they have finished, ask: **How is this passage organized?** (by main idea and details) Direct students to complete the strategy practice activity. Then have them complete the skill practice activity and review the answers together.

DAY 2

Remind students of the *Organization* strategy. Read aloud the first paragraph of the passage. Say: **The beginning of this passage asks whether pigs are smart. Let's see if the author includes information to answer the question.** Have students finish reading the passage independently and complete the strategy practice activity. Then ask: **What other ways could the author have organized the information in the passage?** (chart, bulleted list) **How would a different organization have changed the passage?** (It would probably have made it less interesting.) Direct students to complete the skill practice activity. Review the answers together.

DAY 3

Remind students of the *Organization* strategy. Say: **Many authors use dates to help readers understand the order of events in their texts. Good readers pay attention to dates and time signal words to help them better understand how things may have changed over time.** After students have finished reading the passage, ask: **What is the primary time period for the information included in the passage?** (the 1200s; the Middle Ages) Then direct students to complete the strategy and skill practice activities. Review the answers together.

DAY 4

Remind students of the *Organization* strategy. Say: **As you read the passage, notice words that indicate sequence, such as *later* and *today*.** Have students read the passage independently. When students have finished reading, direct them to complete the strategy practice activity. Remind students to place events on their timelines in chronological order. Then direct students to complete the skill practice activity. Review the answers together.

DAY 5

Remind students of the *Organization* strategy. Review the different ways that texts can be organized, such as by cause and effect, by problem and solution, by main idea and details, or sequentially. Have students read the directions at the top of the page and the passage independently. When students have finished reading, ask: **How is this passage organized?** (by main idea and details) Then direct students to complete the strategy and skill practice activities. Review the answers together.

Daily Reading Comprehension • EMC 3457 • © Evan-Moor Corp.

As you read, pay attention to the title and the headings.

Wild Diet Crazes

Watching what you eat and getting plenty of exercise can be difficult. Many wild diets claim to help people lose weight quickly or in miraculous ways. Here are some unusual diet crazes from the past.

The Tapeworm Diet

In the early 1900s, dieting ads appeared for pills containing tapeworms. Tapeworms are parasites that can live in a person's digestive system. The belief at the time was that the tapeworms would consume some of the food that was in a person's digestive tract, which would cause the person to lose weight. There was no evidence to support this idea, but there was plenty of evidence showing that tapeworms were dangerous. They made people sick and could even cause death.

Diet Sunglasses

Sunglasses with dark blue lenses do not protect your eyes from the glare of the sun, but from the attraction of ice cream. The idea behind this Japanese invention is that if food looks disgusting, people will eat less of it. Do you think people would drink fewer vanilla milkshakes if they looked dark blue? Since they were invented in 2008, thousands of shoppers each year have answered yes.

Ear Stapling

This diet, first introduced in 2000, is a real pain. Dieters have a staple put in their ear cartilage, which is the stiff, flexible part of the outer ear. This is supposed to decrease their appetite. Whether or not this is true, the dieters can definitely get an infection or even suffer nerve damage.

STRATEGY PRACTICE How do the headings help organize the passage?

_____

_____

SKILL PRACTICE Read each question. Fill in the bubble next to the correct answer.

1. The order of diet crazes mentioned in the passage from oldest to most recent is _____.
   Ⓐ tapeworms, sunglasses, ear stapling
   Ⓑ tapeworms, ear stapling, sunglasses
   Ⓒ ear stapling, tapeworms, sunglasses
   Ⓓ sunglasses, ear stapling, tapeworms

2. Which detail supports the idea that tapeworms were dangerous?
   Ⓐ They were sold in the early 1900s.
   Ⓑ They ate food in digestive systems.
   Ⓒ They caused people to get sick.
   Ⓓ They were eaten in pills.

3. Because of the risk of nerve damage and infection, the author believes that _____.
   Ⓐ ear stapling is worth the risk
   Ⓑ dieting has many side effects
   Ⓒ some diets can affect your senses
   Ⓓ ear cartilage should not be stapled

4. A person who is easily affected by the color of food might try which way to lose weight?
   Ⓐ tapeworms
   Ⓑ ear stapling
   Ⓒ diet sunglasses
   Ⓓ exercising

READ THE PASSAGE   Think about the evidence the author presents to support the ideas in the passage.

Babe: Could It Really Happen?

In Dick King-Smith's novel *Babe: The Gallant Pig,* a pig herds sheep better than dogs do. Could that happen in real life? Are pigs as smart as dogs? According to Farm Forward, an advocacy group for sustainable family farms, pigs can do anything dogs can. In support of this conclusion, they point out that the makers of the movie *Babe* did not use any tricks in making the film. They just taught the pig to do the things that they wanted it to do.

How intelligent are pigs? Pretty smart, according to Dr. Stanley Curtis of Penn State University. The scientist taught pigs to play a video game by operating the joystick with their snout. Remarkably, they learned the game more quickly than chimpanzees. Giving human gamers a run for their money, the pigs hit their game targets 80% of the time! Farm Forward also tells of a successful study in which pigs were taught to adjust thermostats.

One pig farmer claims that a sow (a mother pig) in a pen with her piglets kept mysteriously escaping from the enclosure. After finding the lonely sow and her piglets back out with the herd several times, her keepers installed a spring-loaded latch, which could be opened only by pressing a ring and lifting a hook. The sow and piglets kept getting out—always when their keepers were not looking. Finally, the keepers hid behind a shed and watched. After looking to see that no one was watching, the sow depressed the ring by biting it, and then raised the hook. If a sow can figure out how to unlatch a gate while no one is looking, herding sheep is a piece of cake.

STRATEGY PRACTICE   How does the author organize the information about pigs?

_____

_____

SKILL PRACTICE   Read each question. Fill in the bubble next to the correct answer.

1. Which source for pig intelligence would scientists be *least* likely to trust?
   Ⓐ the results of pig training for the movie *Babe*
   Ⓑ the results of Dr. Curtis's experiment
   Ⓒ the study that taught pigs to adjust thermostats
   Ⓓ the statement from the pig farmer with the sow

2. Just before opening the latch, the sow _____.
   Ⓐ escaped from the enclosure
   Ⓑ rejoined the herd
   Ⓒ checked for people watching
   Ⓓ hid behind a shed

3. Why did the sow unlatch the gate?
   Ⓐ to escape from the farmer
   Ⓑ to be with the herd
   Ⓒ to find her piglets
   Ⓓ to find food

4. The evidence in the passage proves the author's idea that _____.
   Ⓐ pigs are clever, social animals
   Ⓑ more movies should include pigs
   Ⓒ farmers do not need to watch all of their animals
   Ⓓ chimpanzees are better at games than humans

READ THE PASSAGE Pay close attention to the organization of the passage.

Grinding Grain Through the Middle Ages

Grinding grain between millstones to produce flour is an ancient practice. Grain, the basis of bread, has always been a very important crop. Grinding grain by hand using millstones was extremely time-consuming. As the population grew and needed more grain, waterwheels came into use around 100 BC to harness the energy of moving water. They helped turn the stones to grind, or "mill," the grain. This was the first use of technology that was not human- or animal-powered. It was the beginning of industrial production. A waterwheel could do the work of 30 to 60 people!

While waterwheel-powered mills greatly benefited those who lived near rivers or oceans, they were not convenient for people who cultivated land that was not near flowing water. Around 1180, the first European windmills appeared, using wooden posts and stones to grind the grain. By the 1200s, windmills were popping up all over Europe.

The first windmill design had one problem—if the wind changed direction, the miller had to turn the entire millhouse to catch the wind. By the end of the Middle Ages, brick and stone tower windmills appeared. Instead of having to turn the entire millhouse when the wind turned, a miller could turn just the cap, or top, of the windmill, making work easier.

These technological advances were just the start, eventually leading to steam power, which fueled the Industrial Revolution. Each advance made life a little easier and freed people up to make better use of their time. They could even stop to enjoy the tasty bread made from milled grain!

STRATEGY PRACTICE Which structure did the author use to relate the history of windmills? Why was it useful?

_____

_____

SKILL PRACTICE Read each question. Fill in the bubble next to the correct answer.

1. What need led to the development of the waterwheel?
   Ⓐ a growing population
   Ⓑ too much running water
   Ⓒ a shortage of millstones
   Ⓓ better access to rivers

2. What led to the invention of the windmill?
   Ⓐ There was too much wind in the fields.
   Ⓑ People had too much free time.
   Ⓒ Bread became a more popular food.
   Ⓓ People wanted to grow grain away from rivers.

3. What caused a problem for early windmills?
   Ⓐ post design
   Ⓑ lack of water
   Ⓒ wind direction
   Ⓓ too much wind

4. Which of these was an effect of industrial production?
   Ⓐ People could spend less time doing difficult tasks.
   Ⓑ The climate in Europe became windier.
   Ⓒ Millers and bakers lost their jobs.
   Ⓓ The amount of steam increased.

READ THE PASSAGE   Think about how each event in vaccine development helped make the next step possible.

The History of Vaccines

Few people enjoy getting shots at the doctor's office. But many of these shots are important vaccines that help prevent us from getting certain diseases or types of infection.

Vaccines got their start in Europe in the 1720s, when a British woman named Lady Mary Wortley Montagu was visiting Turkey. She saw Turkish doctors purposefully inoculating, or infecting, people with small amounts of smallpox. Smallpox is a painful, deadly disease that had no cure at the time. But Lady Montagu was amazed that the patients not only recovered, but then proved to be immune to the disease!

Lady Montagu quickly returned to England, excited to share this new procedure. But inoculation took many years to catch on. One problem was that no one had a precise way of inoculating people safely. Occasionally, patients would become fully infected and then begin spreading the disease. However, inoculation eventually saved enough people for it to become the common practice for preventing smallpox.

Some years later, a scientist named Edward Jenner discovered that people who had been infected with a disease called cowpox became resistant to smallpox. Cowpox was much less harmful than smallpox. Jenner convinced doctors to inoculate people with cowpox, which led to a very safe vaccine and far fewer outbreaks of smallpox. Finally, a French scientist named Louis Pasteur realized that Jenner's idea could be used to treat other diseases. Since then, vaccines have been made for many other diseases, such as polio, tetanus, and rabies.

Today, scientists and doctors continue to create new vaccines that could potentially save millions of lives worldwide.

STRATEGY PRACTICE   Draw a timeline that shows the sequence of events in the passage.

SKILL PRACTICE   Read each question. Fill in the bubble next to the correct answer.

1. Vaccines were first used by _____.
   - Ⓐ Edward Jenner
   - Ⓑ Lady Montagu
   - Ⓒ Turkish doctors
   - Ⓓ Louis Pasteur

2. What happened after Edward Jenner discovered a connection between cowpox and smallpox?
   - Ⓐ Louis Pasteur used Jenner's idea to make vaccines for other diseases.
   - Ⓑ Lady Montagu brought the idea to England.
   - Ⓒ Cowpox became much less harmful than smallpox.
   - Ⓓ Inoculations became common in England.

3. Edward Jenner improved medical science because he _____.
   - Ⓐ was immune to smallpox
   - Ⓑ inspired Lady Montagu
   - Ⓒ helped improve the smallpox vaccine
   - Ⓓ discovered a disease called cowpox

4. What is the main idea of the passage?
   - Ⓐ Edward Jenner discovered that cowpox was similar to smallpox.
   - Ⓑ Multiple vaccines were created after the smallpox vaccine.
   - Ⓒ Turkish patients were treated with early forms of vaccines.
   - Ⓓ The first successful vaccines were created over many years.

Look for important details about the Cowal Highland Gathering.

The Great Games of Scotland

Every August in the Scottish town of Dunoon, over 3,500 people travel from across the world to compete in the Cowal Highland Gathering. Like a cross between a music festival and the Olympics, the Cowal Highland Gathering features musical events, a dancing competition, exhibition tents, local food, and sporting events. Supporters of the gathering say events such as this are important for celebrating Scottish culture.

For over 100 years, pipers have competed for top honors at Cowal. Pipe bands and solo performers play the traditional Scottish instrument—the bagpipe. Fans of the event say the music is breathtaking. However, critics say that when all the bands perform as a single group—with over 3,000 pipers—it sounds like every goose in Scotland has flown to Dunoon to complain of a bellyache.

The Cowal Highland Gathering is also home to the Scottish Highland Dancing National Championships. Hundreds of dancers in kilts and ornately patterned socks jig, fling, and leap for the honor of being the country's best dancer.

Sports fans also flock to the Cowal Highland Gathering. Tossing the caber, a log approximately 19 feet long, is a popular Scottish sport. Men and women who compete heave the huge log end-over-end to make it land as straight as possible. The traditional wrestling event also sees participants from around the world.

From dancing to piping to tossing giant logs, the Cowal Highland Gathering is one of Scotland's most entertaining and popular summer events.

STRATEGY PRACTICE Why do you think the author chose to organize the passage this way?

_____

_____

SKILL PRACTICE Read each question. Fill in the bubble next to the correct answer.

1. What is the passage mostly about?
   Ⓐ what the dancers wear
   Ⓑ the many kinds of events
   Ⓒ how to toss a caber
   Ⓓ what the music sounds like

2. Because a caber is a 19-foot log, people who toss it must be _____.
   Ⓐ fast
   Ⓑ popular
   Ⓒ Scottish
   Ⓓ strong

3. Some people say the Cowal Highland Gathering is important because it _____.
   Ⓐ celebrates Scottish culture
   Ⓑ determines Scotland's best dancers
   Ⓒ features a bagpipe competition
   Ⓓ showcases many events

4. Where can you find evidence that not everyone appreciates the Cowal Highland Gathering?
   Ⓐ first paragraph
   Ⓑ second paragraph
   Ⓒ third paragraph
   Ⓓ fourth paragraph

Determine Important Information

When readers determine important information, they identify the type of text they are reading and then concentrate on finding the essential ideas, events, or details in that text. For nonfiction, determining the important information often means finding the main idea. For fiction, it means understanding essential plot points, themes, or character actions.

DAY 1

Introduce the *Determine Important Information* strategy to students. Explain: **Good readers look for the most important information in a text.** Point to the image on the right side of the ad. Say: **This image is nice to look at, but it doesn't tell me any specific information about Camp Brown Hawk. When you read an ad, look for the main points that help you understand what the ad is trying to sell.** Direct students to read the instructions at the top of the page and then the ad. Then have students complete the strategy practice activity. Review the most important information in the ad, including the activities, history, price, and contact information. Then have students complete the skill practice activity and review the answers together.

DAY 2

Remind students of the *Determine Important Information* strategy. Point out the image and text on the page. Say: **Some authors include diagrams or images to help readers better understand a text. For this experiment, it is helpful to see exactly how the author wants the materials placed. However, you cannot understand the experiment by studying the image alone. Look for important information in the text that explains what you need to do in order to have a successful experiment.** Have students read the directions at the top of the page. Then have students read the experiment and study the image. When students have finished, direct them to complete the strategy and skill practice activities. Review the answers together.

DAY 3

Remind students of the *Determine Important Information* strategy. Point out the introductory text. Ask: **Do you think the chart will make sense if you do not read the passage?** (no) **As you read the passage, look for the most essential information, or main idea. Then think about how that main idea is reflected or further explained in the chart.** Have students read the text and study the chart. When students have finished, have them complete the strategy and skill practice activities. Review the answers together.

DAY 4

Remind students of the *Determine Important Information* strategy. Have students read the directions at the top of the page and then the passage. Ask: **Which information from the passage was more important—the fact that there is a reality show about crab fishing or the fact that workers can be swept overboard?** (swept overboard) **Why is this information more important?** (It shows how dangerous crab fishing can be.) **When you read a passage, focus on finding the most important details that would allow you to share the main idea with others.** Direct students to complete the strategy and skill practice activities. Review the answers together.

DAY 5

Remind students of the *Determine Important Information* strategy. Ask: **Do you ask your friends for their opinions about movies, games, or restaurants? Why are their opinions important to you?** Review how opinions can also be known as "testimonials." Explain: **Businesses often share positive customer testimonials as a persuasive technique.** Have students read the instructions at the top of the page and then the poster. Direct students to complete the strategy practice activity. Discuss why the testimonials might be very important to some people and not important to others. Then have students complete the skill practice activity and review the answers together.

READ THE AD   Read the ad carefully to learn about Camp Brown Hawk.

Spend the summer at Camp Brown Hawk!
Camp is located on beautiful Lake Echo!

Counselors lead campers in these activities:

- hiking on beautiful trails
- swimming
- canoeing and kayaking
- doing crafts such as pottery and woodcarving
- doing fun, nature-based science activities
- singing songs around the campfire

About Camp Brown Hawk:

- We're 80 years old this year.
- All camp staff are trained and experienced.
- Each cabin houses eight boys or girls.
- Kids from ages 6 to 16 are welcome.

(Reserve a space)

Send a check for $50.00 to the address below. All checks must be received by May 15.

Camp Brown Hawk Office

32 Lake Road
Echo Valley, CT, 06421

STRATEGY PRACTICE   What is the most important information you would tell a friend about Camp Brown Hawk? Why?

_____

_____

SKILL PRACTICE   Read each question. Fill in the bubble next to the correct answer.

1. Under which heading would you look to find out if the camp offers bird-watching?
   - Ⓐ Camp is located on beautiful Lake Echo!
   - Ⓑ Counselors lead campers in these activities
   - Ⓒ About Camp Brown Hawk
   - Ⓓ Reserve a space

2. Which evidence best supports the idea that the camp is fun?
   - Ⓐ The camp is 80 years old.
   - Ⓑ Kids between 6 and 16 years old can attend.
   - Ⓒ It costs $50 to reserve a space.
   - Ⓓ There are hiking trails for campers to use.

3. Which evidence best supports the idea that the camp is safe?
   - Ⓐ There are eight kids per cabin.
   - Ⓑ The camp is on a lake.
   - Ⓒ The counselors are trained.
   - Ⓓ Campers sing songs.

4. Why does the ad include a picture?
   - Ⓐ to make the lake look appealing
   - Ⓑ to show exactly what the camp looks like
   - Ⓒ to illustrate the camp's activities
   - Ⓓ to show how to get to the lake

Read each part of the experiment carefully.

Water in Motion

What You Need:

- clear glass tray
- lukewarm water
- large cup with 200 ml of very hot water
- large cup with 200 ml of ice water
- red and blue liquid food coloring

Directions:

1. Fill the tray with lukewarm water.

2. Set the tray on top of the two cups, with the hot cup under one end and the cold cup under the other.

3. Add four drops of red food coloring to the water above the hot cup and four drops of blue food coloring to the water above the cold cup. Add both colors at the same time.

Results:

Color	Water	Observations
blue	cold	sinks and stays together; moves slowly toward hot side in a band of color; spreads out over the hot cup
red	hot	spreads quickly across the top; covers whole top in 1–2 minutes, then starts to sink

Why are the materials and the directions in two separate lists?

_____

Read each question. Fill in the bubble next to the correct answer.

1. Which information is included in the drawing that is *not* listed in the experiment?
   - Ⓐ adding lukewarm water
   - Ⓑ labeling hot and cold water
   - Ⓒ placing the tray on the cups
   - Ⓓ putting food coloring in the water

2. The numbered list tells the _____.
   - Ⓐ steps to take during the experiment
   - Ⓑ materials needed for the experiment
   - Ⓒ results of the experiment
   - Ⓓ reasons to conduct the experiment

3. This experiment is the most similar in writing style to _____.
   - Ⓐ an ad
   - Ⓑ a recipe
   - Ⓒ a magazine article
   - Ⓓ an illustrated story

4. How does the red water move differently from the blue water?
   - Ⓐ It spreads more slowly across the top.
   - Ⓑ It sinks below the blue water more quickly.
   - Ⓒ It moves in a narrower band across the surface.
   - Ⓓ It moves more quickly and spreads out more.

READ THE PASSAGE   Read the passage and study the chart.

What Causes Earthquakes?

Scientists study earthquakes with a tool called a seismometer, which records movements in the ground. In 1935, a scientist named Charles Richter invented a system of measuring earthquakes. It is called the Richter scale. The current method for measuring earthquakes is consistent with this scale. An earthquake is assigned a number between 1 and 10 to describe how much energy it releases, or its magnitude. A magnitude 1.0 earthquake is so weak that it is never felt, while an 8.0 causes severe damage.

Magnitude	Average Number of Earthquakes	Earthquake Effects
2.0–2.9	1,300,000 per year	Rarely felt but are recorded on seismometers
3.0–3.9	130,000 per year	Barely noticeable; hanging objects may swing
4.0–4.9	13,000 per year	Most people notice them; buildings shake
5.0–5.9	1,300 per year	Everyone notices them; windows may break
6.0–6.9	134 per year	Walls may crack; chimneys may fall
7.0–7.9	18 per year	Ground cracks; weak buildings fall down
8.0–8.9	1 per year	Many buildings fall; bridges collapse
9.0–9.9	1 per 20 years	Complete devastation over a wide area
10.0+	Extremely rare	Never recorded

STRATEGY PRACTICE   How is the introductory passage important to understanding the chart?

_____

_____

SKILL PRACTICE   Read each question. Fill in the bubble next to the correct answer.

1. Where is information about the frequency of earthquakes measuring 4.0–4.9?
   Ⓐ in the chart's "Earthquake Effects" column
   Ⓑ in the introductory paragraph
   Ⓒ in the chart's "Average Number of Earthquakes" column
   Ⓓ in the chart's "Magnitude" column

2. Compared to a magnitude 6.0 earthquake, a magnitude 5.0 earthquake is more _____.
   Ⓐ common
   Ⓑ destructive to chimneys
   Ⓒ noticeable
   Ⓓ detectable by seismometers

3. Detailed information about what happens during an 8.0 earthquake is located _____.
   Ⓐ in the chart's "Earthquake Effects" column
   Ⓑ in the introductory paragraph
   Ⓒ in the chart's "Average Number of Earthquakes" column
   Ⓓ in the chart's "Magnitude" column

4. According to the chart, as earthquakes increase in magnitude, _____.
   Ⓐ they are more quickly measured
   Ⓑ they occur more frequently
   Ⓒ they cause more damage
   Ⓓ they are more likely to occur in cities

READ THE PASSAGE   Think about why the writer uses bulleted information.

The Most Dangerous Job

It has been called the deadliest job in the world. In fact, there is even a reality television series about it. But why is Alaskan king crab fishing considered so life-threatening?

People catch king crabs in the Gulf of Alaska and the Bering Sea. These are frigidly cold waters, even at the height of summer. The Alaskan king crab fishing season runs for a few weeks in the fall and winter. Crab fishers drop huge steel cages filled with bait into the sea and then haul them up when crabs climb in. The cages are heavy, the seas are rough, and workers can be swept overboard into the freezing water.

The season is short, so workers must put in long hours during very few weeks, often working in the dark. Add to that the frequent storms and the physical exhaustion, and the job becomes incredibly risky. The positive side of such dangerous work is the possibility of making a large amount of money in a short period of time—but only if you survive the season!

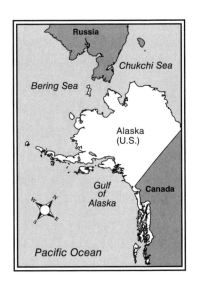

The Good and the Bad

- In 2006, $127 million worth of crab was caught.
- Crew members make between $27,000 and $50,000 per season.
- Fishing shifts last for 18 to 20 hours.
- Between 20 and 40 boats overturn each year.

STRATEGY PRACTICE   Describe a situation when the information from "The Good and the Bad" would be important or useful.

_____

_____

SKILL PRACTICE   Read each question. Fill in the bubble next to the correct answer.

1. **Which evidence best supports the idea that crab fishing is dangerous?**
   Ⓐ the existence of a reality television show
   Ⓑ descriptions of fishing conditions
   Ⓒ a description of how crabs are caught
   Ⓓ how much money fishermen make

2. **Which evidence best supports the statement that crab fishing is life-threatening?**
   Ⓐ The cages are heavy.
   Ⓑ Workers put in long hours.
   Ⓒ Workers can be swept overboard.
   Ⓓ The season takes place in fall and winter.

3. **Compared to most other professions, king crab fishing _____.**
   Ⓐ is difficult and risky
   Ⓑ has better working conditions
   Ⓒ pays less money
   Ⓓ happens in a warmer area

4. **What kind of information is given in the bulleted list?**
   Ⓐ reasons crab fishing is dangerous
   Ⓑ a timeline of crab fishing events
   Ⓒ statistics on crab fishing sales
   Ⓓ crab-fishing data

    Daily Reading Comprehension • EMC 3457 • © Evan-Moor Corp.

READ THE POSTER   Think about how the writer organized the information in the poster.

Spend the Night at the Baseball Hall of Fame in Cooperstown, New York!

With your class or organization, you can

- spend the night in the Hall of Fame Plaque Gallery
- watch a baseball game in the Bullpen Theater
- see the film "The Baseball Experience" in the Grandstand Theater
- explore the museum after regular hours

This opportunity allows young baseball enthusiasts to learn about their sport in a unique way.

Testimonials

- "Spending the night at the Hall of Fame was awesome— it was total immersion in baseball history." – Juan S., age 13, Tupelo, Mississippi
- "I never really appreciated baseball before, but seeing all the exhibits after dark, without other tourists, was amazing." – Leo B., age 13, Queens, New York

- "The best thing about the trip was sleeping in the Plaque Gallery under the pictures of all the greatest ballplayers in history." – Ming W., age 14, Honesdale, Pennsylvania
- "The exhibit on women in baseball was great, and I loved the movie. I felt like I learned so much—but it was really fun, too." – Susan L., age 12, Portland, Oregon

STRATEGY PRACTICE   How is each section of the poster important for convincing people to visit the Baseball Hall of Fame?

_____

_____

SKILL PRACTICE   Read each question. Fill in the bubble next to the correct answer.

1. Which evidence best supports the idea that the overnight trip is fun?
   - Ⓐ facts about the Hall of Fame
   - Ⓑ visitors' testimonials
   - Ⓒ details about the gallery
   - Ⓓ the name of the film

2. Which of these things can groups do on the overnight trip?
   - Ⓐ discuss the museum with daytime tourists
   - Ⓑ talk to famous baseball players
   - Ⓒ explore the museum after regular hours
   - Ⓓ eat dinner in the Hall of Fame

3. The visitors' testimonials include _____.
   - Ⓐ quotations from young visitors
   - Ⓑ baseball statistics
   - Ⓒ directions to the museum
   - Ⓓ historical information

4. According to the poster, the people who can spend the night at the Hall of Fame are _____.
   - Ⓐ kids and their families
   - Ⓑ professional baseball players
   - Ⓒ museum members
   - Ⓓ organizations or classes

Ask Questions

By asking questions, readers can set a purpose for reading or make sure they understand what they have read. Good readers ask questions to involve themselves with the text and often ask questions before they read, while they read, and after they read.

DAY 1

Introduce the *Ask Questions* strategy to students. Explain: **Good readers ask questions to engage with the text they are reading. They ask questions about why the author wrote the text, events that happen throughout the text, and things they still wonder about when they have finished reading.** Read aloud the title of the passage. On the board, write: "Who is Huck? Who is 'Me'?" Tell students to think about these questions as they read the passage. When they have finished, have partners discuss the answers to the questions and how they figured them out. Then direct students to complete the strategy and skill practice activities. Review the answers together.

DAY 2

Remind students of the *Ask Questions* strategy. Say: **When we have questions during reading, we can write these questions down and look for the answers later on in the text. Asking questions as we read keeps us connected to the passage.** Tell students to think of a question as they read the first paragraph. Direct students to write their question in the space provided for the strategy practice activity before they finish reading the passage. Have students read the rest of the passage and then invite volunteers to share their questions. Discuss which questions were able to be answered with information from the text and how to find answers to questions that were not. Then have students complete the skill practice activity. Review the answers together.

DAY 3

Remind students of the *Ask Questions* strategy. Say: **You can ask questions before you read to help you set a purpose for reading.** Read aloud the title of the passage. Write on the board: "What is 'canyon country'? Why is it special? What happens there?" Model the strategy: **My purpose for reading will be to answer these questions.** After students have read the passage, review the answers to your pre-reading questions. Then direct students to complete the strategy and skill practice activities. Review the answers together.

DAY 4

Remind students of the *Ask Questions* strategy. Say: **Remember to think of questions you have before, during, and after reading. Mark places within the text wherever you have a question.** Have students read the passage independently and complete the strategy practice activity with a partner. Then direct students to complete the skill practice activity and review the answers together.

DAY 5

Remind students of the *Ask Questions* strategy. Build background by explaining that proverbs are figures of speech or common sayings that are designed to convey important life lessons. Review the meanings of a few familiar proverbs, such as "Don't count your chickens before they hatch." Say: **As you read, write down any questions you have about the proverbs in the chart in the strategy practice activity section.** When they have finished, discuss which questions were able to be answered with information from the text and how to find answers to questions that were not. Then have students complete the skill practice activity independently. Review the answers together.

Daily Reading Comprehension • EMC 3457 • © Evan-Moor Corp.

READ THE PASSAGE As you read, think of a question you have about the passage.

Huck and Me

What started as a normal summer day relaxing outside in Dad's hammock with a copy of *The Adventures of Huckleberry Finn* turned into something, well, very bizarre. You might think a 13-year-old boy reading an actual book on a beautiful Missouri day is weird enough, when he could have been playing ball with his friends or swimming in Mark Twain Lake, but you haven't heard the rest of my story. I had just read the part where Huck escapes from his father, having faked his own death, when I must've fallen asleep.

I awoke to this repetitive metallic sound. Was Dad banging pots together? And why did his hammock feel hard beneath me? Wait, this wasn't a hammock. I was on a raft, surrounded by heavy fog. Boatmen were banging pots to announce their presence nearby.

Sitting up, I saw a strong African American man across from me. His husky voice sounded oddly comforting. "You been out a while," he said, nodding at me.

A keelboat drifted by, barely visible through the fog. "Jim?" I asked.

"Yes, Huck," the man replied.

"We haven't passed the mouth of the Ohio, have we?" I inquired.

"Fog's just liftin'. Cain't hardly tell."

I had no idea if we'd passed the river that we were going to take north to where Jim would be a free man, and I was clueless as to how I'd left the twenty-first century and become Huck Finn. But floating free on the smooth early-morning Mississippi, back in the 1880s with a friend whose company I'd first come to enjoy on a printed page, seemed like a real fine place to be.

STRATEGY PRACTICE Write a question you have about the passage. Discuss it with a partner.

_____

_____

SKILL PRACTICE Read each question. Fill in the bubble next to the correct answer.

1. What is the author's purpose in this passage?
   Ⓐ to inform
   Ⓑ to express
   Ⓒ to persuade
   Ⓓ to entertain

2. The setting at the beginning contrasts with the setting at the end because _____.
   Ⓐ it starts in the morning, then continues in the afternoon
   Ⓑ it is in modern time at first, then in the 1880s
   Ⓒ it starts on a raft, then continues in a hammock
   Ⓓ it is foggy at first, then the fog lifts

3. How are the narrator and Huck alike?
   Ⓐ They enjoy Jim's company.
   Ⓑ They escaped from their fathers.
   Ⓒ They live near a river.
   Ⓓ They like to read books.

4. One theme of this story is _____.
   Ⓐ getting revenge
   Ⓑ the loss of innocence
   Ⓒ the joy of reading
   Ⓓ fear of the unknown

Ask yourself questions as you read the passage.

Dance Company on Wheels

Mary Verdi-Fletcher was born with spina bifida, a disease that causes weakness in the legs and spine. Undiscouraged, she was not about to be told what she could or could not do. She dreamed of dancing and was determined to make her dream a reality. While still young, Verdi-Fletcher—dancing in her wheelchair— entered a dance contest with a friend. They won first prize. She entered and won more contests, refusing to listen to people who said to her "You can't dance if you're in a wheelchair" or "Dancing in a chair is not really dancing."

However, Verdi-Fletcher was not satisfied with personal success alone. She wanted to make dance available to others with disabilities. In 1980, she founded a dance company called Dancing Wheels. Based in Cleveland, Ohio, Dancing Wheels performs all over the world. In productions like "The Snowman," sit-down (seated) dancers perform with stand-up (standing) dancers. Dazzling lighting designs, fanciful sets and props, melodious music, and festive costuming draw audience members into fairy tales and other stories.

In one show, a young stand-up dancer named Devin played "The Brother Who Cannot See" while a young sit-down dancer named Jenny (now an adult member of the company) performed the role of "The Sister Who Cannot Walk." It was a lovely way to express a theme Verdi-Fletcher has embodied all through her life: We all have disabilities. Some disabilities may be more visible, but hard work and dedication to our dreams can make the seemingly impossible become a reality.

STRATEGY PRACTICE   Write one question you thought of while reading the passage. What is the answer?

_____

_____

SKILL PRACTICE   Read each question. Fill in the bubble next to the correct answer.

1. The author wrote this passage mainly to _____.
   Ⓐ entertain with the story of "The Snowman"
   Ⓑ teach people how to dance in wheelchairs
   Ⓒ provide details about spina bifida
   Ⓓ persuade readers to believe in their dreams

2. The author quotes what people said to Mary Verdi-Fletcher to tell readers _____.
   Ⓐ that no one can dance in a wheelchair
   Ⓑ the wisdom of the people who are quoted
   Ⓒ that wheelchair dancing is not real dancing
   Ⓓ to ignore discouraging opinions

3. The main difference between Dancing Wheels and other dance companies is that most companies _____.
   Ⓐ present elaborate productions
   Ⓑ accompany dance with music
   Ⓒ have only stand-up dancers
   Ⓓ perform all over the world

4. The main theme of this passage is that _____.
   Ⓐ dancing is the best form of art
   Ⓑ with dedication dreams can become reality
   Ⓒ dancing is great exercise for children
   Ⓓ diseases can cause disabilities

READ THE PASSAGE   Ask yourself questions to make sure you understand what you read.

Canyon Country

Canyon Country, Utah. Sarah had wanted to hike there ever since she'd seen pictures of it. Finally, she'd talked her parents into camping there in their RV. But now it seemed all they did was eat, sleep, watch movies, and roast marshmallows. The marshmallows were fine, but while her parents slept in after staying up late to watch the latest Tom Cruise film, Sarah rose with the birds. One morning, she gazed around. Gorgeous! She wasn't about to miss another early morning hike; she'd have to go alone.

Sarah opened the RV door and called for her dog. "Kip!" The chocolate Lab ambled over to the steps. "Let's go hiking!" Kip whimpered and stared longingly at the RV door. "Cassie's not coming," Sarah explained, referring to her little Scottish terrier. "She's still sleeping with Mom and Dad. Besides, you're big, so you can frighten away wild critters."

The rocky trail spiraled through canyons, then up to an outcropping that intrigued Sarah. "Are those native ruins up there?" she wondered. The pair had climbed hardly a quarter of a mile when they stopped short. Some 50 yards ahead, a cougar stood in the middle of the trail. Kip trembled at Sarah's side. What to do? Make yourself look big! That's all she could remember from what she'd read in nature books.

Suddenly, Cassie appeared out of nowhere, barking her tiny head off. Whether the cougar was startled or just not hungry, Sarah didn't know. The cougar hurried up the cliff into a thicket of manzanita bushes.

"So I guess my parents are awake now," said Sarah, hugging Cassie as they followed the scent of coffee. "Glad you're up!" she said, arriving at camp. "Cassie scared away a cougar!"

STRATEGY PRACTICE   How did asking questions before reading help you better understand the passage?

_____

_____

SKILL PRACTICE   Read each question. Fill in the bubble next to the correct answer.

1. What is the author's main purpose?
   Ⓐ to entertain
   Ⓑ to express
   Ⓒ to inform
   Ⓓ to persuade

2. How did Sarah's dogs react differently to the cougar?
   Ⓐ Kip was scared; Cassie acted bravely.
   Ⓑ Kip frightened the cougar; Cassie made noise.
   Ⓒ Kip made himself look big; Cassie looked tiny.
   Ⓓ Kip startled the cougar; Cassie chased it up a cliff.

3. What lesson does Sarah probably learn?
   Ⓐ Nature is most beautiful at sunrise.
   Ⓑ You can accomplish a lot if you start early.
   Ⓒ It is important to be prepared for anything.
   Ⓓ Reality is not as good as what you expect.

4. Which proverb is a theme of this passage?
   Ⓐ Let sleeping dogs lie.
   Ⓑ Beauty is only skin deep.
   Ⓒ A bird in the hand is worth two in the bush.
   Ⓓ Don't judge a book by its cover.

READ THE PASSAGE   Think of a question as you read. Look for the answer in the passage.

Frida Kahlo and Diego Rivera

Mexico has produced many excellent artists, but two of its best known are Frida Kahlo and Diego Rivera. Interestingly, they were married to each other. Both were intensely tied to their Mexican heritage.

Diego Rivera painted pictures on canvases and murals on walls, so he can be called both a painter and a muralist. Many of his murals, boldly painted in earth colors, take up entire walls. Most show common people in everyday scenes—selling flowers on a sidewalk or working in a factory—but the common images carry powerful messages. Studying his paintings, you come away understanding the dignity of hard work, the daily life of native people, and the humble beauty of flowers. Rivera's paintings are personal because they represent the people and the culture around him—the culture of Mexico.

Frida Kahlo's paintings are likewise personal—perhaps more personal than those of Rivera because they reflect her inner world. "I paint self-portraits because I am the person I know best," she once said. Even though she was born into a wealthy family, Kahlo did not enjoy an easy life. As a child, she contracted polio. The disease shrank one leg and led to merciless teasing by schoolmates. When she was 18 years old, she was in a horrific bus accident. For the remainder of her life, Kahlo was in constant physical and emotional pain. She painted 55 self-portraits, the majority of them reflecting her pain.

Like his paintings, Rivera lived large and bold. Beside him, Kahlo looked tiny. Yet her presence, life, and paintings, like his, have always demanded attention.

STRATEGY PRACTICE   Write a question about information from the passage. Ask a partner to answer it.

_____

_____

SKILL PRACTICE   Read each question. Fill in the bubble next to the correct answer.

1. Frida Kahlo's paintings contrast with Diego Rivera's because they _____.
   Ⓐ are self-portraits
   Ⓑ tell about her marriage
   Ⓒ focus on the beauty of flowers
   Ⓓ do not reflect her Mexican identity

2. Which word from the passage signals that the couple's paintings are alike in some way?
   Ⓐ interestingly
   Ⓑ boldly
   Ⓒ likewise
   Ⓓ many

3. What is one theme of Kahlo's paintings?
   Ⓐ the beauty of ordinary people
   Ⓑ the complications of polio
   Ⓒ Mexico's wealthy class
   Ⓓ the pain she felt in body and soul

4. Which best represents the author's purpose?
   Ⓐ to give information about two famous painters
   Ⓑ to tell about how painters work
   Ⓒ to teach the importance of painting
   Ⓓ to persuade readers that one painter was more important than the other

READ THE PASSAGE   If something you read does not make sense to you, write a question about it.

Cultural Proverbs

Many of us grow up hearing sayings repeated over and over. These pieces of wisdom are passed down from one generation to the next in proverbs. Proverbs often use metaphors that apply to many situations, some of which are not literal. Variants of the same ideas appear in many cultures, using different metaphors. Benjamin Franklin collected American proverbs in his book *Poor Richard's Almanack*. Here are some proverbs from two other cultures. How are they like sayings you have heard?

Italian Proverbs	Irish Proverbs
• Don't say four if you don't have them in the sack.	• A trout in the pot is better than a salmon in the sea.
• To each bird, his nest is beautiful.	• To the raven, her own chick is white.
• You can catch more flies with honey than with a barrel of vinegar.	• Soft words butter no parsnips, but they won't harden the heart of the cabbage, either.
• Fine words don't feed cats.	• Mere words do not feed the friars.
• Since the house is on fire, let us warm ourselves.	• When the sky falls, we'll all catch larks.
• Like father, like son.	• As the hound is, so will the pup be.

STRATEGY PRACTICE   Write one question you had while reading the passage. If you learned the answer, write it down.

_____

_____

SKILL PRACTICE   Read each question. Fill in the bubble next to the correct answer.

1. Which best represents another way to express the proverb "To each bird, his nest is beautiful"?
   Ⓐ Many hands make light work.
   Ⓑ Absence makes the heart grow fonder.
   Ⓒ Beauty is in the eye of the beholder.
   Ⓓ A watched pot never boils.

2. What is the meaning of the proverb "When the sky falls, we'll all catch larks"?
   Ⓐ There's a positive side to everything.
   Ⓑ Disaster is just around the corner.
   Ⓒ Bad things happen to everyone.
   Ⓓ Beware of falling birds.

3. The proverbs are arranged to _____.
   Ⓐ appear in order of length
   Ⓑ show similar proverbs from different cultures
   Ⓒ compare Italian people to Irish people
   Ⓓ show which proverbs are the oldest

4. What is the main purpose of the passage?
   Ⓐ to persuade people to read proverbs
   Ⓑ to inform people about wise sayings
   Ⓒ to entertain with humor
   Ⓓ to explain how proverbs are collected

Main Idea and Details

Students look for the central idea or message of a passage or story. They also find details that best support the main idea.

Sequence

Students look for the order of events or steps in a process.

DAY 1

Remind students that the main idea of a passage or paragraph is the most important idea. Details are smaller pieces of information that support the main idea. Say: **Some passages start with a main idea paragraph and each paragraph thereafter includes the supporting details. Other passages include paragraphs that contain their own main ideas and details.** Have students read the instructions at the top of the page. Say: **This passage will have separate main ideas and details in each paragraph.** Then remind them of the *Monitor Comprehension* strategy (Week 1). Tell students to read slowly and think about what they are reading. Then direct students to complete the skill practice activity. Review the answers together. For the strategy practice activity, encourage students to reread only the parts of the passage that were difficult to understand.

DAY 2

Remind students of the *Main Idea and Details* skill. Tell students that the main idea of a passage often appears in the opening paragraph, but they need to pay attention as they read because it may be located elsewhere. Encourage students to keep track of ideas as they read in order to figure out the most important information. Then remind students of the *Visualization* strategy (Week 3). Say: **As you read, make a mental image of the submarine described in the passage. This will allow you to better understand what the passage says about submarines.** Have students read the passage independently and direct them to complete the skill practice activity. Review the answers together. Then have students complete the strategy practice activity and share their sketches with the group.

DAY 3

Introduce the *Sequence* skill to students. Say: **Sequence refers to order, which can be time order or the order of steps in a process.** Review sequence signal words, such as *before, after, next,* and *last.* Say: **As you read, pay attention to when Natasha has different activities throughout the week.** Then remind students of the *Monitor Comprehension* strategy. Say: **As you read, you may wish to make notes in the margins to help you remember what is scheduled each day.** Have students read the instructions at the top of the page and then the passage. When students have finished, direct them to complete the skill practice activity. Review the answers together. Then have students complete the strategy practice activity and compare their chart with a partner's.

DAY 4

Remind students of the *Sequence* skill. Then say: **The passage you are about to read includes specific instructions for two different bear attack scenarios. Pay attention to the advice given for each type of situation.** Then remind students of the *Visualization* strategy. Say: **Visualizing how you should react if you encounter a bear could help you if it ever happens in real life. Try to picture exactly what you would do.** Have students read the instructions at the top of the page and then the passage. Then direct students to complete the skill and strategy practice activities. Review the answers together.

DAY 5

Tell students they will practice both the *Main Idea and Details* and *Sequence* skills. Remind students of the *Monitor Comprehension* strategy. Say: **As you read the passage, take notes on the steps. Underline any parts that you do not understand so you can read them again after you finish.** Have students read the instructions at the top of the page and then the passage. Then direct students to complete the skill and strategy practice activities. Review the answers together.

READ THE PASSAGE   Think about the main idea of each paragraph.

Hidden Cities Beneath Our Feet

In big cities, people dig all the time. Construction workers dig to make foundations for new buildings and homes. Utility companies dig to access broken water pipes or bad electrical wires. City governments dig to make the land more usable. Often while digging, people find items from the past, such as old shoes, bottles, or plates. Although these items can be interesting, they are usually not extraordinary.

In 1978, electric company workers in Mexico City, Mexico, made an amazing discovery. They were digging in the middle of the city when they uncovered a monumental carved stone disk that was 500 years old. The object weighed more than eight tons and showed the image of the striking Aztec moon goddess, Coyolxauhqui.

As surprising as the discovery was, it was only the beginning. The disk turned out to be one small part of the ruins of the ancient capital of the Aztec empire, Tenochtitlan. Historians knew that Tenochtitlan had been destroyed in 1521 when Spanish conquerors tore down buildings and began to build new structures on top of the ruins. But no one knew exactly where the ruins were, nor how much still existed. Despite years of searching, the ancient city's location remained a mystery until those lucky electricians unearthed the first huge clue.

After the discovery of the carved disk, workers uncovered more remains of the city, including a large pyramid-shaped temple that was a ceremonial center of Tenochtitlan. Today, visitors to Mexico City can tour the original site and visit the Templo Mayor Museum. The museum has eight halls featuring thousands of objects that have been excavated, or dug up, from beneath the modern city. This vast treasure includes shells, carved figures, skeletons, ceramics, mosaics, weapons, and statues.

SKILL PRACTICE   Read each question. Fill in the bubble next to the correct answer.

1. The first paragraph is mostly about _____.
   - Ⓐ tools used by ancient Aztecs
   - Ⓑ how workers find old objects
   - Ⓒ the unexpected discovery of a stone disk
   - Ⓓ how scientists learn about other cultures

2. Why were historians surprised to find the ruins of Tenochtitlan?
   - Ⓐ They thought the ruins had been completely destroyed.
   - Ⓑ They believed the city was buried much deeper underground.
   - Ⓒ They thought the ruins were somewhere else.
   - Ⓓ They had never known where the city was located.

3. Which detail best supports the idea that the ruins of Tenochtitlan are a "vast treasure"?
   - Ⓐ The stone disk weighed more than eight tons.
   - Ⓑ Tenochtitlan had been destroyed in 1521.
   - Ⓒ The temple was shaped like a pyramid.
   - Ⓓ Thousands of ancient objects were discovered.

4. Which of these statements best tells the main idea of the passage?
   - Ⓐ Tenochtitlan was destroyed in 1521.
   - Ⓑ Many people visit Mexico City to see the ruins of the Aztec people.
   - Ⓒ Construction workers helped Mexico City discover its ancient past.
   - Ⓓ Coyolxauhqui was an Aztec moon goddess who is represented on an ancient stone disk.

STRATEGY PRACTICE   Underline any parts you did not understand. Reread only those parts.

READ THE PASSAGE   Look for good details in the passage that help you picture submarines.

Submarine Basics

Submarines are boats that are designed to operate and travel underwater. Because they are full of air, like a balloon, submarines do not sink. The air makes them less dense than the water around them. Many kinds of boats use "ballast," which is any material that adds weight to make the boat more stable. Ballast can be anything from metal plates to rocks, but submarines use water to make them dense enough to dive deep into the ocean.

In order to store the water it takes in, a submarine has large ballast tanks, which can hold different amounts of water. To make the submarine dive, special operators pump water into the ballast tanks. Once the controllers have pumped in enough water, the submarine can begin its journey into the ocean depths. The speed at which the submarine dives is partially controlled by how quickly the ballast tanks take in water.

When the submarine is underwater, operators maintain a steady depth by pumping some air back into the ballast tanks. In this state, known as "neutral buoyancy," a submarine can travel around without rising or falling. In order to move through water, the submarine has propellers. The propellers are curved in such a way that they push water forward or backward depending on which way the propellers are spinning. The faster the propellers spin, the faster the submarine will travel. Navigators use special equipment that helps pilots steer submarines safely in dark or murky waters.

To return the submarine to the surface, air is pumped into the ballast tanks, which pushes all of the water out. As the amount of ballast in the submarine decreases, the craft once again becomes less dense and begins to rise.

SKILL PRACTICE   Read each question. Fill in the bubble next to the correct answer.

1. **What is the passage mostly about?**
   Ⓐ ocean density and buoyancy
   Ⓑ how to navigate a submarine
   Ⓒ different kinds of ballast
   Ⓓ how submarines operate

2. **Which of the following is an example of using water as ballast?**
   Ⓐ spinning propellers to move forward
   Ⓑ pumping in water to become more dense
   Ⓒ navigating through underwater obstacles
   Ⓓ measuring the density of ocean water

3. **A submarine can sink when it _____.**
   Ⓐ is denser than ocean water
   Ⓑ is navigating through dark water
   Ⓒ turns on its propellers
   Ⓓ is pumped full of air

4. **When a submarine is at "neutral buoyancy," it _____.**
   Ⓐ pumps air to rise to the surface
   Ⓑ stays at the same depth underwater
   Ⓒ adds water to become faster
   Ⓓ is easy to navigate through the dark

STRATEGY PRACTICE   Visualize what you read about. On a separate sheet of paper, sketch a submarine, including its ballast tanks.

Pay attention to the order of events in the passage.

Running Late

Natasha ran as fast as she could to the tennis courts. The yearbook meeting had run long, and practice was already starting. Coach Parks made the players who showed up late collect all the tennis balls after practice was over. "Great," Natasha thought as she tightened the laces on her tennis shoes, "that means I'll be late for my guitar lesson." The day had been a blur of activities, classes, clubs, and projects. Natasha felt sure there was something she was forgetting.

When practice was over, Natasha raced around the court, scooping the fuzzy yellow tennis balls into a large plastic bucket. Her mind was already working on the apology for her guitar teacher, Mr. Takanawa, when she heard the familiar honk of her mother's car horn.

Natasha returned the balls and bucket to the equipment room and hopped in the front seat. "Do you think Mr. Takanawa will be upset that I'm late?"

"We moved your guitar lesson to next Monday," Mom said, smiling. "Did you forget what day it is today, sweetie?"

Natasha thought back carefully. "Well, yesterday was science club and swim practice, and tomorrow is dance class and then volunteer time at the library, so that means today is Wednesday. I didn't forget."

"You're right, it is Wednesday. Wednesday the 18th. Which means . . ."

Natasha's face flushed bright red. "Oh no! How could I forget my own birthday dinner? Well, at least this means I won't have to apologize to Mr. Takanawa for being late!"

SKILL PRACTICE   Read each question. Fill in the bubble next to the correct answer.

1. According to the passage, when does Natasha usually have guitar lessons?
   Ⓐ Tuesday, after swim practice
   Ⓑ Wednesday, before yearbook club
   Ⓒ Wednesday, after tennis practice
   Ⓓ Tuesday, before science club

2. Which of Natasha's activities happens latest in the week?
   Ⓐ guitar lesson
   Ⓑ dance class
   Ⓒ tennis practice
   Ⓓ volunteer time at the library

3. Which event caused Natasha to be late for tennis practice?
   Ⓐ a canceled guitar lesson
   Ⓑ a long yearbook meeting
   Ⓒ cleaning up the tennis equipment
   Ⓓ attending her birthday dinner

4. On which day of the week does Natasha have the most activities?
   Ⓐ Monday
   Ⓑ Tuesday
   Ⓒ Wednesday
   Ⓓ Thursday

STRATEGY PRACTICE   On a separate sheet of paper, make a chart of Natasha's weekly schedule. Then compare your chart to a partner's.

READ THE PASSAGE   As you read, visualize each step the author gives for surviving a bear attack.

How to Survive a Bear Attack

Thousands of nature lovers see black bears and grizzly bears each year, and most walk away with exciting memories and photographs. But for the unlucky few, bear encounters can lead to serious injury or death. If you come upon a bear in its natural setting, your first instinct may be to panic. But staying safe depends on acting carefully and calmly.

There are many theories about how a person should react when faced with a giant bear. Some people would suggest running away, but bears can run much faster than humans can. Others say a person should drop to the ground, curl up, and play dead. That turns out to be good advice in some situations but not in others. It is best to be as educated as possible about different bear behaviors before you head into the wild.

If a bear is coming toward you, you must first determine if the bear attack is defensive (such as when defending cubs) or predatory (such as when hunting). Black bears and grizzly bears tend to attack for different reasons. Most grizzly bear attacks are defensive. When a bear is defensive, it is feeling threatened. Dropping to the ground is an effective way to show the bear that you are not a threat.

Black bears do not often challenge humans, but when they do, their attacks are usually predatory. Bears do not feel threatened when they are hunting, so playing dead will not help you stay safe. During a predatory bear attack, the first thing you should do is drop any food you have and back away. If the bear still comes toward you, make as much noise as possible by shouting and banging objects. Your own aggressive behavior can convince the bear to back down. You can also use pepper spray during a bear attack. Always bring it with you in the wild, and have it ready to use immediately.

SKILL PRACTICE   Read each question. Fill in the bubble next to the correct answer.

1. If a bear is coming toward you, the first thing you need to do is determine _____.
   - Ⓐ whether you have pepper spray
   - Ⓑ how far away the bear is
   - Ⓒ if the attack is defensive or predatory
   - Ⓓ where the nearest hiding place is

2. At what point is it a good idea to drop down and play dead?
   - Ⓐ after determining that the bear is defensive
   - Ⓑ at the first sign that a bear is nearby
   - Ⓒ after trying to run away
   - Ⓓ before making noise

3. What should you do before hiking in an area where you might encounter bears?
   - Ⓐ learn to identify black bears and grizzly bears
   - Ⓑ practice dropping to the ground and playing dead
   - Ⓒ act aggressively, making loud noises
   - Ⓓ train yourself to run very quickly

4. During a predatory bear attack, you should make loud noises _____.
   - Ⓐ while looking for pepper spray
   - Ⓑ before dropping down and playing dead
   - Ⓒ while running for safety
   - Ⓓ after dropping any food you have

STRATEGY PRACTICE   Write three details from the passage that were easy for you to visualize.

_____

_____

READ THE PASSAGE   Think about the order of steps used to create stop-motion animation.

Stop-Motion Animation

Stop-motion animation uses multiple photos of real objects to create the appearance of movement. To make your own stop-motion movie, you will need a digital camera, a tripod (camera stand), one or more background sets, editing software, and your story's characters. Your characters can be anything you can move: action figures, stuffed animals, or clay creatures of your own design.

First, place your camera on a tripod to keep the camera still. Even though you are creating the illusion of movement, the camera should not move at all. With the camera in place, set up your first background set.

You will take about 10 pictures for each second of your animation. Think about the movements you want to create and the story you want to tell. To begin shooting, place your character and take a picture. Then move the character a small amount and snap another picture. Keep repeating this process, and you will have a series of photos that you can upload into your editing software. Remember that the speed your characters move during the animation will be determined by how much you moved them in between photos. For example, if you want a character to walk from one side of the screen to the other in two seconds, you will need to break the movement into 20 pictures.

When you are editing your movie, you can add dialogue, sound effects, and music. You can also add titles and special effects, such as zooming in on a character. When you have finished, you can share your masterpiece with the world.

SKILL PRACTICE   Read each question. Fill in the bubble next to the correct answer.

1. The passage is mostly about _____.
   Ⓐ the history of stop-motion animation
   Ⓑ how to use movie-editing software
   Ⓒ using the movie setting on a digital camera
   Ⓓ how to make a stop-motion movie

2. To make a stop-motion movie, which of the following should you do first?
   Ⓐ move your character a small amount
   Ⓑ put your camera on a tripod
   Ⓒ upload photos into editing software
   Ⓓ add special effects

3. What should you *always* try to do while taking the pictures?
   Ⓐ use action figures
   Ⓑ add music and special effects
   Ⓒ keep the camera from moving
   Ⓓ zoom in on characters

4. One of the final steps in making a stop-motion movie is adding _____.
   Ⓐ a title
   Ⓑ movement
   Ⓒ characters
   Ⓓ a background

STRATEGY PRACTICE   Did you understand the directions for making a stop-motion movie? Why or why not?

_____

_____

Author's Purpose
Students identify the author's reasons for writing about a subject.

Evaluate Evidence
Students practice evaluating evidence by identifying the author's main idea and examining the evidence the author uses to support that idea.

DAY 1

Introduce the *Author's Purpose* skill to students. Say: **Authors write texts to give information, to entertain readers, to try to persuade readers to think or feel a certain way, or to teach readers how to do something. As you read, ask yourself:** *Why did the author write this passage?* Then remind students of the *Determine Important Information* strategy (Week 5). Point out that identifying important information can help you identify an author's purpose. Have students read the instructions at the top of the page and then the passage. When students have finished reading, direct them to complete the skill and strategy practice activities. Review the answers together.

DAY 2

Remind students of the *Author's Purpose* skill. Say: **When good readers identify an author's purpose, they are better able to understand the author's main points.** Then remind students of the *Ask Questions* strategy (Week 6). Direct students to read the first paragraph, pause, and write a question they have in the strategy practice activity section. Guide them to look for the answer as they continue reading. Then have students complete the skill practice activity and review the answers together.

DAY 3

Introduce the *Evaluate Evidence* skill to students. Say: **When an author makes a claim, it is important to evaluate the evidence that the author includes to support that claim. Sometimes, the author is credible, or believable. Other times, an author may include inaccurate or questionable material. It's up to you as a reader to decide whether or not an author is trustworthy.** Then remind students of the *Determine Important Information* strategy. Say: **As you read, think about each claim the author is making. Decide which information is the most important in relation to whether or not you trust the author.** Then direct students to read the passage before completing the skill and strategy practice activities. Review the answers together.

DAY 4

Remind students of the *Evaluate Evidence* skill. Say: **When an author gives a main idea, he or she will provide specific details that support the main idea. These details are evidence that support the author's claims.** Read aloud the title of the passage, and say: **This passage is about the effects of birth order. Pay attention to the evidence the author gives that supports the conclusions about first, last, and middle children.** Then remind students of the *Ask Questions* strategy. Say: **When you are finished reading, think about questions you had while reading the passage and whether or not you were able to locate the answers.** Direct students to read the passage and to complete the skill and strategy practice activities. Review the answers together.

DAY 5

Tell students they will practice both the *Author's Purpose* and *Evaluate Evidence* skills. Tell them they will read about the dream lives of dogs and humans. Say: **As you read, think about why the author wrote the passage. Also look for the claims that the author is making and the evidence given to support these claims.** Then direct students to read the passage and to complete the skill practice activity. Review the answers together. Then have students independently complete the strategy practice activity and compare what they underlined with a partner.

READ THE PASSAGE   Think about why the author wrote the passage and what it is mostly about.

The Battle at Kruger

In September 2004, tourist David Budzinski visited Kruger National Park in South Africa. The eight-minute video that he recorded became an Internet sensation and has been viewed by millions of people all over the world.

The video begins with a herd of Cape buffaloes approaching a watering hole. Nearby, a group of lions wait, hiding from their prey. As soon as the lead buffalo spots the lions, it turns, and the chase is on. The lions separate a small Cape buffalo calf from its mother and knock it into the water. The lions surround the calf and work slowly to pull it back out of the water. Before they are successful, however, a hungry crocodile comes by and grabs the calf's back leg with its powerful jaws. Now the lions are trying to fight off the crocodile!

It may sound like the poor calf was doomed, but what happens next is the reason this video went viral and has had over 64 million hits since it was uploaded in 2007.

As the lions and crocodile are fighting over the calf, the other Cape buffaloes regroup and charge the lions! One buffalo flips a lion into the air with its large horns, and the others stomp and snort at the now-frightened lions. The calf, though injured, manages to stand up and return to its mother in the herd. The angry Cape buffaloes then chase the lions away from the watering hole.

The video of "The Battle at Kruger" is a powerful example of why you should never give up hope, even in the face of a seemingly hopeless situation.

SKILL PRACTICE   Read each question. Fill in the bubble next to the correct answer.

1. The author's main purpose for the passage is to _____.
   Ⓐ describe Kruger National Park
   Ⓑ explain how videos become viral
   Ⓒ give information about Cape buffalo
   Ⓓ inspire readers with an exciting story

2. Which word best describes the author's attitude about the video of "The Battle at Kruger"?
   Ⓐ enthusiastic
   Ⓑ horrified
   Ⓒ curious
   Ⓓ amused

3. The author would probably agree that the video is popular because _____.
   Ⓐ the calf was saved
   Ⓑ there were lions involved
   Ⓒ the video is short
   Ⓓ there are many videos online

4. Which word best describes the author's intended message?
   Ⓐ fear
   Ⓑ hope
   Ⓒ defense
   Ⓓ caution

STRATEGY PRACTICE   What information does the author give to show the supposed hopelessness of the situation?

_____

_____

Name: _____

READ THE PASSAGE   As you read, think about why the author wrote the passage.

A Tale of Two Toxins: The Difference Between Venom and Poison

You have probably heard the words "venomous" and "poisonous" used to describe an animal that uses toxins, or harmful substances, to hunt other animals or defend itself. But these words have specific meanings, and they are not exact synonyms. To find out when a toxin is a poison and when it is venom, read on.

Venom

Venom refers to toxins that an animal stores in one particular place. Snakes such as rattlesnakes, water moccasins, or cobras are venomous because they have toxins stored in glands that connect to their fangs. Spiders, scorpions, jellyfish, and hornets are all examples of venomous creatures.

Poison

Poison refers to toxins that are found throughout an animal's body. The most colorful example of this type of creature is the poison dart frog. These frogs eat insects that are also poisonous (though not to the frogs), and the poisons in the insects then become part of the thin layer of slime that coats the frogs' bodies. Many insects and even some mammals, such as the slow lorax, are examples of poisonous creatures.

A New Purpose

Whether venomous or poisonous, animals use toxins to defend themselves and to help them hunt for food. But these toxins may have another purpose, too. Scientists are using some toxins to help fight diseases in humans.

SKILL PRACTICE   Read each question. Fill in the bubble next to the correct answer.

1. The author's main purpose for writing the passage is to _____.
   Ⓐ explain how animals defend themselves with toxins
   Ⓑ describe how scientists use venom and poison
   Ⓒ inform readers about the difference between venom and poison
   Ⓓ tell readers how to protect themselves from toxic creatures

2. Why does the author include headings in the passage?
   Ⓐ to list the types of toxic animals
   Ⓑ to show the topic of each section
   Ⓒ to compare humans and toxic animals
   Ⓓ to convince readers that toxins are dangerous

3. Why does the author include information about the poison dart frog?
   Ⓐ to explain why they have slime
   Ⓑ to give an example of a poisonous creature
   Ⓒ to link color with being poisonous
   Ⓓ to tell how scientists are using frog toxins

4. What is the author explaining in the section titled "A New Purpose"?
   Ⓐ how toxins may benefit people
   Ⓑ how toxins cause disease
   Ⓒ how each toxin works
   Ⓓ how each type of toxin is different

STRATEGY PRACTICE   Write one question you had while reading the passage.

_____

_____

READ THE FLIER   Look for evidence that supports the author's claims.

The **Academy** of **Goose Defense**

**Dozens of people every year are bitten by rampaging geese.
Don't be a victim! Protect yourself from these feathered bullies!**

**Take my goose
self-defense
class today!**

Don't let the creeps of the
bird world ruin your next
park outing. Be the hero of
your next picnic by standing
up to the geese or running
away calmly. Take my class
at the Academy of Goose
Defense today!

At the Academy of Goose Defense,
here is what you will learn:

• **stern and serious commands** for telling a goose
to leave you alone. My own studies have shown that geese respond
well to specific phrases, such as, "Please take your business
elsewhere," and "I do not appreciate it when you hiss like that."

• **secret techniques** to dodge an angry goose. By studying dozens
of martial-arts movies, I have created a series of jumps and tumbles
that will probably keep you safe from some geese.

• **ways to flee** from a goose without looking like a chicken. When
a goose hisses and flaps its wings, it is telling you that it's getting
ready to hurt you. I know how to leave the scene safely, without
the other geese laughing at me—and I'll teach you, too.

SKILL PRACTICE   Read each question. Fill in the bubble next to the correct answer.

1. Which words from the second bullet point suggest
that the "secret techniques" might not be very
effective?
   Ⓐ "secret" and "dodge"
   Ⓑ "probably" and "some"
   Ⓒ "jumps" and "tumbles"
   Ⓓ "studying" and "created"

2. Why does the author include the paragraph in the
lower-left corner?
   Ⓐ to share information about the academy
   Ⓑ to explain why geese can be dangerous
   Ⓒ to give examples of martial arts techniques
   Ⓓ to persuade people to take the class

3. According to the evidence in the flier, it appears
that the Academy of Goose Defense _____.
   Ⓐ is not a worthwhile class
   Ⓑ offers proven self-defense techniques
   Ⓒ is taught by a well-trained instructor
   Ⓓ has been taken many times

4. Which phrase from the flier provides the best
evidence that geese can be dangerous?
   Ⓐ looking like a chicken
   Ⓑ creeps of the bird world
   Ⓒ bitten by rampaging geese
   Ⓓ geese laughing at me

STRATEGY PRACTICE   Which information in the flier is the most important for determining whether you
trust the author? Why?

_____

_____

READ THE PASSAGE   Think about the evidence the author presents to support the passage's main points.

Where Is Your Place in the Family?

Birth order—does it matter? Are you different because you are the first, second, or third child in your family—or maybe the last of nine?

A Norwegian study found that first-borns have an average IQ that is three points higher than people who fall into a different place in the birth order, perhaps because first-borns often mentor younger brothers and sisters, which reinforces their own skills. In 2007, an international organization of CEOs found that 43% of CEOs are first-borns, 33% are middle children, and 23% are last-borns. First-borns are more likely to be surgeons and astronauts and earn higher salaries. Additionally, MSNBC cites a study showing that nearly all of the U.S. presidents have been the first-born child or the first-born son in their families.

If first-borns are more successful, last-borns are generally more agreeable. They are also more likely to be funny, possibly to get attention from all the bigger people at the dinner table. Mark Twain and Stephen Colbert were both the youngest in large families, and Jim Carrey was the youngest of four. According to a 2007 *Time* magazine article, "The Power of Birth Order," last-borns are more adventurous and more likely to be artists and entrepreneurs.

Then there are the middle children; we have not ignored them! Many middle children lack one-on-one time with their parents. They often feel short-changed: the oldest gets more privileges, and the youngest is "spoiled." Ignored they may be, but middle children tend to grow into well-adjusted, easygoing adults.

Many factors, including genetics, income, and education, make us who we are, but if the research is correct, birth order may be one of the most important factors.

SKILL PRACTICE   Read each question. Fill in the bubble next to the correct answer.

1. Which evidence supports the idea that first-borns may be smarter than their younger siblings?

   Ⓐ Last-borns tend to be more adventurous than their brothers and sisters.

   Ⓑ Middle children sometimes feel neglected.

   Ⓒ First-borns have a higher average IQ than those born later.

   Ⓓ Middle children tend to be well-adjusted adults.

2. Which would be the best evidence that last-borns are likely to be funny and agreeable?

   Ⓐ facts and statistics

   Ⓑ the number of siblings each last-born has

   Ⓒ giving information about last-born IQs

   Ⓓ supporting opinions

3. Which kind of evidence is given about last-born children?

   Ⓐ statistics

   Ⓑ IQ

   Ⓒ a research study

   Ⓓ a magazine article

4. Which idea could use more evidence to support it?

   Ⓐ CEOs are more often first-born.

   Ⓑ Birth order can affect IQ.

   Ⓒ Middle children are easygoing.

   Ⓓ Last-borns are more likely to be artists.

STRATEGY PRACTICE   Write one question you thought of while reading the passage. What is the answer?

_____

_____

READ THE PASSAGE   Think about why the author wrote the passage.

Do Dogs Dream?

Many people feel that dreams are a uniquely human experience, but just as many dog owners will likely disagree. Commonly reported signs of doggy dreams include shaking legs, muffled barks, and snorting.

Scientists confirm that dogs probably do dream. It turns out that dog brains and human brains have many similarities during sleep cycles. Researchers used special machines to measure electrical activity in a dog's brain and a human's brain. Scientists already knew that when humans dream, a certain part of the brain is active during sleep. Researchers discovered that the same part of the brain is active in sleeping dogs. Scientists have other data that back up these findings.

Many people dream that they are trying to move but cannot. Interestingly, part of that experience is not a dream. When people sleep, the brain releases a chemical that causes the dreamer to become temporarily paralyzed. Researchers think this happens so that people cannot physically act out dreams while they are sleeping. Dog brains release the same chemical. In one study during which this chemical was blocked, sleeping test dogs performed physical activities, such as standing up, sniffing around the room for imaginary rabbits, or chasing phantom tennis balls.

Because of these similarities, researchers believe that the content of a dog's dream might come from the same source as a human's dream. "People's dreams are usually based on things they did that day," says Dr. Samantha Hudspith. "So there's reason to believe that dogs dream about the things they've done that day. Of course, there will never be a way to prove this. Dogs cannot describe their dreams the way that humans can."

SKILL PRACTICE   Read each question. Fill in the bubble next to the correct answer.

1. The author's main purpose for the passage is to _____.
   A. interpret the meaning of dreams
   B. entertain dog owners with a fun story
   C. explain what happens when humans and dogs sleep
   D. persuade people that dogs and humans are exactly alike

2. Which of these provides evidence that human and dog brains paralyze the body during sleep?
   A. data showing that brains are active during sleep
   B. Dr. Samantha Hudspith's statement about the content of dreams
   C. researchers measuring electrical activity during dreams
   D. the study blocking a chemical in the brain during sleep

3. Which of these statements would the author most likely agree with?
   A. There is much evidence to support the idea that dogs dream.
   B. The evidence to support the idea that dogs dream is unreliable.
   C. Scientific ideas are not worth considering.
   D. Animal dreams are too difficult to explain.

4. Which statement best supports the idea that dog and human brains are similar during sleep?
   A. Researchers measured brain activities of dogs and humans.
   B. Dog and human brains release a paralyzing chemical.
   C. Dogs and humans dream about what they did that day.
   D. Dogs and humans sleep every night.

STRATEGY PRACTICE   Locate and underline the most important information in each paragraph.

Compare and Contrast

Students practice comparing and contrasting by looking at the similarities and differences between two or more people or things.

Make Inferences

Students practice making inferences by using clues in a passage to understand what is being implied.

DAY 1

Introduce the *Compare and Contrast* skill to students. Say: **To compare, we tell how two or more things are alike. To contrast, we tell how they are different. Looking for similarities and differences between topics in a text can help you better understand the author's points.** Remind students of the *Make Connections* strategy (Week 2). Say: **As you read, make a text-to-self connection. Think about how you would have liked living in feudal Japan.** Have students read the instructions at the top of the page and then the passage. When students have finished reading, direct them to complete the skill and strategy practice activities. Review the answers together.

DAY 2

Remind students of the *Compare and Contrast* skill. Then tell students they are going to read about dragon stories from two different cultures. Remind students of the *Organization* strategy (Week 4). Say: **As you read, pay attention to how each paragraph is organized. Also pay attention to the overall organization of the passage.** Have students read the instructions at the top of the page and then the passage. When students have finished reading, direct them to complete the skill and strategy practice activities. Review the answers together.

DAY 3

Introduce the *Make Inferences* skill to students. Say: **You can think of making inferences as "reading between the lines," or looking for information that is not directly stated in the text. Good readers use clues from the text and their own prior knowledge or experiences to make inferences while reading.** Remind students of the *Make Connections* strategy. Say: **You can use prior knowledge to infer information that is hinted at within a passage.** Direct students to read the passage and to complete the skill and strategy practice activities. Review the answers together.

DAY 4

Remind students of the *Make Inferences* skill. Say: **When we make inferences, we use our own background knowledge and clues from the text to fill in information that we have not been told directly.** Remind students of the *Organization* strategy. Say: **Some authors organize information to create suspense or drama. Look for this type of organization as you read about a famous painting, *Mona Lisa*, and what happened when it was stolen.** Then have students read the passage. Direct them to complete the skill and strategy practice activities, and review the answers together.

DAY 5

Tell students they will practice both the *Compare and Contrast* and *Make Inferences* skills by reading about the typical diets of nobility and peasants during the Renaissance. Then remind students of the *Make Connections* strategy. Say: **As you read, make text-to-world connections by thinking about similarities and differences between the past and the present.** When students have finished reading, direct them to complete the skill and strategy practice activities. Review the answers together.

READ THE PASSAGE   Think about how the groups of people in feudal Japan were alike and different.

Leaders in Feudal Japan

In feudal Japan, from roughly 1200 to 1900, there were two main groups that made up the class system—nobles and peasants. The nobles were made up of the wealthiest and most powerful people. In descending order, the nobles consisted of emperors, shoguns, daimyos, and samurai. People from the higher class could punish people in the lower class for not showing proper respect. It was very important to know about and recognize members of each group.

The emperor was in charge of feudal Japan in name, but he actually held very little military power. While the emperor was the wealthiest person in the country and was the religious leader, he was a figurehead, or false leader. The emperor received money and goods from all of Japan, but he lacked the authority to make military decisions.

The leader of the feudal Japanese military was called the shogun. The shogun had power over all of Japan's warriors, who protected Japan's land and interests. Even though the shogun title was usually passed down in a family line, some shoguns seized power through force.

The daimyos were the next most important group. Daimyos built imposing castles, bought and sold land, and employed vast groups of people to work on their properties. People could easily identify daimyos because of their colorful clothing, which included specific colors determined by rank and wealth.

Even though many modern people are familiar with Japanese samurai, they were at the bottom of the ruling class in feudal Japan. Samurai were powerful warriors who fought for the military. They were cared for by the people of Japan, but they served under the daimyos, shoguns, and emperors.

SKILL PRACTICE   Read each question. Fill in the bubble next to the correct answer.

1. How was the emperor different from other leaders in feudal Japan?
   - Ⓐ He was the most powerful daimyo.
   - Ⓑ He led armies of samurai.
   - Ⓒ He was the country's spiritual leader.
   - Ⓓ He was an important military leader.

2. How were the emperors and shoguns alike?
   - Ⓐ They both fought battles in the military.
   - Ⓑ They both built large, imposing castles.
   - Ⓒ They both wore clothes with special colors.
   - Ⓓ They were both members of the noble class.

3. Shoguns and samurai were alike because both were _____.
   - Ⓐ religious leaders
   - Ⓑ involved in the military
   - Ⓒ given titles through family lines
   - Ⓓ employed by daimyos

4. Which group had the most wealth?
   - Ⓐ emperors
   - Ⓑ samurai
   - Ⓒ daimyos
   - Ⓓ shoguns

STRATEGY PRACTICE   If you were a noble in feudal Japan, which group would you most want to be part of? Why?

_____

_____

READ THE PASSAGE   Look for details that tell how Chinese and European dragons are alike and different.

Dragons of China and Europe

Dragons appear in fictional stories from around the world, but not all dragons are alike. The dragons that appear in myths from European countries are huge, terrifying, fire-breathing creatures that are shaped like reptiles with wings. They serve as a force of evil and, in famous stories dating from ancient times, must be slain by the heroes of their tales. Legendary heroes such as Hercules, St. George, and Beowulf all fought and killed evil dragons in order to prove their worth.

The dragons that appear in Chinese stories, however, are generally symbols of spiritual power. Similar creatures exist in myths from other countries throughout Asia. Chinese dragons symbolically serve as protection against evil forces in the world. They are shaped like long snakes; they do not have wings or breathe fire. Because of their power, these dragons were historically associated with the emperors of China. The symbol of the dragon is still used today on buildings, on monuments, and even on the clothing of powerful people. During Chinese New Year celebrations, men and boys carry huge dragon puppets and dance with them in parades.

Though the mythical dragons of Asia and Europe are different, they may have a common source. Some experts claim that dragon stories were originally created because ancient people found dinosaur fossils. Because they lacked knowledge about what the dinosaurs were, these people imagined the kind of animal the bones could have come from—huge reptilian dragons.

SKILL PRACTICE   Read each question. Fill in the bubble next to the correct answer.

1. How are Chinese dragons different from European dragons?
   Ⓐ They have appeared in stories for centuries.
   Ⓑ They must be slain by a hero.
   Ⓒ They breathe fire.
   Ⓓ They are a symbol of spiritual power.

2. What do European dragons have that Chinese dragons do not have?
   Ⓐ wings
   Ⓑ heads
   Ⓒ large bodies
   Ⓓ great power

3. According to the passage, European and Chinese dragons both appear _____.
   Ⓐ in parades
   Ⓑ on buildings
   Ⓒ on clothing
   Ⓓ in stories

4. The source of both European and Asian dragons might be _____.
   Ⓐ symbols
   Ⓑ snakes
   Ⓒ dinosaurs
   Ⓓ monuments

STRATEGY PRACTICE   How does the author organize the information about the two kinds of dragons?

_____

_____

Name: _____

READ THE PASSAGE   Use clues from the passage to make inferences about the peppered moth.

The Peppered Moth

Natural selection is the process by which one type of animal within a species thrives because of certain characteristics that make it more likely to live than others in its group. The history of the peppered moth is an example of the natural selection process.

In nineteenth-century England, certain types of peppered moths were able to better blend into their surroundings. During that time period, great changes were happening in Great Britain. The Industrial Revolution was part of this change, and with it came air pollution. Natural selection often takes hundreds or even thousands of years to occur. For the peppered moth, this process occurred relatively quickly.

At the beginning of the Industrial Age, most peppered moths in England were light-colored and speckled with black markings, although a few moths had dark-colored wings. Because the light-colored moths blended into the light-colored bark on the trees, they could not be easily seen by birds that would eat them. As the air grew more polluted, however, tree trunks became covered with soot and became darker. The light-colored moths became easy for birds to see against the dark tree trunks. Since the dark-colored moths now had the advantage, their numbers grew. Within 50 years, the peppered moth went from being mostly light-colored to being mostly dark-colored.

In the twentieth century, the air significantly cleared up, and the peppered moth population changed again. As tree trunks lightened due to less soot in the air, light-colored moths once again had an advantage. Their numbers increased as soot levels declined. Depending on their environment, the coloration of the moths helped them to be "naturally selected" to survive.

SKILL PRACTICE   Read each question. Fill in the bubble next to the correct answer.

1. What can you infer about the peppered moth's natural selection process?

Ⓐ It was normal for the time period.

Ⓑ The length of time was unusual.

Ⓒ The soot levels in England did not affect it.

Ⓓ This type of color change is typical for moths.

2. Which statement is most likely true?

Ⓐ Dark-colored moths were originally easy to see on trees.

Ⓑ Both kinds of moths were decreasing in number.

Ⓒ The color of the moths was not important.

Ⓓ Birds prefer the taste of light-colored moths.

3. Which would mostly likely happen if soot darkened England's trees again?

Ⓐ Birds would eat fewer moths.

Ⓑ Light-colored moths would become a problem.

Ⓒ Moths would not be able to stay alive.

Ⓓ The population of dark-colored moths would increase.

4. You can infer from the passage that the birds in England _____.

Ⓐ did not like the taste of the pepper moth

Ⓑ were always able to find enough moths to eat

Ⓒ were dangerously affected by the soot levels

Ⓓ changed colors to adapt to their environment

STRATEGY PRACTICE   Describe an experience that natural selection reminds you of.

_____

_____

READ THE PASSAGE   Think about how the author organizes the events in the passage.

Stealing *Mona Lisa*

Leonardo da Vinci's *Mona Lisa* is perhaps the most famous painting in the world. The mysterious smile of the woman in the portrait has intrigued viewers for hundreds of years and has drawn millions of visitors to the museum in which it hangs—the Louvre in Paris, France.

About a hundred years ago, in August of 1911, *Mona Lisa* was stolen from the Louvre. The people of France were distraught, fearing that the painting had been destroyed. The police had few leads in the case and made only one arrest. They believed that Guillaume Apollinaire, a famous poet and art critic, might have stolen the painting, but he was quickly released. While in custody, he tried to blame another famous artist for the theft—Pablo Picasso.

As it turned out, neither man was involved with the infamous theft. Two years after *Mona Lisa* was stolen, a man who claimed to have the painting contacted an Italian art dealer. This man, Vincenzo Peruggia, offered the painting to the art dealer. There was just one condition—the art dealer would have to keep the painting in Italy instead of sending it back to France. Even though the art dealer believed that Peruggia might not have the painting, he contacted the police anyway. When the art dealer met Peruggia, he found that the man's story was true. Peruggia, a former handyman at the Louvre, had stolen the painting. He was quickly arrested and convicted of the crime. *Mona Lisa* survived intact and was returned to the Louvre in Paris, where it is still on display.

SKILL PRACTICE   Read each question. Fill in the bubble next to the correct answer.

1. You can infer that the police quickly released Guillaume Apollinaire because they _____.
   Ⓐ believed he was guilty
   Ⓑ did not have enough evidence to charge him with the crime
   Ⓒ believed Pablo Picasso stole the painting
   Ⓓ thought if they released him, he would lead them to the real thief

2. What can you infer from the fact that the police made only one arrest before Vincenzo Peruggia?
   Ⓐ The police had few clues to work with.
   Ⓑ The police were not concerned about the theft.
   Ⓒ Peruggia was good at hiding from the police.
   Ⓓ The art dealer kept information from the police.

3. Why did the Italian art dealer contact the police?
   Ⓐ He wanted *Mona Lisa* to stay in Italy.
   Ⓑ He was working with Apollinaire.
   Ⓒ He wanted to help return the painting to the Louvre.
   Ⓓ He wanted to sell the painting to the police.

4. Which was most likely Peruggia's main motive for the theft of the painting?
   Ⓐ to gain money
   Ⓑ to give it to Italy
   Ⓒ to become famous
   Ⓓ to help the Louvre

STRATEGY PRACTICE   How does the author use the passage's organization to make the story exciting?

_____

_____

READ THE PASSAGE Think about how Renaissance diets were alike and different.

Renaissance Diets: Peasant vs. Noble

During the sixteenth and seventeenth centuries, a time period known as the Renaissance, the most common food in England for both rich and poor was bread. Grains such as rye and barley were ground and baked to form heavy loaves. People used the bread to hold meat (if they were lucky enough to have meat) and to soak up grease, such as lard, used in cooking. The nobility and peasants alike did not eat many raw vegetables, believing that raw fruits and vegetables could make them sick. They did, however, use some vegetables and herbs, such as onions and garlic, in their cooking.

Members of wealthy families had access to more types of food than the poor did. Once explorers landed in the New World (North and South America), they brought back samples of many fruits and vegetables that were new to Europe, such as melons, oranges, lemons, potatoes, and tomatoes. Nobles then grew these foods in their gardens and served them to guests. Along with these imports, sugar cane from the New World provided the rich with a new sweetener for foods and beverages. They also feasted on many types of meat and fish.

Peasants during the Renaissance had a much less varied diet. They did not eat nearly as much meat (or nearly as much of anything) as their wealthy counterparts. For the most part, they ate bread and simple soups or stews. As with other periods in history, people's economic status had a significant impact on their diet—and their health.

SKILL PRACTICE Read each question. Fill in the bubble next to the correct answer.

1. Unlike wealthy members of society, peasants during the Renaissance ate mostly _____.
   Ⓐ tomatoes and potatoes
   Ⓑ bread, soups, and stews
   Ⓒ foods from the New World
   Ⓓ roasted meats and fish

2. Because mainly the nobles used sugar, you can conclude that sugar was probably _____.
   Ⓐ expensive
   Ⓑ simple
   Ⓒ nutritious
   Ⓓ important

3. Both the rich and the poor ate a lot of _____.
   Ⓐ fruits
   Ⓑ vegetables
   Ⓒ bread
   Ⓓ meats

4. What can you infer about the foods of the nobility during the Renaissance?
   Ⓐ People took great pride in foods from their homeland.
   Ⓑ The foods that people ate were all the same.
   Ⓒ Simple foods were highly valued.
   Ⓓ Having foods from the New World showed their status.

STRATEGY PRACTICE Do you think the diets of wealthy and poor people are as different today as they were during the Renaissance? Explain.

_____

_____

Character and Setting

Students practice analyzing character and setting by looking at the traits and motivations of a character and where and when a passage's events take place.

Theme

Students practice identifying the theme by looking for the central message or lesson in a passage.

DAY 1

Introduce the *Character and Setting* skill to students. Say: **Characters are the people, animals, or creatures in a fictional story. In nonfiction passages, the characters are real people. You can learn more about a character by thinking about the character's actions and words. The setting is where and when a passage or story takes place.** Tell students they are going to read about a real-life long-distance swimmer. Say: **Think about *why* Diana Nyad challenges herself to swim so far and so often.** Then remind students of the *Monitor Comprehension* strategy (Week 1). Say: **As you read, pause briefly to think about what you have learned.** Have students read the instructions at the top of the page and then the passage. When students have finished, direct them to complete the skill and strategy practice activities. Review the answers together.

DAY 2

Remind students of the *Character and Setting* skill. Say: **You are going to read about Vlad Dracula, who was a real person. As you read, you can compare him to what you already know about the fictional Dracula.** Then remind students of the *Visualization* strategy (Week 3). Say: **As you read, visualize what Vlad Dracula's castles may have looked like.** Have students read the passage. When students have finished, direct them to complete the skill and strategy practice activities. Review the answers together.

DAY 3

Introduce the *Theme* skill to students. Say: **Many fictional stories have been shared throughout time as a way to teach readers certain lessons, or morals. A theme is a message or lesson that is embedded within a passage. You may often understand the theme only after you have read the entire passage and paused to think about what you have read.** Then remind students of the *Monitor Comprehension* strategy. Say: **Stay focused as you read the passage. If you are distracted, pause and go back a few sentences to ensure you did not miss anything.** When students have finished, direct them to complete the skill practice activity. Review the answers together. Then have students complete the strategy practice activity, and discuss the theme of the passage as a group.

DAY 4

Remind students of the *Theme* skill. Say: **When you look for a theme in a nonfiction passage, focus on the author's main point or message. Ask: *What is the author trying to teach me?*** Then remind students of the *Visualization* strategy. Say: **As you read, visualize the observation cages. Imagine how they look and how the sharks approach them.** Have students read the passage. Then direct students to complete the skill and strategy practice activities. Review the answers together.

DAY 5

Tell students they will practice both the *Character and Setting* and *Theme* skills by reading about an important moment in baseball history. Encourage students to focus on Joe DiMaggio's actions and words in order to understand his personal character and the passage's theme. Then remind students of the *Monitor Comprehension* strategy. Say: **Note any parts of the passage that you have difficulty understanding and read them again after you have finished.** Have students read the passage. When students have finished, direct them to complete the skill and strategy practice activities. Review the answers together.

Name: _____

READ THE PASSAGE   Look for details in the passage about Diana Nyad and her accomplishments.

Diana Nyad, Marathon Swimmer

Diana Nyad, born in 1949, is one of the world's greatest long-distance swimmers. She started as a speed swimmer, winning races in high school and dreaming of the Olympics. However, Nyad fell ill with heart disease before she could compete in the 1968 Olympic Games and had to spend three months in bed. By the time Nyad was better, she was unable to swim as fast as she had previously.

Nyad then turned from speed swimming to distance swimming. Her first race was 10 miles in the cold waters of Lake Ontario. Even though she came in tenth place, she was the first woman ever to complete the course. In 1974, Nyad set a record while swimming a 22-mile race in the Bay of Naples, Italy. That same year she tried to swim back and forth across Lake Ontario, a total of 64 miles. Nyad successfully made it across the giant lake, but on the return trip, she lost consciousness and had to be pulled from the water. In 1975, she swam around Manhattan Island, a distance of 28 miles, in a record 7 hours and 57 minutes. Three years later she swam 102 miles from the Bahamas to Florida.

In 2010, at the age of 61, Nyad announced she would swim from Cuba to Florida. In order to train, Nyad spent as many as 14 hours a day swimming in the ocean. The swim from Cuba to Florida would last at least 60 hours and cover 103 miles. Unfortunately, bad weather forced Nyad to wait until the next year. In 2011, Nyad attempted the swim but was blown off course after being in the water for 29 hours. Nyad attempted the swim again a few months later, but she had to stop because of multiple jellyfish stings.

Despite these setbacks, Nyad continues to persevere and plans to eventually make the Cuba-to-Florida swim. She has vowed to never stop swimming and wants other older Americans to understand that it is never too late to make one's dreams come true.

SKILL PRACTICE   Read each question. Fill in the bubble next to the correct answer.

1. When Diana Nyad turned from speed to distance swimming, it showed that she _____.
   Ⓐ did not want to go to the Olympics
   Ⓑ never found success as a speed swimmer
   Ⓒ liked distance races better than speed races
   Ⓓ was devoted to the sport of swimming

2. What was the world of competitive swimming probably like in the early 1970s?
   Ⓐ There were few female distance swimmers.
   Ⓑ Distance swimmers competed only in the U.S.
   Ⓒ Many Olympic records were being broken.
   Ⓓ Distance swimming was more popular than speed swimming.

3. Why was the Bahamas–Florida swim probably easier to complete than the swim across Lake Ontario and back?
   Ⓐ She was younger then.
   Ⓑ It was before she became ill.
   Ⓒ The water was warmer.
   Ⓓ It was a shorter distance.

4. Which word best describes Nyad?
   Ⓐ reckless
   Ⓑ determined
   Ⓒ sickly
   Ⓓ imaginative

STRATEGY PRACTICE   Did you understand Diana Nyad's need to challenge herself? Why or why not?

_____

_____

READ THE PASSAGE   Think about whom the passage is about and where the events took place.

The Real Dracula

You have probably heard of the fictional vampire named Dracula. Did you know he may have been based on a real person? Vlad Dracula ruled in Walachia (located in present-day Romania) during the mid-1400s. He was the second son of Vlad Dracul, who got his surname from being in the Order of the Dragon. When Vlad Dracula's father and older brother were killed, Vlad Dracula assumed leadership in Walachia. Because the rural farming society was frequently invaded by neighboring principalities, he spent his life trying to keep the Hungarian kingdom and the Ottoman (Turkish) Empire from taking over his homeland. Following his death, he became known as Vlad Tepes, which translates to Vlad the Impaler.

Vlad Dracula was known for his exceptional cruelty, which he showed to peasants, noblemen, friends, and enemies alike. His nickname, Vlad the Impaler, came about because of his favorite way to execute people—by painfully impaling them on stakes and placing them in public view. It is estimated that Vlad Dracula killed between 40,000 and 100,000 people in his lifetime.

Although exact information about Vlad Dracula's homes has been lost to history, tourists still flock to the legendary fortresses where it is believed he lived. One of his likely residences, Castle Poenari, is a ruin now. It stands high on a cliff overlooking a deep gorge and is said to be haunted. Visitors to the ruin must climb almost 1,500 steps to reach it. Another castle, Castle Bran, is called Dracula's Castle and is a major tourist attraction in Romania. It has been renovated several times in its 600-year history, but it still looks like something out of a fairy tale.

In 1897 author Bram Stoker wrote a novel about a vampire named Dracula. Stoker chose the name believing it was the Romanian word for "devil." Stories began to circulate that Vlad Dracula, like the fictional Dracula, had been a vampire. From then on, the legends of the ruler grew greater—and bloodier—than ever before.

SKILL PRACTICE   Read each question. Fill in the bubble next to the correct answer.

1. Which word best describes Vlad Dracula?
   Ⓐ ghostly
   Ⓑ creative
   Ⓒ brutal
   Ⓓ resourceful

2. Stories about Vlad Dracula being a vampire began because _____.
   Ⓐ he really was a vampire
   Ⓑ he killed so many people
   Ⓒ his origins were so mysterious
   Ⓓ a fictional vampire had the same name

3. Where can tourists see Vlad Dracula castles?
   Ⓐ Romania
   Ⓑ Turkey
   Ⓒ Hungary
   Ⓓ Dracul

4. Why is Vlad Dracula also known as Vlad the Impaler?
   Ⓐ because that was also his father's name
   Ⓑ because of the way he executed people
   Ⓒ because of Bram Stoker's *Dracula*
   Ⓓ because of the names of Romanian castles

STRATEGY PRACTICE   Underline words or phrases from the passage that help you visualize the setting.

READ THE FOLK TALE   Think about the moral, or lesson, of the story.

Too Small, Too Loud

Once there was a man who lived in a house that he despised. He thought his house was far too loud. His neighbors lived nearby, and he could hear them shouting through the walls. The birds outside made a terrible racket. Even the sound of the wind blowing and the rain falling on the roof bothered the man. He also believed that his house was not large enough: it had very few rooms, and the furniture made it seem cramped and crowded. Finally, fed up, the man went to the wise woman of the village and asked her what to do.

"I have the answer," she replied. "You must bring your chickens, your sheep, your goats, and your cow to live in your house with you. Only then will you be able to solve the problem you are facing."

The man thought this advice was very peculiar and went home thinking he had wasted his time. But as the days passed and the man's discomfort grew, he finally decided to follow the wise woman's advice. He brought all the animals indoors. Now, he could barely move without tripping over a goat or a sheep, and the noise from the cackling chickens and mooing cow was unbearable. He went back to see the wise woman.

"Your advice has made the situation worse," the man cried. "What should I do now?"

The woman smiled and nodded sagely. "Yes, that is exactly what I thought would happen. This is very good. Now go home and empty your house of all the livestock. Put the animals back in their pens."

The man went home and did as the wise woman suggested. As soon as the last chicken had been ushered out of the house, the man was astonished by how big and quiet it now seemed.

SKILL PRACTICE   Read each question. Fill in the bubble next to the correct answer.

1. **What is the man's complaint?**
   - Ⓐ He thinks his house is too big.
   - Ⓑ He feels his house is too tiny and noisy.
   - Ⓒ He is very lonely and bored.
   - Ⓓ He does not know what to do with his animals.

2. **What happens when the man brings his animals inside?**
   - Ⓐ The house seems smaller and louder.
   - Ⓑ The wise woman gives the man advice.
   - Ⓒ The animals do not like living inside.
   - Ⓓ The neighbors complain about the noise.

3. **The wise woman tells the man to put the animals back outside so he will _____.**
   - Ⓐ stop bothering her with his silly problem
   - Ⓑ find new ways to organize his house
   - Ⓒ spend more time with his neighbors
   - Ⓓ realize the house seems large and peaceful without them

4. **Which of the following best describes the passage's theme?**
   - Ⓐ Silence is golden.
   - Ⓑ Animals belong outside.
   - Ⓒ Everything is relative.
   - Ⓓ Every house has problems.

STRATEGY PRACTICE   Do you understand the point the author is trying to make? Why or why not?

_____

_____

READ THE PASSAGE Think about the message of the passage.

Swimming with the Sharks

Marine biologist Luke Tipple has spent a lot of time in shark cages. People use shark cages, which are underwater structures with metal bars, to observe and study dangerous sharks, especially great white sharks. The practice of using shark cages is very controversial; the sharks are lured with bait so that scientists or tourists inside the very large cages can watch them. Despite some people's objections, Tipple feels that shark cages are a safe, effective way to study great whites.

One argument against using shark cages is that baiting sharks interferes with the natural world and may make sharks more likely to attack humans in the wild. An incident from 2007, in which a great white shark attacked a shark cage off Guadalupe Island, Mexico, is often cited as evidence for this claim. Tipple feels that in that case, the bait was badly positioned, causing the shark to crash into the cage and get caught in its bars. He believes the shark did not attack at all—it was just trying to escape.

Tipple now runs a shark diving company. He points out that the practice of using shark cages has benefits for both humans and sharks. Shark cages allow scientists to study sharks up close in their natural environment, especially the endangered great white shark. And it gives non-scientists a way to observe and understand sharks, which are generally feared. This contact between human and shark makes it far more likely, in Tipple's view, that people will support shark conservation.

SKILL PRACTICE Read each question. Fill in the bubble next to the correct answer.

1. Why do some people object to using shark cages?
   Ⓐ They feel that feeding the sharks will make them rely on people.
   Ⓑ They believe the cages can kill sharks.
   Ⓒ They feel that luring sharks interferes with nature.
   Ⓓ They do not believe that people should study sharks.

2. Luke Tipple thinks shark cages are beneficial for scientists because the cages _____.
   Ⓐ help scientists study sharks in nature
   Ⓑ allow scientists to capture wild sharks
   Ⓒ show scientists how sharks react to metal
   Ⓓ allow scientists to get funding from tourists

3. Tipple approves of using shark cages for tourists so they will _____.
   Ⓐ learn to fear sharks
   Ⓑ help to feed sharks
   Ⓒ better understand sharks
   Ⓓ stay away from sharks

4. One theme of the passage is that _____.
   Ⓐ scientists should be careful when doing research
   Ⓑ wild animals can be tamed with bait
   Ⓒ sharks are not dangerous creatures
   Ⓓ greater understanding can lead to greater protection

STRATEGY PRACTICE Imagine you are observing sharks from inside a shark cage. Describe your visualization.

_____

_____

READ THE PASSAGE   Pay attention to the people, events, and locations in the passage.

Batter Up!

It is May 15, 1941. The New York Yankees baseball team is playing the Chicago White Sox at Yankee Stadium in New York City. The Yankees are in fourth place in the American League. Ted Williams has been leading the Boston Red Sox with an incredible batting average. In contrast, Yankees centerfielder Joe DiMaggio has been in a hitting slump. But on this day, he hits a single. The Yankees lose the game, but the world's greatest hitting streak has begun.

Between May 15 and July 16, the Yankees play 56 games. In each one, DiMaggio hits the ball and gets safely to first base at least once. In game after game, he makes one, two, or three base hits. Encouraged by the streak, the Yankees do better and better and are soon on their way to the World Series.

Then on July 17, everything changes. DiMaggio takes a taxi to the ballfield in Cleveland, Ohio. The cabdriver tells the ballplayer that he has a strange feeling the hitting streak will end that day. DiMaggio is thrown out on his first turn at bat, walks on his second, is thrown out on his third, and hits into a double-play on his fourth at-bat. The streak is over. Despite the end of the hitting streak, the Yankees go on to beat the National League's Brooklyn Dodgers in the World Series later that year.

To this day, Joe DiMaggio is considered one of the greatest ballplayers of all time. He is widely praised for the amazing 1941 streak in which he had 91 hits out of 223 at-bats, exceeding Williams's batting average. Years later, when asked whether he felt the cabdriver had jinxed him on that last day of the streak, DiMaggio replied, "I told him he hadn't. My number was up."

SKILL PRACTICE   Read each question. Fill in the bubble next to the correct answer.

1. Where did Joe DiMaggio's hitting streak begin?
   Ⓐ New York City
   Ⓑ Cleveland
   Ⓒ Chicago
   Ⓓ Boston

2. DiMaggio's attitude toward the cabdriver shows that DiMaggio was _____.
   Ⓐ resentful
   Ⓑ embarrassed
   Ⓒ good-natured
   Ⓓ angry

3. On the day the hitting streak began, the Yankees _____.
   Ⓐ beat the White Sox
   Ⓑ were in fourth place
   Ⓒ were in the World Series
   Ⓓ took a taxi to the ballfield

4. The 1941 Yankee performance illustrates the theme that _____.
   Ⓐ one person can inspire many others
   Ⓑ baseball is the world's best sport
   Ⓒ words can affect someone's fortune
   Ⓓ sports bring strangers together

STRATEGY PRACTICE   List two important facts from the passage about Joe DiMaggio.

_____

_____

Cause and Effect

Students practice identifying cause-and-effect relationships by looking for what happens (the effect) and why it happens (the cause).

Prediction

Students practice using clues from a passage to predict what will happen next.

DAY 1

Introduce the *Cause and Effect* skill to students. Say: **You can find causes and effects by thinking about what happens and why. You are going to read about different kinds of baseball pitches. As you read, think about why a pitcher would use a certain pitch and what effect that pitch might have.** Remind students of the *Ask Questions* strategy (Week 6). Say: **As you read, pause to think about any questions you have about the content.** Have students read the instructions at the top of the page and then the passage. Tell students to write any questions they have in the strategy practice activity section while they are reading. When students have finished, direct them to complete the skill practice activity. Review the answers together.

DAY 2

Remind students of the *Cause and Effect* skill. Remind them that some passages include one cause-and-effect relationship while others may have multiple causes and effects. Tell students they are going to read about why insects can be a beneficial part of a person's diet. Then remind students of the *Make Connections* strategy (Week 2). Say: **You can make a text-to-world connection by thinking about how various world populations are different from your own.** Have students read the passage. When students have finished, direct them to complete the skill and strategy practice activities. Review the answers together.

DAY 3

Introduce the *Prediction* skill to students. Say: **When you read a nonfiction passage, you can make predictions about things that might happen in the future based on what you read. Look for details within the passage that offer clues about future probabilities.** Then remind students of the *Ask Questions* strategy. Say: **Asking questions about what you have read is a good way to check that you understood everything in the passage.** Have students read the passage. When students have finished, direct them to complete the skill practice activity. Review the answers together. For the strategy practice activity, have partners work together to ask and answer questions.

DAY 4

Review the *Prediction* skill with students. Explain that they are going to read a passage about Africanized honeybees, which are often referred to as African killer bees. Tell students to use what they know and what they read to predict how people or bees might react in certain situations. Remind students of the *Make Connections* strategy. Say: **Make a personal connection to the text by thinking about how you feel about the bees after you have read the passage.** Then have students read the instructions at the top of the page and the passage. When students have finished reading, direct them to complete the skill and strategy practice activities. Review the answers together.

DAY 5

Tell students that they will practice both the *Cause and Effect* and *Prediction* skills by reading a passage about how cellphones have changed over time. Then remind students of the *Ask Questions* strategy. Say: **As you read, note any questions you have about the passage's content.** Then have students read the passage. When students have finished, direct them to complete the skill and strategy practice activities. Review the answers together.

READ THE PASSAGE   Think about the different types of pitches detailed in the passage.

A Pitcher's Secret Weapons

Fastballs, breaking balls, and changeups—these are the three types of pitches that good pitchers throw during baseball games. Pitchers know that the key to pitching a good game is being unpredictable. By learning a variety of pitches, pitchers can keep batters guessing—and missing!

Fastballs The fastball is the most common type of pitch in baseball. Pitchers throw fastballs with backspin, which means the ball spins backward while it moves forward through the air. Backspin helps the ball travel faster through the air because the seams on the baseball whip the air as the ball spins, moving it out of the way. Pitchers use fastballs in order to make the balls simply too fast for batters to hit. Fastballs are also easier on a pitcher's arm than some other types of pitches.

Breaking Balls You may have heard of curveballs or sliders, two types of breaking ball pitches. Breaking balls "break," or move left, right, up, or down, as they travel. The direction that a breaking ball moves depends on how the pitcher holds the ball and how the pitcher uses his or her arm, shoulder, and wrist. Pitchers like breaking balls because they are difficult for batters to follow, but they are hard on a pitcher's arm and can cause serious injury if the pitch is thrown poorly.

Changeups Changeups are sometimes called "slow balls" because they travel more slowly than most other pitches. A changeup is thrown just like a fastball, which usually makes the batter think a fast pitch is coming. But the ball is held in the pitcher's hand differently, which is why it travels more slowly than a fastball would. Pitchers use changeups to throw a batter's timing off. Batters often swing early at changeups.

SKILL PRACTICE   Read each question. Fill in the bubble next to the correct answer.

1. Pitchers like to throw breaking balls because they _____.

   Ⓐ are too fast for batters to hit

   Ⓑ confuse a batter's timing

   Ⓒ are hard for batters to track

   Ⓓ are easy to throw

2. One reason pitchers might throw more fastballs than breaking balls is because _____.

   Ⓐ fastballs are harder for batters to hit

   Ⓑ throwing breaking balls is harder on a pitcher's arm

   Ⓒ batters are not used to swinging at fastballs

   Ⓓ breaking balls are the most common type of pitch thrown

3. What is the main reason pitchers learn to throw many kinds of pitches?

   Ⓐ to keep batters confused during the game

   Ⓑ to show off their athletic abilities

   Ⓒ to keep fans interested in the game

   Ⓓ to prevent their throwing arm from getting tired

4. A changeup travels more slowly than a fastball because of _____.

   Ⓐ the direction that the ball spins

   Ⓑ how the ball slides left or right

   Ⓒ how the batter swings at the ball

   Ⓓ how the pitcher holds the ball

STRATEGY PRACTICE   Write one question you thought of while reading the passage.

_____

_____

READ THE PASSAGE   Think about why some people include insects in their diet.

Bugs for Dinner

How is this for a menu: an appetizer of beetle larvae followed by fried caterpillars and then chocolate-covered grasshoppers for dessert. In many countries around the world, insects are part of the everyday diet. In fact, many people who are concerned about nutrition and future supplies of food think people should take a second look at eating insects.

Around 2,000 different species of insects are edible. Insects often contain more protein, fat, and carbohydrates than fish or beef. They can provide more energy than other sources of protein. Many also have high levels of vitamins and minerals necessary for good health. In addition, insects are easy to raise and use fewer resources, so they are a cheaper and more sustainable food source than processed foods. Valuing insects as food could eventually lead to the protection of the wild habitats where they live. Raising insects for food can create new jobs and income in places where there is great poverty and low employment.

The main problem in promoting insects as food is known as the "ick factor," the squeamishness that many people feel when they consider eating bugs. But opinions about food, like many things, are determined by the culture. For example, shrimp is a beloved food in the United States, but in some parts of Africa, people think shrimp is disgusting compared to a juicy and delicious red ant.

SKILL PRACTICE   Read each question. Fill in the bubble next to the correct answer.

1. Which of these is determined by culture?
   Ⓐ the cost of insects
   Ⓑ insects' nutritional value
   Ⓒ the popularity of a food
   Ⓓ job creation

2. How might eating more insects lead to protection of the habitats where insects live?
   Ⓐ If people value the insects, they will want to protect areas where the insects live.
   Ⓑ If people value insects, the government will make it illegal to gather them in the wild.
   Ⓒ People will decide to move closer to areas with the most insects, which will lead to protection.
   Ⓓ People will need protection because the habitats might become dangerous.

3. People in some parts of Africa eat red ants because they _____.
   Ⓐ like the taste of red ants
   Ⓑ have nothing else to eat
   Ⓒ cannot get shrimp
   Ⓓ want to create more jobs

4. According to the passage, eating insects might be better than eating beef because _____.
   Ⓐ insects taste better than beef
   Ⓑ most insects are edible
   Ⓒ people can get jobs raising insects
   Ⓓ insects have more nutrients than beef

STRATEGY PRACTICE   Think of a food you eat that is not eaten in another culture or population. Why do you think this difference in diet exists?

_____

_____

Look for clues in the passage that can help you make predictions about the future of Tasmanian devils.

The Plight of the Tasmanian Devil

You may have seen cartoons featuring the Tasmanian devil—a crazed, snarling beast that spins in a furious circle when it is angry. Real Tasmanian devils do have rather nasty personalities. They will bare their sharp teeth and growl when defending themselves. Tasmanian devils are in terrible trouble, though, and despite their bad reputation, these animals need help.

In 1996, scientists began noticing large tumors on the faces of Tasmanian devils. The tumors are caused by a cancer that, unlike other cancers, is spread through bites. Only Tasmanian devils get the disease, which is known as devil facial tumor disease, or DFTD.

The facial tumors caused by DFTD make it nearly impossible for the animals to eat. If a Tasmanian devil does not die from DFTD, it will instead starve to death. Sightings of these creatures in their natural habitats have declined by as much as 70%, and the Tasmanian devil was added to the endangered species list in 2009.

The Save the Tasmanian Devil Program (STTDP) has been working with zoos to capture the animals and isolate healthy ones in outdoor, free-range enclosures. Zoos are also breeding Tasmanian devils and are slowly increasing healthy populations. Despite these efforts, DFTD continues to spread in the wilds of Tasmania, and scientists have been unable to find a treatment or a cure.

SKILL PRACTICE Read each question. Fill in the bubble next to the correct answer.

1. What would probably happen if a Tasmanian devil was threatened by another animal?
   Ⓐ It would bare its teeth and growl.
   Ⓑ It would die of starvation.
   Ⓒ It would contract DFTD.
   Ⓓ It would run to safety.

2. Which of these would probably happen if an infected Tasmanian devil bit another Tasmanian devil?
   Ⓐ The first animal would survive.
   Ⓑ The second animal would get DFTD.
   Ⓒ The second animal would kill the first.
   Ⓓ Both animals would die in the fight.

3. If a Tasmanian devil with DFTD were able to eat, it would probably _____.
   Ⓐ survive with its tumors
   Ⓑ die of the disease
   Ⓒ starve to death
   Ⓓ become cured

4. In the future, Tasmanian devils will probably _____.
   Ⓐ become extinct
   Ⓑ learn how to survive DFTD
   Ⓒ live and thrive only in zoos
   Ⓓ double their population numbers

STRATEGY PRACTICE Write a question that can be answered with information from the passage. Then have a partner answer the question.

_____

_____

Use information from the passage to make predictions about Africanized honeybees.

March of the Killer Bees

The African killer bee sounds like a pretty scary insect, but its real name—Africanized honeybee—is not quite as frightening. In the 1950s, African honeybees and European honeybees were bred together in Brazil, and the so-called killer bees were created.

Bee breeders were attempting to develop a honeybee that was better suited to warm climates. Unfortunately, some colonies of these new bees escaped, and the bees have since moved northward at a rate of 100 to 300 miles per year. Once the bees left Brazil, they moved quickly into the lower regions of the United States. They have currently spread through the southern parts of California, Nevada, Arizona, New Mexico, Utah, Texas, Oklahoma, Louisiana, and Florida. Recently, however, their movement has decreased. Some scientists believe Africanized honeybees will do well only in warm climates.

Africanized honeybees do not actively seek out victims. They are easily disturbed, however, especially by the vibration of motors. They are also more likely to attack than other bee species. Once disturbed, swarms of Africanized honeybees may chase an intruder for a quarter of a mile and are 10 times more likely than other bees to sting when provoked.

Like all honeybees, Africanized honeybees can sting only once before they die. Their swarming tendencies, however, have caused the United States government to issue this warning to those attacked: "RUN away quickly! Do not stop to help others. Continue to RUN!"

SKILL PRACTICE Read each question. Fill in the bubble next to the correct answer.

1. What would probably happen if a person drove a tractor near a hive of Africanized honeybees?

   Ⓐ The bees would ignore the tractor.

   Ⓑ The driver would not notice the bees.

   Ⓒ The bees would move their hive to a new place.

   Ⓓ The bees would become upset and attack.

2. If you tried to help someone who was being attacked by Africanized honeybees, you would probably _____.

   Ⓐ also be attacked

   Ⓑ escape unharmed

   Ⓒ hurt the person involved

   Ⓓ destroy the bee colony

3. What is probably the best way to keep from being stung by Africanized honeybees?

   Ⓐ chase them away by running motors

   Ⓑ stay inside on warm days

   Ⓒ move to another state

   Ⓓ avoid bothering them

4. If the climate in the United States becomes much warmer, Africanized honeybees will most likely _____.

   Ⓐ move back south

   Ⓑ die off

   Ⓒ move farther north

   Ⓓ stop their movement

STRATEGY PRACTICE How do you feel about honeybees? Why?

_____

_____

READ THE PASSAGE   Think about how phones have changed and how they could change in the future.

The Super Computer in Your Pocket

In 2000, very few cellphones could connect to the Internet, and most could only make phone calls or send basic text messages from black and white screens. People who bought phones at that time were mostly concerned about the phone's size, not what it could do. In about a decade, however, cellphones were transformed into much different tools.

By 2012, the majority of cellphones could connect to the Internet, and most ran "apps," or applications, such as games, social networking tools, or programs with the ability to create and share creative projects. For example, a new phone in 2012 allowed users to shoot videos, edit the videos into movies, add sound effects, and publish the final product on video-sharing sites. People who bought phones in 2012 worried about how fast their phones were and how quickly they could perform tasks. People were no longer concerned with just making phone calls.

So what will phones be like in 2024? No one knows for sure, but you can make some good guesses. Even though phones change, their improvements are based on similar goals. For example, most companies want to make phones that are easier to use. Early phones had number buttons you had to push, later phones had touch screens, and even later phones had voice commands—no touching required. Phone companies also try to make phones that can do things older phones could never do. Over the years, cellphones went from having no cameras to being able to record high-definition videos.

Phone companies are always looking for people with exciting new ideas. If you can think of a better way to make phones, you might be able to help invent the next superphone!

SKILL PRACTICE   Read each question. Fill in the bubble next to the correct answer.

1. **Which of these will most likely be true in 2024?**
   Ⓐ Phones will no longer make calls.
   Ⓑ Phones will have even more features.
   Ⓒ People will not use phones as much.
   Ⓓ Companies will sell the same number of phones.

2. **By 2012, people were worried about phone speed because _____.**
   Ⓐ people spoke more quickly
   Ⓑ people wanted their phones to do complex tasks
   Ⓒ slow phones were easier to use
   Ⓓ fast phones played videos too quickly

3. **Which of these will likely disappear from phones in the future?**
   Ⓐ number buttons
   Ⓑ voice commands
   Ⓒ cameras
   Ⓓ video-making programs

4. **Many people in 2000 did not choose a phone based on its features because most phones _____.**
   Ⓐ were connected to the Internet
   Ⓑ were too large to carry
   Ⓒ had the same limited features
   Ⓓ had unlimited apps

STRATEGY PRACTICE   Write a question you thought of while reading the passage. What is the answer?

_____

_____

Nonfiction Text Features

Students practice identifying and comprehending common features of nonfiction text.

Visual Information

Students examine and evaluate information that is depicted visually.

DAY 1

Introduce the *Nonfiction Text Features* skill to students. Say: **Nonfiction passages often include special features, such as headings, captions, lists, visual elements, footnotes, or special fonts.** Explain to students that they will be reading a flier for the Underground Railroad Bicycle Route. Say: **Good readers use nonfiction text features to help them better understand a text.** Then remind students of the *Determine Important Information* strategy (Week 5). Say: **Not all information in a text is critically important to understanding the main idea. Look for the most important information as you read.** Then have students read the instructions at the top of the page and the passage. When students have finished, direct them to complete the skill and strategy practice activities. Review the answers together.

DAY 2

Remind students of the *Nonfiction Text Features* skill. Say: **This passage includes a chart. The author has organized information about past medical practices in a way that makes them easy for readers to understand.** Review how charts are structured by pointing out the rows, columns, and headings. Then remind students of the *Organization* strategy (Week 4). Say: **As you read, think about how the chart's organization affects how easy it is to find information.** When students have finished reading, direct them to complete the skill and strategy practice activities. Review the answers together.

DAY 3

Introduce the *Visual Information* skill to students. Say: **Authors can use visual information to help readers better understand the content of their texts. Sometimes it can be difficult to understand the written description of a process that has multiple steps. Visual elements can show the reader an example of what is being discussed in a passage.** Then remind students of the *Determine Important Information* strategy. Say: **Combine what you read in the passage with what you see in the visual information to determine the most important information the author is trying to convey.** When students have finished reading the passage and studying the diagram, direct them to complete the skill and strategy practice activities. Review the answers together.

DAY 4

Review the *Visual Information* skill with students. Say: **Something as simple as a drawing can help readers better understand the written information in a passage.** Tell students they are going to read a passage and study a drawing about how to make a lean-to shelter. Then remind students of the *Organization* strategy. Say: **This passage has been organized to show the steps in a process. Think about how adding step numbers makes the instructions easier to understand.** Have students read the passage and study the drawing. When students have finished, direct them to complete the skill and strategy practice activities. Review the answers together.

DAY 5

Tell students they will practice both the *Nonfiction Text Features* and *Visual Information* skills by reading a passage and studying a diagram about bogs. Then remind students of the *Organization* strategy. Say: **As you read, think about why the author organized the passage into three distinct sections. How does this organization help readers?** When students have finished reading, direct them to complete the skill and strategy practice activities. Review the answers together.

READ THE FLIER   Think about what you would need to know to plan a trip on the Underground Railroad Bicycle Route.

The Underground Railroad Bicycle Route
Explore African American History by Bike!

See the Path, Feel the Courage:
- Travel along some of the same routes that African Americans used during their journey north.
- Explore famous sites used by African Americans during their escape from slavery.
- Visit museums and parks dedicated to preserving the story of the Underground Railroad.

Difficulty of Route:
Each leg of the trip is moderately difficult. This tour is for cyclists who ride regularly. Riders should expect rolling hills on some legs.

Recommended Number of Miles to Travel per Day:
Legs are 45–65 miles, depending on cyclist's level of fitness and amount of gear being carried.

Lodging Options:
Campsites and hotels are both available.

For more information, visit our website.

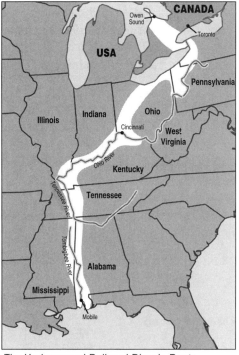

The Underground Railroad Bicycle Route spans 2,000 miles.

SKILL PRACTICE   Read each question. Fill in the bubble next to the correct answer.

1. Which section or feature would you look at to find out how long each leg of the route is?
   - Ⓐ the map
   - Ⓑ See the Path, Feel the Courage
   - Ⓒ Difficulty of Route
   - Ⓓ Recommended Number of Miles to Travel per Day

2. What information does the caption give?
   - Ⓐ the difficulty of the route
   - Ⓑ the start and end points of the route
   - Ⓒ the length of the route
   - Ⓓ where to find other information about the route

3. The bulleted list tells you _____.
   - Ⓐ points of interest along the route
   - Ⓑ benefits of traveling the route
   - Ⓒ rules to follow when traveling the route
   - Ⓓ places to stay along the route

4. Who is the intended audience of this flier?
   - Ⓐ students studying the Civil War
   - Ⓑ bicyclists who like history
   - Ⓒ bicyclists who are new to cycling
   - Ⓓ people with little time for vacation

STRATEGY PRACTICE   What is one important thing to know in order to plan a ride along this bicycle route?

_____

_____

READ THE PASSAGE   Look for information that tells you how the chart is organized.

Strange Medicine

Science and medicine have come a long way over the past 1,000 years. Doctors understand a lot about how the body works, how diseases begin, and how to treat many diseases. But doctors were not always on the right track. Here are some of the strangest medical practices in history. As you can see, some of them worked, and some of them were the result of strange thinking!

Name of the Practice	Description of the Practice	When Was It First Used?	Does It Work?
Leeching	Doctors first placed leeches on patients in order to draw out the bad spirits, or "humors," in a person. Today, leeches are used to remove blood in order to reduce swelling and aid circulation.	Around 400 BC	Doctors have used leeches for over 2,000 years. In the right conditions, leeches are quite helpful at removing blood from wounds.
Trepanation (treh-pan-AY-shun)	Patients have a hole drilled, scraped, or hammered into their skull, allowing the brain tissue to be permanently exposed.	Evidence suggests that trepanation was used 10,000 years ago.	No. Your skull protects the brain from injury, exposure, and infection.
Maggot therapy	Maggots are poured into a wound. The maggots eat diseased and rotting tissue but allow healthy tissue to remain.	Eleventh century	Maggot therapy is effective in cleaning wounds.
Mercury therapy	Liquid mercury was used to clean wounds and as a treatment for many diseases.	Second century	Mercury is highly toxic. It is used in some medicines today in very small doses.

SKILL PRACTICE   Read each question. Fill in the bubble next to the correct answer.

1. Which section gives the chart's purpose?
   Ⓐ Leeching
   Ⓑ When Was It First Used?
   Ⓒ the introduction
   Ⓓ Description of the Practice

2. The information in parentheses under "Trepanation" helps you _____.
   Ⓐ define the word
   Ⓑ pronounce the word
   Ⓒ know the word's part of speech
   Ⓓ alphabetize the word

3. Under which heading would you look to find which practice is the oldest?
   Ⓐ Name of the Practice
   Ⓑ Description of the Practice
   Ⓒ When Was It First Used?
   Ⓓ Does It Work?

4. Under which heading would you look to find which practice involves surgery?
   Ⓐ Name of the Practice
   Ⓑ Description of the Practice
   Ⓒ When Was It First Used?
   Ⓓ Does It Work?

STRATEGY PRACTICE   How does the chart make the information easier to understand?

_____

READ THE PASSAGE   Use the diagram to learn more about the main ideas of the passage.

The Supply Chain

All of the things we use and enjoy, from computers to bicycles to the clothes we wear, would not exist without help from a lot of people.

Think about a bicycle, for example. The metal for the bicycle's frame comes from a supplier. The supplier sends the metal to a manufacturer, where workers then turn the metal into bicycle parts. The manufacturer then puts the bicycle together and sends it to a distributor. The distributor then sends the bicycles out by truck to the many stores, or retailers, across the country. The retailers then sell the bicycles to customers. Each link in the chain is connected by logistics, which transports goods from one stage to the next. From supplier to customer, the chain of people and places that help make and sell things like bicycles is called the supply chain.

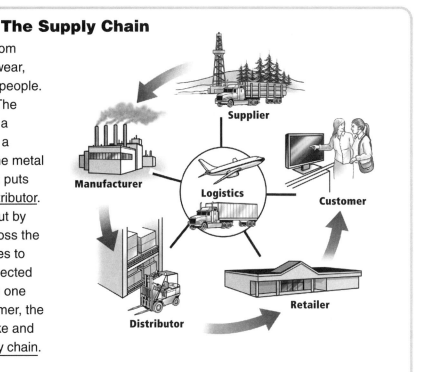

SKILL PRACTICE   Read each question. Fill in the bubble next to the correct answer.

1. What is the last stage of the supply chain?
   Ⓐ customer
   Ⓑ supplier
   Ⓒ distributor
   Ⓓ retailer

2. Which of these is an example of a retailer?
   Ⓐ a factory that makes television screens
   Ⓑ a person who wants to buy a new chair
   Ⓒ a store that sells athletic shoes
   Ⓓ a warehouse that holds new guitars until ordered

3. A blizzard that shuts down highways would disrupt which part of the supply chain the most?
   Ⓐ the retailer
   Ⓑ logistics
   Ⓒ the supplier
   Ⓓ the manufacturer

4. A customer ordering a bed online directly from a distributor would cut out which part of the supply chain?
   Ⓐ the supplier
   Ⓑ the distributor
   Ⓒ the manufacturer
   Ⓓ the retailer

STRATEGY PRACTICE   What key information do the passage and the diagram convey?

_____

_____

READ THE PASSAGE   Think about what information the illustration adds.

A Shelter in Minutes

Stranded in the wilderness without a tent, tarp, or RV? No problem. With some sticks and leaves and a piece of rope or vine, you can build a lean-to. A lean-to is one of the most basic forms of shelter.

Step 1: Find two trees that are growing close together.

Step 2: Find two thick, straight sticks or branches long enough to touch both trees.

Step 3: With a rope or vine, tie one of the sticks or branches to the trees as high as you can. Lay the other stick on the ground parallel to the first one.

Step 4: Lay more sticks or branches perpendicular to the first two and tie them. This is the frame for your lean-to.

Step 5: Cover the frame with leaves, grass, or other materials to block the wind and rain.

SKILL PRACTICE   Read each question. Fill in the bubble next to the correct answer.

1. The illustration shows how to _____.
   Ⓐ find good trees for making a lean-to
   Ⓑ cover the lean-to frame with leaves
   Ⓒ choose vines to tie the sticks
   Ⓓ make a shelter in the wilderness

2. What can you learn from the passage that you cannot see in the illustration?
   Ⓐ the order in which to assemble the materials
   Ⓑ the fact that you need sticks or branches
   Ⓒ how the sticks form the frame
   Ⓓ how to fill in the frame

3. The illustration adds information by showing _____.
   Ⓐ a completed lean-to
   Ⓑ the lean-to's measurements
   Ⓒ where to build a lean-to
   Ⓓ how to sleep inside a lean-to

4. According to the illustration, a lean-to is most like a _____.
   Ⓐ tree
   Ⓑ tent
   Ⓒ truck
   Ⓓ bathroom

STRATEGY PRACTICE   Why is giving an illustration with instructions more effective than just listing the instructions by themselves?

_____

_____

READ THE PASSAGE Look at the diagram before you read the passage. Then look at the diagram as you read.

A Bog Develops

What Are Bogs?

A bog is a spongy wetland filled with highly acidic water and partially decomposed plant material. Bogs are usually found in cold northern areas such as Ireland, Scandinavia, and Siberia.

Formation

Bogs form in cool areas where rain falls faster than it can evaporate. As water sits in a lake or other depression, moss accumulates on the surface. There, the moss decays very slowly until it sinks into the bog. A new layer of moss builds on the surface again, restricting oxygen and blocking heat below. This further slows decomposition. Eventually, the partly decomposed plant material becomes peat—a product that has long been used in northern Europe as fuel. Left undisturbed for millions of years, peat becomes coal.

Deceptive Ground

A bog may look solid when the peat mat spreads across the surface, but underneath it contains water, a false bottom (actually a layer of decomposing plant debris), and a true bottom. Occasionally an unwary walker falls through the top layer of a bog and drowns. Today, as in the past, wooden boardwalks are sometimes laid across bogs to provide safe passage.

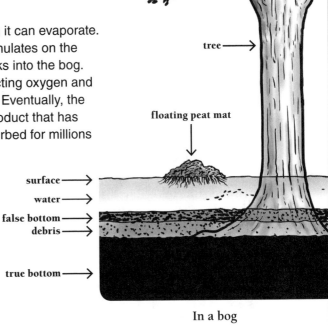

In a bog

SKILL PRACTICE Read each question. Fill in the bubble next to the correct answer.

1. In which section would you find how land becomes a bog?

   Ⓐ What Are Bogs?

   Ⓑ Deceptive Ground

   Ⓒ the diagram

   Ⓓ Formation

2. The diagram helps readers understand the text by _____.

   Ⓐ mapping locations of dangerous bogs

   Ⓑ illustrating how to walk safely on a bog

   Ⓒ showing the layers of a typical bog

   Ⓓ demonstrating how to use bog peat for fuel

3. In the diagram, what is on the surface of a bog?

   Ⓐ a tree

   Ⓑ a false bottom

   Ⓒ debris

   Ⓓ a floating peat mat

4. What can you find out in the "Deceptive Ground" section?

   Ⓐ the definition of a bog

   Ⓑ the dangers of bogs

   Ⓒ how a bog decomposes

   Ⓓ how bog peat is used

STRATEGY PRACTICE How did referring to the diagram as you read help you understand the information?

_____

_____

Main Idea and Details

Students look for the central idea or message of a passage or story. They also find details that best support the main idea.

Sequence

Students look for the order of events or steps in a process.

DAY 1

Review the *Main Idea and Details* skill with students. Say: **Good readers look for a main idea in each paragraph of a text. The paragraphs will also include details that support the main ideas.** Read aloud the first paragraph of the passage. Draw a Main Idea and Details cluster on the board: *Main Idea: Giant ground sloth one of the largest mammals; Detail: Central and South America; Detail: Extinct; Detail: Died out 10,000 years ago.* Direct students to look for the main ideas and details in the rest of the passage. Then remind students of the *Monitor Comprehension* strategy (Week 1). Say: **As you read, you can underline, circle, or make notes near the main ideas and details to keep track of what you have learned.** Have students read the passage. When students have finished, direct them to complete the skill and strategy practice activities. Review the answers together.

DAY 2

Review the *Main Idea and Details* skill with students. Say: **Details give additional information about the main idea. You can think of them as individual pieces of a puzzle that go together to create a complete image.** Tell students to look for key details about the titan arum plant as they read. Then remind students of the *Visualization* strategy (Week 3). Say: **As you read about the plant, think about what it looks and smells like. Make a picture in your mind of this unusual plant.** Have students read the passage. When students have finished, direct them to complete the skill and strategy practice activities. Review the answers together.

DAY 3

Review the *Sequence* skill with students. Say: **The sequence in a passage tells the order of events or steps in a process. As you read the passage, look for the sequence of steps Wilbur Scoville used to determine the hotness of peppers.** Then remind students of the *Monitor Comprehension* strategy. Say: **You can write the sequence of steps, such as 1, 2, or 3, within the passage to remind you of the order. By keeping these notes, you can easily locate the information after you have finished reading.** Have students read the passage. Then direct them to complete the skill and strategy practice activities. Review the answers together.

DAY 4

Review the *Sequence* skill with students. Say: **Authors who are giving directions will often place them in order to help readers fully understand a process. You can look for sequence signal words, such as *first, then,* or *next,* as you read.** Tell students to look for sequence signal words as they read about flamenco dancing. Then remind students of the *Visualization* strategy. Say: **As you read, imagine you are the student who is learning the dance. Think about what you need to do in order to be successful, and create a visualization of that experience.** Have students read the passage. When students have finished, direct them to complete the skill and strategy practice activities. Review the answers together.

DAY 5

Tell students they will practice both the *Main Idea and Details* and *Sequence* skills. Tell them they are going to read about the Northwest Passage. Remind students of the *Monitor Comprehension* strategy. Say: **Sometimes, you can miss important details the first time you read something. Rereading will help you fully understand the information in the passage and how it fits together.** Have students read the passage. When students have finished, direct them to complete the skill and strategy practice activities. Review the answers together.

     Daily Reading Comprehension • EMC 3457 • © Evan-Moor Corp.

READ THE PASSAGE   As you read, think about each paragraph's main idea.

Gigantic Prehistoric Sloths

One of the largest mammals to ever walk the earth was the prehistoric giant ground sloth. Giant ground sloths lived primarily in South and Central America until they became extinct, or died out completely. Giant ground sloths became extinct about 10,000 years ago, during the end of the Ice Age.

The scientific name for the prehistoric giant ground sloth is Megatherium, which means "gigantic beast." And indeed, giant ground sloths were massive creatures. Bigger than most elephants, they weighed around five tons. When standing on their powerful hind legs, giant sloths were about 20 feet tall, or about twice the height of a basketball hoop stand.

Megatheriums had huge, 12-inch claws on each of their front paws. They used these claws primarily for reaching and removing choice leaves from trees and bushes. The sloths also had claws on their back paws, but the size of those claws was much less threatening. Despite the power of the sloths' claws, most scientists believe they were most likely used only for gathering food.

Giant ground sloths were very slow-moving animals that ate only plants. When they were standing, the sloths used their muscular tails for balance. Otherwise, they walked very slowly on all four feet. Modern-day sloths are small tree-hanging animals that are roughly the size of small dogs. They are also extremely slow-moving, but they are much smaller and less dangerous than their awesome ancestors. The prehistoric giant ground sloths were far too large to dwell in trees as their modern-day relatives do. Most likely, they could have easily reached the tops of most trees by simply standing up and reaching out with their enormous claws.

SKILL PRACTICE   Read each question. Fill in the bubble next to the correct answer.

1. **What is the passage mostly about?**
   Ⓐ large mammals
   Ⓑ the Ice Age
   Ⓒ giant ground sloths
   Ⓓ prehistoric animals

2. **Prehistoric ground sloths were different from modern-day sloths because prehistoric ground sloths _____.**
   Ⓐ were bigger
   Ⓑ were slower
   Ⓒ ate fewer plants
   Ⓓ did not become extinct

3. **How did giant ground sloths balance themselves when they were standing up?**
   Ⓐ with their claws
   Ⓑ with their tails
   Ⓒ with their front legs
   Ⓓ with tree branches

4. **Which detail supports the idea that giant ground sloths were huge animals?**
   Ⓐ They moved very slowly.
   Ⓑ Their claws were powerful weapons.
   Ⓒ They could stand on their hind legs.
   Ⓓ They weighed around five tons.

STRATEGY PRACTICE   Did you understand the main ideas the author presented? Why or why not?

_____

_____

Name: _____

READ THE PASSAGE   Look for details that help you visualize what the titan arum looks like.

The Smelliest Plant

Here is one flower you would not want to give as a gift—at least not to anyone you like! It is the smelliest member of the plant kingdom, and it is called the titan arum. The word "titan" describes something gigantic, and this plant certainly lives up to its name.

The titan arum grows in the tropical forests of Sumatra, Indonesia. When the plant is in bloom, its stem is about 10 feet tall, and its "flower" spans a diameter of three to four feet. The bloom is actually a funnel-shaped leaf that opens, giving access to hundreds of tiny flowers inside. Visitors flock to botanical gardens in the United States to see these gigantic plants in bloom, but their noses should also be prepared for a unique experience. Besides its enormous size, the titan arum is also known for its hideous smell.

The titan arum's odor, which is strongest at night, can be smelled from a distance of a half mile away. People describe the terrible odor as the smell of rotting flesh, a stench that creates huge, stomach-turning waves of nausea in those who get a whiff. Because of its similarity to decaying flesh, the titan arum is best known by its common name—the corpse flower.

What is the point of this plant's horrible smell? The answer is surprisingly simple. The small beetles and flies that pollinate, or fertilize, the plant love its stinky smell. These insects smell the odor, think it is actual decaying flesh, are attracted to it, and end up pollinating the plant. The titan arum needs its awful smell to survive. Without the smell and the insects it attracts, the titan arum might not be able to continue as a species.

SKILL PRACTICE   Read each question. Fill in the bubble next to the correct answer.

1. Which characteristic gives the titan arum its nickname of "corpse flower"?
   Ⓐ It comes from tropical forests.
   Ⓑ It is a gigantic plant.
   Ⓒ It is pollinated by small beetles.
   Ⓓ It has a terrible odor.

2. When a titan arum is in bloom, how tall is the stem?
   Ⓐ 10 feet
   Ⓑ 3 to 4 feet
   Ⓒ 7 feet
   Ⓓ 20 feet

3. At which time of day is the odor of the titan arum the strongest?
   Ⓐ at night
   Ⓑ early in the morning
   Ⓒ early in the afternoon
   Ⓓ in the early evening

4. Which detail supports the idea that there is a reason the titan arum has such a horrible smell?
   Ⓐ The plant smells like rotting flesh.
   Ⓑ The insects that pollinate the plant are attracted by its smell.
   Ⓒ The plant can be smelled from a distance of a half mile.
   Ⓓ Human beings do not like the smell.

STRATEGY PRACTICE   Which details from the passage helped you best visualize a titan arum?

_____

_____

READ THE PASSAGE   Pay attention to the series of steps involved in measuring a pepper's heat.

How Hot Is That Pepper?

You are at a party and are sampling the munchies. You pop a harmless-looking pepper into your mouth, chew it, and swallow it. Yikes! As the pepper burns every part of your mouth, you look frantically for water, ice, or something sweet to make the burning stop.

Some peppers are so hot that they can lead to vomiting, digestive problems, and hospitalization. The simplest way to check the hotness of a pepper is to taste it. There is, however, a safer way to tell in advance how hot a pepper will be: find out where it rates on the Scoville scale.

The Scoville scale, the classic way to determine the hotness of a pepper, was developed by an American chemist, Wilbur Scoville, in 1912. The chemical that causes the sensation of heat in a pepper is called capsaicin, and Scoville discovered a method for measuring the amount of it. Since the amount of capsaicin did not mean much to pepper consumers, Scoville devised a method of rating peppers.

To rate peppers, Scoville followed a series of steps. First, he blended ground peppers in a solution of sugar and water. Then, he had a panel of trained tasters sample the solution. If the tasters found the solution hot, the solution was diluted with additional water and sugar. The tasters continued with this process until they no longer felt the sensation of heat. The Scoville scale measures the number of times the solution needs to be diluted for the tasters to sense no heat at all. The number of dilutions is the number of heat units. Scoville then listed the peppers tested in order by their heat unit range.

The next time you are hungry and are thinking about eating a random pepper, be sure to check the Scoville scale first. Your tongue and your stomach will thank you.

SKILL PRACTICE   Read each question. Fill in the bubble next to the correct answer.

1. What should a person do before eating a random pepper?
   Ⓐ drink a glass of water
   Ⓑ check the pepper's Scoville rating
   Ⓒ make a solution of water and sugar
   Ⓓ find a group of trained testers

2. What did Wilbur Scoville learn before he decided to develop his scale?
   Ⓐ how to dilute peppers
   Ⓑ how to train pepper tasters
   Ⓒ the number of times a pepper must be diluted
   Ⓓ the amount of capsaicin in peppers

3. What did Scoville do first to rate the hotness of peppers?
   Ⓐ He diluted a pepper solution.
   Ⓑ He created an easy-to-use scale.
   Ⓒ He ground up peppers with sugar and water.
   Ⓓ He had tasters eat a pepper solution.

4. What is the last step in rating the hotness of a pepper?
   Ⓐ checking the amount of capsaicin
   Ⓑ blending the pepper with sugar and water
   Ⓒ recording when the solution no longer tastes hot
   Ⓓ having tasters taste the solution

STRATEGY PRACTICE   Which parts of the passage best helped you understand the Scoville scale?

_____

_____

READ THE PASSAGE   Pay attention to the steps involved in learning flamenco dancing.

Learning Flamenco Dancing

So you want to learn to dance the highly expressive Spanish dance form, flamenco. This is not a dance you can master in a day or even in a week. Learning flamenco dancing takes time, patience, determination, and a certain amount of personal flair.

The first step is to find a good teacher. Research lesson prices and the qualifications of the teacher. Talk with people who have already taken lessons from the teacher to find out if they were satisfied customers.

Once you have chosen your teacher or class, you will then need to purchase dancing shoes. Female dancers also need a practice skirt.

In your classes, you will learn how to move your whole body the flamenco way. The dance style includes intricate hand and arm movements, the *zapateado* (stepping movements that create distinctive tapping sounds), and specific body movements. It takes a lot of practice to learn flamenco dance steps and to perform them rapidly with the precise rhythm the dance requires.

As the movements become more familiar, you must learn what is by far the most important aspect of flamenco—dancing with heart! The flamenco dancer must have a deep understanding of the music and dance with passion and emotion.

Once you are ready to perform, you will need a costume. In addition to dancing shoes, female dancers usually wear a long ruffled dress. Male dancers often wear tight pants and long-sleeved shirts. If you are in doubt about your costume choice, check with your teacher to find out what he or she recommends. To win over the crowd, you will need more than a costume—you must have the courage to let your passion for the dance shine.

SKILL PRACTICE   Read each question. Fill in the bubble next to the correct answer.

1. **What do you need to do first to learn flamenco dancing?**
   Ⓐ dance with emotion
   Ⓑ learn specific steps
   Ⓒ buy a dancing costume
   Ⓓ find a good teacher

2. **What do you need to buy before your first lesson?**
   Ⓐ a performance costume
   Ⓑ dancing shoes
   Ⓒ a long-sleeved shirt
   Ⓓ practice music

3. **According to the passage, what is the last thing you must learn to properly dance flamenco?**
   Ⓐ to dance with rhythm
   Ⓑ to learn specific movements
   Ⓒ to dance with heart
   Ⓓ to learn the *zapateado*

4. **What do you need after you are ready to perform?**
   Ⓐ the proper costume
   Ⓑ intricate arm movements
   Ⓒ passion and emotion
   Ⓓ a good sense of rhythm

STRATEGY PRACTICE   Were you able to visualize people doing flamenco dancing? Why or why not?

_____

_____

READ THE PASSAGE   If you do not understand the main idea in a paragraph, reread the paragraph slowly.

The Northwest Passage

At the end of the fifteenth century, Western explorers began looking for the Northwest Passage—a water route through the Arctic that is north of the Canadian mainland and connects the Atlantic and Pacific oceans. Early in the nineteenth century, a passage was discovered, but it proved to be ice-bound and impossible to navigate. Recently, however, the situation has begun to change.

In August 2007, scientists confirmed that Arctic sea ice had shrunk to its lowest levels since records have been kept. As a result, the entire length of the Northwest Passage was ice-free and navigable for the entire month that August. Why did this happen? The answer is believed to be global warming. The planet's rising temperatures caused Arctic ice to thaw at a rate faster than scientists had predicted.

Because sea ice is white and reflective, most of the sun's rays bounce off its surface. When sea ice melts, however, dark ocean waters are exposed. These dark waters absorb the sun's light instead of reflecting it, which causes the water to warm. In warmer water, new ice has trouble forming, which then causes more ice to melt and less ice to form in the years to come.

Scientists are not predicting that the Northwest Passage with be open year-round in the foreseeable future. Global warming has no effect on the tilt of Earth's axis, which is what makes winter in the Arctic extremely harsh. But if global warming continues, sailors of the future may one day be able to claim the Northwest Passage for good.

SKILL PRACTICE   Read each question. Fill in the bubble next to the correct answer.

1. What is the passage mostly about?
   - Ⓐ why the Northwest Passage opened in 2007
   - Ⓑ the expeditions of Western explorers
   - Ⓒ what causes global warming
   - Ⓓ the long search for the Northwest Passage

2. Which event happened after the Arctic sea ice shrank to its lowest level?
   - Ⓐ The Northwest Passage was ice-free and navigable for an entire month.
   - Ⓑ The presence of sea ice began increasing at alarming rates.
   - Ⓒ Global warming began to affect Earth's axis.
   - Ⓓ Explorers tried unsuccessfully to find and navigate the Northwest Passage.

3. How did Arctic sea ice change in 2007?
   - Ⓐ It blocked the passage from the Atlantic to the Pacific Ocean.
   - Ⓑ It melted more than it had since measuring began.
   - Ⓒ It started reflecting the sun's rays.
   - Ⓓ It opened the Northwest Passage for good.

4. What happens after dark ocean waters are exposed?
   - Ⓐ The water reflects more of the sun's light.
   - Ⓑ New ice forms deep in the ocean.
   - Ⓒ The water absorbs the sun's energy and gets warmer.
   - Ⓓ Winters in the Arctic become harsher.

STRATEGY PRACTICE   Describe something in the passage that you better understood after rereading it.

_____

_____

Author's Purpose

Students identify the author's reason for writing about a subject.

Evaluate Evidence

Students practice evaluating evidence by identifying the author's main idea and examining the evidence the author uses to support that idea.

DAY 1

Review the *Author's Purpose* skill with students. Say: **An author's purpose is *why* the author wrote a text. Think about the author's motive for writing the passage as you read.** Tell students they are going to read about a fire in Centralia, Pennsylvania. Say: **Think about why the information in the passage was important enough to the author to share it with readers.** Then remind students of the *Determine Important Information* strategy (Week 5). Say: **As you read, think about how the fire has affected the community and how it could affect others in the future.** When students have finished reading the passage, direct them to complete the skill and strategy practice activities. Review the answers together.

DAY 2

Review the *Author's Purpose* skill with students. Say: **Authors write to entertain, persuade, teach, or inform. Look for clues within a text that hint at the author's purpose, such as the steps for directions or persuasive language.** Then remind students of the *Ask Questions* strategy (Week 6). Say: **When you begin reading a passage, you can ask a question about what you want to learn. Look for the answer as you continue reading. Sometimes, you will still have questions when you have finished. You can look for the answers in books, on the Internet, or by asking a teacher or expert. Asking and answering questions will help you better understand what you have read.** Have students read the passage. When students have finished, direct them to complete the skill and strategy practice activities. Review the answers together.

DAY 3

Review the *Evaluate Evidence* skill with students. Say: **Good writers offer evidence to support their claims.** Read the first paragraph of the passage aloud. Explain: **The author says the Sphinx is "an enormous sculpture." What evidence is given to support this claim?** (It is 241 feet long and 66 feet high.) Remind students to look for facts that can be verified by other sources when reading nonfiction texts. Then remind students of the *Determine Important Information* strategy. Say: **Not all information that is included in a passage is truly important to supporting a claim.** Direct students to read the passage and complete the skill and strategy practice activities. Review the answers together.

DAY 4

Review the *Evaluate Evidence* skill. Then tell students they will read about coral reefs in the world's oceans and how some of them can help—or hurt—sea life. Students should look for evidence of these claims. Review the *Ask Questions* strategy. Say: **When you ask questions after you read, you can confirm that you understood the information in a text.** Direct students to read the passage and to complete the skill practice activity. Review the answers together. Then have partners complete the strategy practice activity to ask and answer questions.

DAY 5

Tell students they will practice the *Author's Purpose* skill and the *Evaluate Evidence* skill as they read a passage about bubonic plague. Say: **As you read, think about why the author wrote the passage and the evidence the author presents.** Then remind students of the *Determine Important Information* strategy. Say: **Think about which information you would share with others if you had to give a summary of this passage.** When students have finished reading, direct them to complete the skill and strategy practice activities. Review the answers together.

READ THE PASSAGE   As you read, think about why the author wrote the passage.

The Endless Fire

Centralia, Pennsylvania, was a coal-mining town for more than 100 years. Every year, the local fire department burned trash at the town dump, but on May 27, 1962, something unexpected happened. The fire found its way into the abandoned mine pits beneath the town. A vein of coal underground caught fire, and firefighters worked tirelessly to drown the flames with water. Despite their valiant efforts, the fire was never completely extinguished.

For the next 20 years, repeated efforts to extinguish the great fire failed. Firefighters dug trenches, flushed the pits with water, and tried filling them with ash, but nothing worked. Every time it seemed the fire was under control or on the verge of going out, the flames erupted once again.

Over time, the fire created public safety and health hazards for the residents of Centralia. Toxic fumes and gases rose up into people's yards, homes, and businesses. Families had to abandon their homes as the fumes and a gas called carbon monoxide became life-threatening.

In 1983, a study revealed that the fire could possibly continue to burn for a century or even more. The federal government became involved, but there was little that officials could do by then. Studies show that the fire could spread to as many as 3,700 acres and endanger other towns in the area. More than 40 million dollars have been spent as a result of this fire, but it keeps on burning under the almost-deserted town. Only about a dozen people continue to live in Centralia today.

SKILL PRACTICE   Read each question. Fill in the bubble next to the correct answer.

1. The author's main purpose was to _____.
   Ⓐ describe life in Pennsylvania towns
   Ⓑ inform people about the Centralia fire
   Ⓒ persuade people to practice fire safety
   Ⓓ predict what will happen as the Centralia fire burns

2. The second paragraph mainly describes _____.
   Ⓐ the firefighters' attempts to stop the fire
   Ⓑ how the fire affected people's health
   Ⓒ what rules firefighters must follow when battling underground fires
   Ⓓ the reasons why fighting the Centralia fire was unsuccessful

3. What is the purpose of the third paragraph?
   Ⓐ to illustrate how long the fire lasted
   Ⓑ to describe the buildings that were burned
   Ⓒ to explain why the residents moved away
   Ⓓ to show what coal mines are like

4. Why does the author mention the 1983 study?
   Ⓐ to show how the government's money was spent
   Ⓑ to explain how the fire started
   Ⓒ to state how long the fire may burn
   Ⓓ to report the town's current population

STRATEGY PRACTICE   Which information from the passage helps you understand the difficulty of fighting the Centralia fire?

_____

_____

READ THE PASSAGE   Think about the author's different reasons for writing the passage.

Mud Bugs: Your Next Best Friend

Do you want a pet that is unusual, is easy to take care of, and could possibly scare your younger sister? If so, then you should consider owning a crawfish. Also known as crayfish, crawdads, and mud bugs, these freshwater crustaceans look a lot like lobsters but are only about the size of jumbo shrimp. These small, fun critters will make a wonderful addition to any home.

Do dogs make you wheeze and cats make you sneeze? Crawfish are nonallergenic except if eaten by people who are allergic to shellfish. They will not fill your home with hairballs or muddy paw prints. Perhaps best of all, crawfish will not create any odors as long as their habitats are kept clean, their water is filtered, and their tanks are well cared for.

Owning a pet can be a huge responsibility. Cats and dogs can live for two decades, and some pets, such as African gray parrots, can live between 50 and 60 years! If you want a pet but not a long commitment, you should get a crawfish. While some crawfish can live up to five years, most live for about two years.

Crawfish are easy to feed, too. A favorite food is shrimp pellets, but crawfish will eat scraps of vegetables, such as potatoes and celery, and they will even eat bits of meat. Their eating habits mean you need to keep them away from fish or expensive plants, however, or they might end up being your crawfish's next meal!

SKILL PRACTICE   Read each question. Fill in the bubble next to the correct answer.

1. The author's main purpose is to _____.
   - Ⓐ entertain people with a story about an unusual pet
   - Ⓑ persuade people to buy crawfish as pets
   - Ⓒ inform people about freshwater crustaceans
   - Ⓓ describe unusual pets for people to own

2. Why does the author list the life spans of multiple types of pets?
   - Ⓐ to give information about animal life spans
   - Ⓑ to convince people that African gray parrots need too much care
   - Ⓒ to remind people that some pets come with long time commitments
   - Ⓓ to persuade people to buy pets that will live the longest amount of time

3. What is the purpose of the second paragraph?
   - Ⓐ to describe the crawfish's habitat
   - Ⓑ to compare the needs of different pets
   - Ⓒ to help readers determine whether they have pet allergies
   - Ⓓ to explain the advantages of keeping crawfish

4. Why does the author include the last paragraph?
   - Ⓐ to give information about crawfish eating habits
   - Ⓑ to warn people not to eat crawfish
   - Ⓒ to list similarities between crawfish and lobsters
   - Ⓓ to explain how to clean crawfish habitats

STRATEGY PRACTICE   What is one question you still have about crawfish? How can you find the answer?

_____

_____

READ THE PASSAGE Look for factual evidence that is given about the Sphinx.

Mystery of the Sphinx

The Great Sphinx of Giza, Egypt, is one of civilization's greatest mysteries. No one knows for sure exactly when, why, or how it was built. It is an enormous sculpture, believed to be the biggest ever created. It measures about 241 feet (73.5 meters) long and 66 feet (20 meters) high. Due to its unknown origin, this massive creation has baffled locals, tourists, historians, and archaeologists for centuries.

The Sphinx has the body of a lion and the head of a man, which gives it the appearance of a mythical creature. It remains mostly intact today, with the exception of its nose. Many legends revolve around the missing nose, but a widely accepted explanation is that a former ruler had the nose carved off at some point after its creation.

Most archaeologists believe that the Sphinx was built about 4,600 years ago by a pharaoh, or ruler, named Khafre. His pyramid, the giant tomb that holds Khafre's body, is located directly behind the Sphinx. Stone blocks cut out in order to carve the Sphinx were used to build the Khafre Valley Temple at about the same time. Some historians also believe the Sphinx's face was modeled after the face of Khafre.

For most of its existence, the Sphinx was buried in sand. One story claims that around 1400 BC, the pharaoh Thutmose IV dreamed that the Sphinx ordered him to clear away the sand in return for the crown of Egypt. The sand soon buried the Sphinx again, however. In the 1850s, the sand was partially cleared, and in the 1930s, the Sphinx was completely exposed. Now, however, wind, humidity, and smog are causing the Sphinx to crumble. Archaeologists must act quickly to preserve this mysterious symbol of Egypt.

SKILL PRACTICE Read each question. Fill in the bubble next to the correct answer.

1. Which evidence supports the idea that Khafre built the Sphinx?
   - Ⓐ Khafre saw the Sphinx in a dream.
   - Ⓑ The Khafre Valley Temple was built with stone from around the Sphinx.
   - Ⓒ Khafre's body is located inside the Sphinx.
   - Ⓓ Documents from that time say Khafre built the Sphinx.

2. Why is the Sphinx considered to be mysterious?
   - Ⓐ It is the biggest sculpture ever made.
   - Ⓑ Wind and smog are causing it to crumble.
   - Ⓒ No one knows why it was built.
   - Ⓓ It was buried in the sand for centuries.

3. Which evidence supports the idea that the Sphinx is an ancient creation?
   - Ⓐ Khafre ruled roughly 4,600 years ago.
   - Ⓑ Tourists still visit the Sphinx today.
   - Ⓒ Some of the sand around the Sphinx was cleared in the 1850s.
   - Ⓓ The Sphinx is roughly 240 feet long.

4. Which evidence best supports the idea that the Sphinx looks like a mythical creature?
   - Ⓐ It does not have a nose.
   - Ⓑ It lives under the sand in Egypt.
   - Ⓒ It appears to people in their dreams.
   - Ⓓ It has the body of a lion and the head of a man.

STRATEGY PRACTICE Which information from the passage would be most useful to someone concerned with saving the Sphinx? Why?

_____

_____

READ THE PASSAGE   Focus on the types of information the author provides about coral reefs.

Coral Fakes

Coral reefs are structures created by corals, which are tiny organisms that live in the world's oceans. Coral reefs are a vital habitat for hundreds of different species of plants and animals. Due to pollution and overfishing, however, many of these reefs are disappearing. The animals and plants that live in and around coral reefs are in danger of losing their habitats.

Earth's oceans are not owned or controlled by any one organization or country. Because of this, lawmakers and scientists are unable to control everything that goes in—or travels through—the world's waters. Despite the obstacles, people still want to help save coral reef populations. Some experts believe the answer is to create artificial reefs. Many artificial reefs have already been created by people sinking objects to the ocean floor, such as old ships, volcanic rock, and even hundreds of old subway cars. Over time, these structures become covered with coral and can create new homes for fish and other living things.

There can be a disadvantage to the creation of artificial reefs, however. In the 1970s, two million tires were tied together and sunk off the coast of Florida to create a new reef. After multiple storms, the tires came loose from one another. They polluted the water and washed up on the beaches. Today, the people who sink objects are more careful about using objects that could become pollutants. However, the metal objects that have been used will eventually break down, so those reefs might crumble over time. As a result, some companies have begun making artificial reefs from materials that will not break down, and these may be more successful in the future.

SKILL PRACTICE   Read each question. Fill in the bubble next to the correct answer.

1. Which of these is evidence that coral reefs are vital habitats?

   Ⓐ They are disappearing.

   Ⓑ They are home to hundreds of species.

   Ⓒ They stop the spread of pollution.

   Ⓓ They can be created artificially.

2. Which evidence best supports the idea that coral reefs are endangered?

   Ⓐ Pollution and overfishing are destroying coral reefs.

   Ⓑ Experts have found ways to create artificial reefs.

   Ⓒ Metal reefs may begin to break down over time.

   Ⓓ Coral reefs are not controlled by any one organization or country.

3. Which evidence supports the idea that metals should not be used to make artificial reefs?

   Ⓐ They will break down over time.

   Ⓑ They become covered with coral.

   Ⓒ They have caused pollution in the past.

   Ⓓ They were tied together and sunk in the 1970s.

4. Which of these is evidence of the disadvantage of artificial reefs?

   Ⓐ storms over the ocean

   Ⓑ objects that have been sunk

   Ⓒ overfishing of habitats

   Ⓓ tires that washed up on beaches

STRATEGY PRACTICE   Write a question that can be answered with information from the passage. Then have a partner answer it.

_____

_____

READ THE PASSAGE   Look for details in the passage that hint at the author's purpose.

Ships of Death

In October 1347, a group of ships from central Asia sailed into the harbor of Messina, Sicily. The people on shore were horrified to see the sailors stagger off the ships, deathly ill, shaking with fever and covered with strange swellings. The disease known as the "Black Death" had arrived. Bubonic plague, the terrifying illness which had already claimed millions of lives in Asia, spread quickly across Italy, France, and Spain, and then moved through the rest of Europe.

Bubonic plague is carried by bacteria that live on the fleas that live on rats. Doctors in the mid-1300s did not know this—they wore masks to protect themselves from "bad air." But they did know that the plague caused painful swellings called buboes, high fevers, and, in many cases, death. When the plague moved into a person's lungs, it was called pneumonic plague and was even more deadly, killing nearly all of its victims.

The people of the Middle Ages had no way to stop the plague. For six years, Europe suffered under the onslaught of the Black Death. When it finally slowed down and then all but stopped in 1353, the world had been changed forever. As much as 30% of Europe's population had died from the plague.

Bubonic plague is still active today. Every year, it continues to infect people in Asia, Africa, South America, and North America. Modern victims are incredibly lucky, however, compared to the victims of the past. When bubonic plague is diagnosed early, it can now be cured with antibiotics.

SKILL PRACTICE   Read each question. Fill in the bubble next to the correct answer.

1. The author's main purpose was to _____.
   Ⓐ give information about the plague's history
   Ⓑ persuade readers to avoid people with the plague
   Ⓒ express ideas about the effects of the plague
   Ⓓ help current victims of the plague survive

2. Why did the author include information about pneumonic plague?
   Ⓐ to describe the swellings called buboes
   Ⓑ to explain a variation of the plague
   Ⓒ to show the number of people who died
   Ⓓ to tell how people survived the plague

3. Which evidence supports the idea that doctors in the 1300s did not know how to treat the plague?
   Ⓐ Doctors identified the plague's symptoms.
   Ⓑ The plague was carried on fleas on rats.
   Ⓒ Doctors wore masks to avoid bad air.
   Ⓓ The plague originated in Asia.

4. Which evidence supports the idea that the bubonic plague is much less deadly today?
   Ⓐ It is in Asia, Africa, and the Americas.
   Ⓑ It causes painful swellings called buboes.
   Ⓒ It is caused by bacteria that do not exist today.
   Ⓓ It can now be treated with antibiotics.

STRATEGY PRACTICE   Which information from the passage would be the most useful for a medical student who is studying the way diseases spread? Why?

_____

_____

Compare and Contrast

Students practice comparing and contrasting by looking at the similarities and differences between two or more people or things.

Make Inferences

Students practice making inferences by using clues in a passage to understand what is being implied.

DAY 1

Review the *Compare and Contrast* skill with students. Say: **Good readers look for how two or more things are alike or different when they compare them.** Tell students they are going to read about two historic flu outbreaks. Encourage them to look for similarities and differences in the two pandemics. Then remind students of the *Make Connections* strategy (Week 2). Say: **When you make a connection, you don't have to have experienced the *exact* same thing an author is writing about. Instead, you can think of a similar situation from your own life and relate it to what you have read.** Have students read the passage. Then direct them to complete the skill and strategy practice activities. Review the answers together.

DAY 2

Remind students of the *Compare and Contrast* skill. Then tell students they are going to read about how different types of rocks are formed. Say: **Look for repeated words or phrases that signal similarities.** Then remind students of the *Monitor Comprehension* strategy (Week 1). Say: **A good way to monitor your comprehension is to briefly pause after each paragraph and ask yourself:** *Could I tell that information to someone else?* **If not, reread the information.** Have students read the passage. When they have finished, direct them to complete the skill and strategy practice activities. Review the answers together.

DAY 3

Review the *Make Inferences* skill with students. Say: **Not all information is directly stated in a text. You can use what you already know and what you read to figure out "hidden" or implied information.** Tell students they are going to read a passage about robots that make music. Remind them to "read between the lines" to make inferences. Then remind students of the *Make Connections* strategy. Say: **As you read, think about the kind of music you enjoy. Compare music you have heard to the sounds that the robots might make.** When students have finished reading, direct them to complete the skill and strategy practice activities. Review the answers together.

DAY 4

Remind students of the *Make Inferences* skill. Then tell students they are going to read about composting. Say: **Over the last decade, much has been written about the benefits of recycling and composting. Use any background information you have about this topic to make inferences as you read.** Then remind students of the *Monitor Comprehension* strategy. Say: **Good readers look for key details within a text. You can underline key details or mark them with stars to keep track of important information.** When students have finished reading, direct them to complete the skill and strategy practice activities. Review the answers together.

DAY 5

Tell students they will practice both the *Compare and Contrast* and *Make Inferences* skills as they read a folk tale. Say: **Look for similarities and differences between the characters in the folk tale. Then think about messages that are not directly stated.** Remind students of the *Monitor Comprehension* strategy. Say: **If you do not understand a word, you can look it up in the dictionary or use context clues to figure out its meaning.** Direct students to read the passage and to complete the skill and strategy practice activities. Review the answers as a group.

READ THE PASSAGE   Look for details that describe the 1918 and 2009 flu viruses.

Flu Pandemics

In 1918, the world suffered one of the worst flu outbreaks in recorded history. A flu pandemic, or worldwide outbreak, infected roughly one in every three people in the world. Recordkeeping was not very accurate at that time, so the final death toll remains unknown. Given what we do know, it is estimated that as many as 100 million people died from the 1918 flu pandemic. It is still considered to be the worst natural disaster in history.

The flu, short for *influenza,* is caused by a virus. When the human body detects any virus, the immune system becomes active in order to fight it. Typically, people with strong immune systems, such as healthy young adults, recover faster from the virus than people who have weak immune systems, such as the elderly or very young children. However, the 1918 flu virus killed more healthy adults than it did the elderly or the very young. The 1918 virus was so deadly that people's bodies overreacted. Strong immune systems then became too aggressive in fighting the virus and actually caused more harm, often killing those infected.

Fortunately, science, recordkeeping, and disaster-response measures have all improved greatly. Today, doctors have better medicines to treat potential outbreaks, and they know more about how viruses spread. In 2009, another flu pandemic broke out. The virus was related to the one in 1918. However, this flu virus was less dangerous and did not cause people's immune systems to overreact. Also, medicines to treat or prevent the flu were stronger, so the 2009 pandemic caused only a tiny fraction of the amount of damage done by the pandemic in 1918.

SKILL PRACTICE   Read each question. Fill in the bubble next to the correct answer.

1. Compared to other natural disasters, the 1918 flu virus was _____.

   Ⓐ not as deadly

   Ⓑ much deadlier

   Ⓒ equally severe

   Ⓓ the least severe

2. How did the 1918 flu virus affect people compared to most other flu viruses?

   Ⓐ It affected people with weaker immune systems the most.

   Ⓑ Elderly people recovered more slowly.

   Ⓒ More young children were affected.

   Ⓓ More victims were healthy young adults.

3. How were the 1918 flu virus and the 2009 flu virus similar?

   Ⓐ Both caused pandemics.

   Ⓑ Both infected the same number of people.

   Ⓒ Both created immune system overreactions.

   Ⓓ Both were untreatable with medicine.

4. Which best explains why fewer people died from the 2009 flu virus than from the 1918 flu virus?

   Ⓐ The 1918 outbreak affected people with weak immune systems.

   Ⓑ Doctors in 1918 did not have the right medicines.

   Ⓒ People's immune systems were stronger in 2009.

   Ⓓ People kept better records in 2009.

STRATEGY PRACTICE   Describe a recent natural disaster that you are familiar with. How was it similar to or different from the 1918 flu pandemic?

_____

_____

Think about the ways different rocks are classified.

Classifying Rocks

Rocks are all around us. They can be found randomly on the ground or as part of beautiful landscaping. Have you ever wondered where all of these rocks come from? Rocks are classified into three main categories based on how they formed. The next time you see a rock, think about its possible origin.

Igneous Rocks

Igneous rocks form when magma (hot, molten rock located deep inside Earth) cools. These rocks are divided into two types. **Intrusive** igneous rocks develop when liquid magma becomes solid inside Earth. **Extrusive** igneous rocks form when lava (magma from a volcano) becomes solid on Earth's surface.

Sedimentary Rocks

All sedimentary rocks form on top of Earth's surface. They form from sand, minerals, and tiny fragments of rocks, seashells, and even plants. Wind, water, and ice deposit the fragments (called sediment) in layers called **strata**. Over time, the strata layers harden into rock, which forms new rocks.

Metamorphic Rocks

Not surprisingly, metamorphic rocks have undergone a metamorphosis, or a change. Metamorphic rocks form when sedimentary or igneous rocks are transformed by heat or pressure. These transformations may occur inside Earth, when magma heats the rocks, or on the surface, when tectonic plates collide during an earthquake. When these thick plates that make up Earth's crust hit each other, they create enormous amounts of pressure, which forms new rocks.

SKILL PRACTICE Read each question. Fill in the bubble next to the correct answer.

1. Igneous rocks differ from sedimentary rocks because igneous rocks form _____.
   - Ⓐ when molten rock cools
   - Ⓑ from layers of sediment
   - Ⓒ from seashells and fossils
   - Ⓓ when rock is transformed

2. How are intrusive and extrusive rocks similar?
   - Ⓐ Both come from volcanoes.
   - Ⓑ Both are found on Earth's surface.
   - Ⓒ Both form from liquid magma.
   - Ⓓ Both form from sand and minerals.

3. How are metamorphic and igneous rocks similar?
   - Ⓐ Both require pressure to form.
   - Ⓑ Both start out as sedimentary rocks.
   - Ⓒ Both form during an earthquake.
   - Ⓓ Both can form inside Earth or on its surface.

4. Which of these do only sedimentary rocks do?
   - Ⓐ change with time
   - Ⓑ form strata
   - Ⓒ react to temperature
   - Ⓓ form inside Earth

STRATEGY PRACTICE Was there any part of the passage that you did not understand right away? How did you figure it out?

_____

_____

READ THE PASSAGE   Use clues from the passage and what you know about music to make inferences.

Music—By Robot?

At England's University of Plymouth, Professor Eduardo Miranda has been programming pairs of robots to compose music. Miranda's robots have simple "vocal cords" and are programmed to sing and to listen to each other. The robots' unique warbling sounds do not perfectly match the human voice, but each machine is definitely sharing music with the other in a new and unique way.

Each robot is equipped with speakers, software that mimics the human voice, a mouth that opens as it "sings," a microphone for ears, and a camera for eyes. The robots also move. Miranda hopes that by studying his robot vocalists, he can discover something about how and why humans create, perform, and listen to music.

When the robots sing, first one robot makes six random sounds. Its partner responds with more vocalizations. The first robot analyzes the sounds to see if their sequences are similar. If they are, it nods its head and commits the sounds to memory, and the second robot notices and "memorizes" the musical sequence, too. If the first robot thinks the sounds are too different, it shakes its head and both robots ignore the sounds. Then the process continues.

Miranda set up an experiment in which he left the two robots alone in his study for two weeks. When he returned, his little warblers had, by imitating each other, not only shared notes but combined them. The product of their collaboration was far from symphonic, but the robots had begun to combine the notes into their own self-developed "songs."

With the help of his warbling robots, one of Miranda's goals is to create music that no human would ever compose. Miranda believes the robots are ideal for this purpose because they would not be influenced by any existing musical styles or rules.

SKILL PRACTICE   Read each question. Fill in the bubble next to the correct answer.

1. Why did Professor Eduardo Miranda leave the robots alone in his study?
   - Ⓐ He was busy teaching classes.
   - Ⓑ He did not want anyone to take the robots.
   - Ⓒ He wanted to see what the robots would do on their own.
   - Ⓓ He had not finished programming the robots.

2. What do Miranda's robots probably have?
   - Ⓐ the skills to create new hardware
   - Ⓑ the desire to print out sheet music
   - Ⓒ the vocalizations needed to create symphonies
   - Ⓓ the ability to create original music

3. During Miranda's experiment, the two robots _____.
   - Ⓐ locked the door
   - Ⓑ interacted with each other
   - Ⓒ learned to sing better than humans
   - Ⓓ refused to cooperate with one another

4. Miranda probably wants his robots to _____.
   - Ⓐ discover new forms of music
   - Ⓑ sing music as well as humans do
   - Ⓒ promote traditional forms of music
   - Ⓓ memorize a variety of music

STRATEGY PRACTICE   What types of music do you enjoy? Why?

_____

_____

READ THE PASSAGE   As you read, think about what you would need to start a composting pile.

Making Soil from Kitchen Scraps

As soon as a plant dies anywhere on Earth, it is quietly attacked by microscopic bacteria along with visible organisms like insects, fungi, and worms. Composting is nature's way of recycling. The process can turn any kind of organic waste—food scraps, manure, grass clippings, leaves, sawdust, and even paper—into dark, rich soil called *humus*. The final product can then be used in gardens to improve natural growth.

Although composting happens naturally, many backyard gardeners create compost heaps to produce humus that will help their plants thrive. It is possible to begin with nothing more than dry leaves, water, air, and kitchen scraps (excluding meat and fat). Protect the compost pile from prowling pets and wildlife, and mix it in proper proportions with dry materials like straw or shredded newspaper. The process will happen naturally, without any extra work from human hands. Professional composters have more fine-tuned processes and often use manure from ranches or parks, but the basic ingredients for professionals and amateurs alike are exactly the same.

It may be hard to imagine a large pile of vegetables or paper turning into soil, but it happens every day. Two of the most productive composters are bacteria and earthworms. Bacteria love compost heaps, and compost heaps love bacteria. Bacteria eat nearly anything and are excellent decomposers. Earthworms ingest soil and organic material, break it down inside their bodies, and then cast it off as rich soil. When extra items are added to a compost pile, such as eggshells or the husks from corncobs, bacteria and earthworms get to work in a flash. If you are a gardener, consider making your own compost pile soon—your garden will reward you.

SKILL PRACTICE   Read each question. Fill in the bubble next to the correct answer.

1. You can infer that humus is _____.
   Ⓐ destroyed by bacteria
   Ⓑ harmful to growing vegetables
   Ⓒ the best soil for a garden plot
   Ⓓ created only by professionals

2. A composter could probably best protect the compost pile from pets and wildlife by _____.
   Ⓐ putting up warning signs
   Ⓑ keeping bacteria out
   Ⓒ adding leftover food to the pile
   Ⓓ building a fence around the pile

3. What can you infer about plants in a garden that contains humus?
   Ⓐ They are larger and healthier than other plants.
   Ⓑ They have been grown in an unnatural way.
   Ⓒ They are less attractive than regular plants.
   Ⓓ They have harmful ingredients in their soil.

4. Which item would be good for a compost pile?
   Ⓐ empty cans
   Ⓑ wilted lettuce
   Ⓒ hamburger
   Ⓓ rocks

STRATEGY PRACTICE   What information from the passage is most important for explaining how scraps become soil?

_____

_____

READ THE FOLK TALE   Underline or make notes about words you do not understand.

The Fish Thief

Although Anil had been fishing in the stream with others since daybreak, no one had caught any fish. As daylight faded, Anil pondered his situation: "Perhaps these others are honest fishers, but I am not." So he packed up his rod and awaited the darkness.

In Anil's part of India, many large estates had lush gardens and beautiful lakes. Wealthy estate owners often left their gates open during the day so that visitors could enjoy the lovely gardens. Occasionally, a wandering holy man entered an estate and meditated there for weeks, but the owners did not mind. At night, the gates were securely closed.

Knowing that a nearby estate's lake was filled with fish, Anil climbed over the estate's walls and cast his net in the private lake. The noise roused the owner's servants, and they began to scour the darkness for the intruder. When Anil heard people searching, he used ashes to disguise himself as a holy man and pretended to meditate. Finding him, the servants reported to the owner that there was no intruder, only a respectable holy man.

The next day, word spread that a great yogi was residing beneath a tree in the estate. People began bringing fruits, naan bread, samosas, and other delicacies and set them at Anil's feet. Some people even left coins. "This is strange," thought Anil. "I am only a pretend holy man, but this life is much nicer than the life of a fish thief." And from that moment on, Anil decided to become a real seeker of truth and spent the rest of his life in peaceful contemplation.

SKILL PRACTICE   Read each question. Fill in the bubble next to the correct answer.

1. Anil was different from the other fishers because they _____.

   Ⓐ were honest, but he was not

   Ⓑ had delicacies to eat, but he did not

   Ⓒ caught fish, but he did not

   Ⓓ owned estates, but he did not

2. The gates of the estate were most likely locked at night because the owner did not want _____.

   Ⓐ yogis living in his garden

   Ⓑ thieves and intruders to enter

   Ⓒ his servants to escape

   Ⓓ others to know about his garden

3. People brought fruits and other foods to Anil because _____.

   Ⓐ no one was catching any fish

   Ⓑ they had respect for holy men

   Ⓒ the servants needed food

   Ⓓ they wanted to honor the owner of the estate

4. How was Anil different at the end of the passage?

   Ⓐ He was a successful fisher.

   Ⓑ He owned a large estate.

   Ⓒ He decided to be a real holy man.

   Ⓓ He became a servant at the estate.

STRATEGY PRACTICE   List one or two words you found confusing and describe how you figured out their meanings.

_____

_____

Character and Setting

Students practice analyzing character and setting by looking at the traits and motivations of a character and where and when a passage's events take place.

Theme

Students practice identifying the theme by looking for the central message or lesson in a passage.

DAY 1

Review the *Character and Setting* skill with students. Say: **You can learn about the character of a real person by thinking about that person's words, actions, and beliefs. The setting in a nonfiction text is where and when events take place.** Then review the *Monitor Comprehension* strategy (Week 1). Say: **Part of monitoring comprehension is being able to paraphrase information from a text, or repeat it in your own words. As you read the passage, think about original ways to explain the key information.** Have students read the instructions at the top of the page and the passage. When students have finished, direct them to complete the skill and strategy practice activities. Review the answers together.

DAY 2

Review the *Character and Setting* skill with students. Say: **You can learn a lot about a character in a story by thinking about how that character changes over time. As you read, also think about how the setting affects the characters.** Remind students to study the characters' actions as they read. Then remind students of the *Visualization* strategy (Week 3). Say: **As you read, make a mental picture of what is happening in the passage. Try to use each of your five senses to create a complete visualization.** When students have finished reading, direct them to complete the skill practice activity. Review the answers. Then have students complete the strategy practice activity and share their sketches with the group.

DAY 3

Review the *Theme* skill with students. Say: **Good readers look for a central message, or theme, within a passage. Often, the theme is not directly stated, but you can figure it out by seeing what the characters learn.** Tell students to look for the theme after they have finished reading the entire passage. Then remind students of the *Monitor Comprehension* strategy. Say: **Rereading is a good way to search for a passage's theme. Reread the passage at least once to help you find the hidden lesson.** Have students read the passage. When students have finished, direct them to complete the skill and strategy practice activities. Review the answers together.

DAY 4

Review the *Theme* skill with students. Say: **When you read a nonfiction passage, look for a theme or message that the author is trying to share. Ask: *What would this author like me to do? How would this author like me to act?*** Instruct students to think about these questions as they read about first impressions. Then remind students of the *Visualization* strategy. Say: **You can visualize events that have happened in your own life and compare them to events or information in a passage.** Have students read the passage. When students have finished, direct them to complete the skill and strategy practice activities. Review the answers together.

DAY 5

Tell students they will practice both the *Character and Setting* and *Theme* skills as they read about a successful cartoonist. Then remind students of the *Monitor Comprehension* strategy. Say: **Remember that you can make notations in the passage to help you remember important information.** Have students read the passage. When students have finished, direct them to complete the skill and strategy practice activities. Review the answers together.

READ THE PASSAGE   Think about the characteristics of people who volunteer to help others.

Building a Home Far from Home

Octavio González Caballero grew up in Paraguay and is going to college in Chile. So how did he end up in Knoxville, Tennessee, putting shingles on the roof of a new home for a poor family? González Caballero is one of the international students who has traveled across the globe to join Habitat for Humanity, a nonprofit organization that brings people together to build homes for families in need.

The idea for Habitat for Humanity began when wealthy businessperson Millard Fuller and his wife, Linda, began looking for ways to help those who were less fortunate. The Fullers partnered with an organization in Georgia that provided homes for poor families. Habitat for Humanity was formed in 1976. Since then, Habitat for Humanity has constructed more than 500,000 houses around the world.

In between hammering, González Caballero takes a break and talks about why the program is so important to him. "I enjoy getting to share this experience with the family. I also wanted to see what Habitat is doing in the United States," he says. "Habitat gives people an opportunity, and families need an opportunity. It's a satisfactory feeling being a part of that."

When he finishes working in Knoxville, González Caballero will visit other U.S. cities to talk about the success of the program in other countries. He will share stories about the 400 homes that have been built back in his home country.

González Caballero wants to finish college, where he is studying to be an engineer. But he does not plan to abandon the Habitat for Humanity philosophy. Upon graduation, González Caballero hopes to work for a nonprofit organization and continue to make a better world for everyone.

SKILL PRACTICE   Read each question. Fill in the bubble next to the correct answer.

1. According to the passage, which word best describes Octavio González Caballero?

   Ⓐ lazy

   Ⓑ optimistic

   Ⓒ cautious

   Ⓓ distant

2. Which of these describes people who volunteer for Habitat for Humanity?

   Ⓐ They come from families in need.

   Ⓑ They want to help others have better lives.

   Ⓒ They come from foreign countries.

   Ⓓ They have backgrounds in engineering.

3. Where is González Caballero currently building a house?

   Ⓐ Paraguay

   Ⓑ Chile

   Ⓒ Georgia

   Ⓓ Tennessee

4. Millard and Linda Fuller can best be described as _____.

   Ⓐ quiet

   Ⓑ cooperative

   Ⓒ generous

   Ⓓ friendly

STRATEGY PRACTICE   Use information from the passage to write one or two sentences that describe Habitat for Humanity.

_____

_____

READ THE PASSAGE   Think about how the setting affects the characters in the story.

A Flimsy Dinghy

The ride so far was spectacular, but as usual, Dad's attention was closely focused on the raft. He clutched the hard rubber side grips while the rest of us paddled. Dad comes on our annual white-water trips only to be with Mom on her birthday—not because he loves plunging downstream in what he always calls "a flimsy dinghy."

Of course, Mom was having a great time, squealing with delight every time the bright yellow raft slapped the surface of the surging river. Caitlin, this year's guide, was doing a superb job. She steered expertly through the rocks, splashes, and sudden drops.

The storm came out of nowhere. Heavy clouds dropped down like a window slamming shut. They quickly blocked out the sun, and the sky turned a dark, ominous gray.

"Hold tight," said Caitlin. "I'll guide us to the next access point where we can dock safely."

Mom and I both looked at Dad, afraid that the sudden change in weather would push him over the edge. But it turns out that there is a spark of adventure in everyone—even Dad.

As the sky erupted, Dad leaned back his head to let the rain splash on his face. Then he laughed and grabbed the fourth paddle—which usually lies untouched on the floor of the raft—stuck it in the choppy water, and began rowing.

The summer rain stopped as quickly as it had started. Mom and I stared in amazement as Dad kept happily rowing, and our flimsy dinghy bounced along under a sparkling, fresh rainbow.

SKILL PRACTICE   Read each question. Fill in the bubble next to the correct answer.

1. **Which of the following best describes how Dad usually acts on white-water rafting trips?**

   Ⓐ cautious and nervous

   Ⓑ adventurous and daring

   Ⓒ uninterested and bored

   Ⓓ excited and enthusiastic

2. **The setting of the story changed when _____.**

   Ⓐ the family arrived at the river

   Ⓑ Caitlin guided the boat in a new direction

   Ⓒ the raft slapped the river

   Ⓓ a sudden storm arrived

3. **Which word best describes how Mom felt at the end of the story?**

   Ⓐ frightened

   Ⓑ nervous

   Ⓒ surprised

   Ⓓ worried

4. **Which of the following best explains Dad's actions at the end of the story?**

   Ⓐ He was pretending to enjoy white-water rafting.

   Ⓑ He felt happy and was able to enjoy himself.

   Ⓒ He was scared and unhappy with his family.

   Ⓓ He was eager to dock and get to safe land.

STRATEGY PRACTICE   On a separate sheet of paper, sketch how the characters and setting looked at the end of the story.

READ THE PASSAGE   Think about the lesson, or moral, of the story.

Compromise in Aisle Five

Beto held one side of the long box, Nick held the other, and neither one showed any sign of letting go any time soon. Suddenly, Sam's Hardware, the only store in town still open at that late hour, was the scene of an epic showdown.

"Drop it!" said Beto, who was used to giving orders to his dog instead of another human being. "I need this heavy-duty foil for my science fair project!"

"I got here first," said Nick, grabbing onto the box even tighter, "and I need it more than you do!"

"I'd let you have it," said Beto, "but it's the last one they have."

Shoppers gathered in the aisle to watch as the two students tugged the long box back and forth.

"No way," shouted Nick. "You're out of luck. I need this foil for my solar oven."

"You have got to be kidding me!" yelled Beto. "Don't tell me you're thinking of making a solar oven out of a pizza box and foil, because that's *my* science fair project, and I spent ages choosing it."

"Well, that's my project, too," said Nick, "and I have no intention of changing my mind."

They stood in the center of the aisle for a few tense moments, staring at each other fiercely and practically growling. Suddenly the solution occurred to both boys at once and they both burst out laughing. The other shoppers applauded as the box fell to the ground.

Two weeks later, Nick and Beto laughed again when their science fair collaboration won the second-place ribbon. It was the beginning of a long and productive friendship.

SKILL PRACTICE   Read each question. Fill in the bubble next to the correct answer.

1. Why is the hardware store setting an important part of the story's conflict?
   Ⓐ It sells dangerous items.
   Ⓑ It is the only store still open.
   Ⓒ The owner dislikes fighting.
   Ⓓ The shoppers are uncomfortable.

2. How did Beto and Nick change during the story?
   Ⓐ They were stubborn at first but then realized they could cooperate.
   Ⓑ They were annoyed at first but then became extremely angry.
   Ⓒ They were friendly at first but then got into a heated argument.
   Ⓓ They were surprised at first but then became very serious.

3. How does the story title relate to the theme?
   Ⓐ Two shoppers come to an agreement.
   Ⓑ Two school rivals argue in public.
   Ⓒ Two boys learn other things to do with foil.
   Ⓓ Two classmates run into each other at the grocery store.

4. What lesson did Beto and Nick learn?
   Ⓐ It is important to stand your ground in an argument.
   Ⓑ Laughter solves all problems.
   Ⓒ Working together gets better results than working against each other.
   Ⓓ Competition makes people improve their game.

STRATEGY PRACTICE   How does rereading help you better understand the story's theme?

_____

_____

READ THE PASSAGE As you read, visualize what it is like to meet someone for the first time.

The First Impression

Have you ever heard the phrase "You never get a second chance to make a first impression"? It may sound like an odd piece of advice, but it is true—the first impression someone has of you when meeting you for the first time will likely affect how that person treats you or reacts to you in the future.

What is even more interesting is that the brain takes in all the information to create that first impression in about three seconds. When you meet someone for the first time, by the time you have stated your name or shaken hands, the other person has already formed an opinion about the type of person you are.

So how do you make a good first impression? All of the things adults tell you—such as dressing nicely, practicing good hygiene, and being polite—are very important. However, the most important tool for making a good first impression is your face. Smiling, being responsive, and looking like you are happy will almost always have a positive effect on people, especially people who do not know you. Humans are wired to want to smile back when we are smiled at.

Additionally, smiling and being in a positive mood helps you better understand and relate to new things. This means that you are likely to be friendlier to people you do not know and to be more creative and able to solve problems more quickly. So if you ever need a reason to be happy, think about the wonderful people you might meet—and impress—with a cheerful smile.

SKILL PRACTICE Read each question. Fill in the bubble next to the correct answer.

1. According to the passage, a good first impression is important because it _____.
   (A) makes people less likely to judge you
   (B) affects how people treat you in the future
   (C) involves having a nice appearance
   (D) forces people to smile more often

2. Which of the following best describes the passage's theme?
   (A) There is never a reason to be sad.
   (B) Being positive has many rewards.
   (C) People judge each other too quickly.
   (D) Smiling is not needed in true relationships.

3. Why do you never get a second chance to make a first impression?
   (A) People decide very quickly what they think.
   (B) You will not see strangers a second time.
   (C) Your brain stops taking in information.
   (D) People change how they react in the future.

4. According to the passage, which of these is the best way to make a good first impression?
   (A) by smelling good
   (B) by shaking hands
   (C) by being well dressed
   (D) by smiling at the person

STRATEGY PRACTICE Visualize a good first impression and a bad first impression you have experienced. How were they different?

_____

_____

READ THE PASSAGE As you read, think about the different ways people can accomplish their dreams.

Quick Draw

When Sergio Aragonés came to New York City from Mexico in 1962, he had only 20 dollars and an art portfolio bulging with his cartoons. He spoke very little English but hoped to make it as a cartoonist for popular magazines in the United States.

Friends told Aragonés that his silly style was perfect for *MAD* magazine. Embarrassed by his poor English, he approached a Cuban cartoonist named Antonio Prohias who worked for the magazine. Unfortunately, it turned out that Prohias spoke even less English than Aragonés did. Still, Prohias enjoyed meeting another Hispanic cartoonist and passed samples of Aragonés's work on to the editors.

MAD's editors loved what they saw and decided to give Aragonés a try. Since he could not write jokes in English, Aragonés created some wordless cartoons that did not need any translation. The editors at *MAD* agreed to publish them, placing them in the margins of the magazine. Aragonés's "marginals" were immediately popular, although the editors suspected that Aragonés would soon run out of ideas. They expected him to last one or two issues at most.

For more than 50 years, this energetic cartoonist has proven the editors wrong. Aragonés's cartoons have appeared in all but one issue of *MAD* since his work first appeared in January 1963—and they were missing that time only because they were lost in the mail. Aragonés's speed, dedication, and consistency have earned him the reputation as the world's most productive cartoonist.

SKILL PRACTICE Read each question. Fill in the bubble next to the correct answer.

1. **What did Sergio Aragonés learn in his career?**
   - Ⓐ It is important to rely on friends for job opportunities.
   - Ⓑ By using your talent and taking a chance, obstacles can be overcome.
   - Ⓒ The United States is the best place to work.
   - Ⓓ Risks always work out for the best.

2. **Aragonés's decision to draw wordless cartoons shows that he was _____.**
   - Ⓐ afraid his jokes were not funny
   - Ⓑ embarrassed by his early cartoons
   - Ⓒ able to draw in only one style
   - Ⓓ uncomfortable writing in English

3. **Aragonés would probably agree that _____.**
   - Ⓐ success depends on hard work and consistency
   - Ⓑ cartoons are not an important art form
   - Ⓒ magazine editors are hard to work with
   - Ⓓ there is no need to learn a second language

4. **Which statement best describes the passage's theme?**
   - Ⓐ Cartoons are easy to create.
   - Ⓑ English is a difficult language to learn.
   - Ⓒ Humor is a universal language.
   - Ⓓ Cartooning is a good way to make money.

STRATEGY PRACTICE Explain how Aragonés's actions reveal his character.

_____

_____

Cause and Effect
Students practice identifying cause-and-effect relationships by looking for what happens (the effect) and why it happens (the cause).

Prediction
Students practice using clues from a passage to predict what will happen next.

DAY 1

Review the *Cause and Effect* skill with students. Say: **Think about what happens—the effect. Then think about why it happened—the cause.** Tell students to look for characters' motivations as causes in a passage about real-life superheroes. Then remind students of the *Ask Questions* strategy (Week 6). Read the directions at the top of the page and say: **Think of a question you have after hearing the directions. Look for the answer within the passage.** When students have finished reading, direct them to complete the skill and strategy practice activities. Review the answers together.

DAY 2

Remind students of the *Cause and Effect* skill. Tell students they are going to learn what caused certain people to accidentally discover new inventions. Say: **Look for what happened and why.** Then remind students of the *Make Connections* strategy (Week 2). Say: **You can make a text-to-world connection by thinking about how what you read in the passage relates to the world around you today.** Have students read the passage. When students have finished, direct them to complete the skill and strategy practice activities. Review the answers together.

DAY 3

Review the *Prediction* skill with students. Say: **Good readers use information from a nonfiction passage and their own personal knowledge to make predictions about what might happen in the future.** Tell students they will read a passage about medical technology. Encourage them to use what they learn to predict what life might be like in 50 years. Then remind students of the *Ask Questions* strategy. Say: **By asking and answering questions, you can check that you understand all of the information in a passage.** Direct students to read the passage and to complete the skill practice activity. Review the answers together. For the strategy practice activity, have partners work together.

DAY 4

Remind students of the *Prediction* skill. Say: **When you read fiction stories, pause briefly after each paragraph to predict what might happen next. When you have finished reading, think about whether or not your predictions were correct and why.** Then remind students of the *Make Connections* strategy. Say: **You can make a text-to-text connection by comparing a passage to another book, article, or story you have read.** When students have finished reading the passage, direct them to complete the skill and strategy practice activities. Review the answers together.

DAY 5

Tell students they will practice both the *Cause and Effect* and *Prediction* skills as they read about ancient tapestries. Say: **Look for causes and effects, and use that information to make predictions about the future.** Remind students of the *Ask Questions* strategy: **You can ask questions before you read, while you read, and after you read. These questions will help you to better understand the text.** Have students read the passage. When students have finished, direct them to complete the skill practice activity. Review the answers together. Then have students complete the strategy practice activity and compare their answers.

Daily Reading Comprehension • EMC 3457 • © Evan-Moor Corp.

READ THE PASSAGE   As you read, think about the arguments for and against real-life superheroes.

Real-Life "Superheroes"

On a cool night in San Francisco, a man calling himself Motor Mouth patrols the streets, looking to lend a hand to anyone needing aid. Dressed in a costume that includes a black mask to cover his face, Motor Mouth is one of a growing number of real-life "superheroes." People belonging to this group do not have actual superpowers, but they do want to help their communities and make the world a safer place.

In 2011, more than 300 people claimed to participate in the real-life superhero movement. Some people, such as Benjamin Fodor, who also uses the name Phoenix Jones when wearing his mask and cape, have received a lot of media attention. However, many of the other real-life superhero participants maintain low profiles. Most prefer to blend in with everyone else.

Do these real-life superheroes actually help? It depends on whom you ask. Phoenix Jones claims to have stopped robberies and fights, but the police say that his actions sometimes interfere with their work. They even had to arrest him once for spraying someone with pepper spray. In general, it is dangerous for people to insert themselves into potentially violent situations such as break-ins or fights. Police claim that regular citizens do not have the training or support to deal with criminals, and they advise would-be heroes to safely gather information about the crime and immediately contact the police instead.

The real-life superheroes and their supporters claim that they are responding to needs in their communities that police officers are unable to meet. They point out that the vast majority of real-life superheroes perform community service work, such as helping to feed the homeless. They also claim that the superheroes are positive symbols for their communities, inspiring others to do good deeds.

SKILL PRACTICE   Read each question. Fill in the bubble next to the correct answer.

1. Benjamin Fodor was arrested because he _____.
   Ⓐ created the superhero movement
   Ⓑ claimed to have superpowers
   Ⓒ sprayed someone with pepper spray
   Ⓓ wanted media attention

2. Police officers believe ordinary people should not try to be superheroes because they _____.
   Ⓐ could replace police officers
   Ⓑ will cause more crime
   Ⓒ lack professional training
   Ⓓ respond to needs in their communities

3. How do many real-life superheroes help their communities?
   Ⓐ by having unique abilities
   Ⓑ by wearing special costumes
   Ⓒ by lowering national crime rates
   Ⓓ by performing community service work

4. Why do some superheroes wear a costume or use a made-up name?
   Ⓐ to call attention to themselves
   Ⓑ to blend in with society
   Ⓒ to pretend to work for the police
   Ⓓ to help them respond when needed

STRATEGY PRACTICE   Write a question you still have about real-life superheroes.

_____

_____

READ THE PASSAGE   Think about what caused each inventor to make a breakthrough discovery.

Accidents That Changed the World

Inventors around the world spend millions of dollars each year trying to create devices, medicines, and other inventions that will make the world a better place to live. For a few lucky people, however, amazing inventions are more like happy accidents.

Vulcanized Rubber

In 1839, Charles Goodyear was looking for a way to make rubber more durable and less likely to melt at high temperatures. He accidentally spilled rubber, sulfur, and lead onto a hot stove. The mixture became harder than normal rubber and could withstand the high heat. Called vulcanized rubber, this accidental invention eventually made tires and sneakers possible.

Pacemakers

A medical pacemaker is inserted into a person's heart to help regulate the speed, or pace, of the heart's beats. But Wilson Greatbatch was not trying to invent this successful medical device in 1956. Instead, he was trying to build a device that would record fast heartbeats. But when Greatbatch accidentally used the wrong part in his device, it began pulsing at the same rate as a healthy heart.

Plastic

During the early 1900s, people needed a way to insulate electronics. They commonly used a material called shellac, which comes from beetles in Asia. However, shellac was expensive and difficult to work with. A chemist named Leo Baekeland wanted to invent an alternative. Instead, the material he ended up producing paved the way for modern plastic.

SKILL PRACTICE   Read each question. Fill in the bubble next to the correct answer.

1. Vulcanized rubber was accidentally invented because Charles Goodyear _____.

Ⓐ tried combining rubber with lead

Ⓑ spilled materials on a hot stove

Ⓒ added higher temperatures to regular rubber

Ⓓ put shellac in a rubber mixture

2. Wilson Greatbatch accidentally invented the pacemaker because he used _____.

Ⓐ a wrong part

Ⓑ electronics insulation

Ⓒ a record of fast heartbeats

Ⓓ higher heat than normal

3. Why did Leo Baekeland try to invent an alternative to shellac?

Ⓐ Shellac was in short supply.

Ⓑ He did not like working with beetles.

Ⓒ Shellac is costly to produce and hard to use.

Ⓓ He was hired to insulate electronics.

4. What caused Goodyear and Baekeland to invent their new materials?

Ⓐ They wanted to make existing products better.

Ⓑ They tried to create original inventions.

Ⓒ They were making medical devices.

Ⓓ They hoped to become famous inventors.

STRATEGY PRACTICE   How would modern life be different without these accidental inventions?

_____

_____

Name: _____

READ THE PASSAGE   Write questions about parts of the passage that interest you.

Bacteria Robots

It might seem like something from a science fiction movie, but scientists today are working on ways to combine certain kinds of bacteria with tiny robots. Scientists want to use these creations to improve the way we administer medicine. They claim that drug therapy, disease diagnosis, and even surgery could be greatly aided by the use of nanobiotechnology. *Nano-* means "tiny," and *bio-* means "life." This tiny technology will use living organisms in combination with electronics.

Electronics makers already use tiny robots to build complex but very tiny circuits. Medical scientists want to use these robots to repair patients' damaged organs or to direct medicines to affect specific cells. For example, tiny robots could be engineered to deliver chemotherapy directly to cancer cells instead of to the entire body.

Existing electronics are the right size, but they lack practical use. Robots that can be built small enough to enter a person's cells would be too tiny to move on their own. Therefore, scientists want to use tiny organisms such as bacteria to act as vehicles for the robots. The bacteria will be "driven" through the bloodstream by magnetic pulses. Once the bacteria are in the correct locations, the robots will be able to do their jobs. In theory, these robots will cause less damage to the body than traditional methods of delivering medicines or performing surgeries.

Nanobiotechnology has yet to be put into practice, but many people already have concerns about its use. Some people worry about the ethics involved with manipulating live organisms—and the possible side effects for their human hosts.

SKILL PRACTICE   Read each question. Fill in the bubble next to the correct answer.

1. Which of these is a reasonable prediction about the future if nanobiotechnology becomes a reality?
   Ⓐ Surgeries will take longer.
   Ⓑ Patients will recover more quickly.
   Ⓒ There will be more infections.
   Ⓓ Doctors will be less likely to diagnose diseases.

2. According to information from the passage, scientists will probably _____.
   Ⓐ continue trying to create nanobiotechnology
   Ⓑ look for new diseases caused by bacteria
   Ⓒ replace doctors with robots in surgery
   Ⓓ ignore all concerns from the public

3. Which of these could be a future benefit of nanobiotechnology?
   Ⓐ medicines that cost less
   Ⓑ superhuman strength
   Ⓒ fewer bacterial diseases
   Ⓓ simplified surgery

4. Due to public concern, it is possible that _____.
   Ⓐ dangerous bacteria will be released to the public
   Ⓑ nanobiotechnology will not be used
   Ⓒ doctors will be replaced by electronics makers
   Ⓓ nanobiotechnology will cure all diseases

STRATEGY PRACTICE   Write a question you would ask a scientist who is working on nanobiotechnology. Discuss your question with a partner.

_____

_____

READ THE PASSAGE   Read slowly and pause after each paragraph.

At the Buzzer

The middle school basketball game was tied in the last minute of the game. The Taylor Tigers were supposed to have easily beaten the Appleville Armadillos. But Jesse Michael, the Armadillos' star player, was having the game of his life. He had scored 25 of his team's 40 points with fantastic jump shots, and he also contributed 11 rebounds. Jesse now had the ball and was charging down the court.

Jesse darted around one Tiger defender, then another. He dribbled and spun to his left as two more Tigers tried to trap him and steal the ball. Jesse had an open view of the hoop—and of the Tigers' number-one defensive player, Robbie "The Robber" Williamson.

Robbie had the most steals of any player in the district. He was also surprisingly fast for his size. He grinned and moved between Jesse and the basket. Jesse stopped, faked like he was going to shoot, and then jumped and launched the ball. Robbie, however, had not been fooled. He waited patiently, and as soon as Jesse shot the ball, he leapt up and tipped it off course. The ball sailed out of bounds, so it was still the Armadillos' ball.

With only 30 seconds left on the clock, Armadillos player Ferdinand Molera threw the ball inbounds to Jesse. But before Jesse could get set, Robbie swooped in and stole the ball! Unfortunately, Robbie had moved too fast and was unable to keep control. Once again, the ball rolled out of bounds.

Now there were only 10 seconds left. The Armadillos got set to throw the ball inbounds again. There would be time for one more shot.

SKILL PRACTICE   Read each question. Fill in the bubble next to the correct answer.

1. Based on what has already happened in the story, what will most likely happen next?
   Ⓐ Ferdinand will throw the ball to Robbie.
   Ⓑ Jesse will pass the ball to Robbie.
   Ⓒ The Armadillos will give the ball to the Tigers.
   Ⓓ Jesse will make a last-second basket.

2. What makes the setting of the story so exciting?
   Ⓐ The Armadillos are from Appleville.
   Ⓑ The game will decide the championship.
   Ⓒ The score is tied near the end of the game.
   Ⓓ The Tigers are on their home court.

3. Based on information from the story, what will Jesse probably do in the future?
   Ⓐ pass the ball to Ferdinand
   Ⓑ continue to be a star player
   Ⓒ not play as well
   Ⓓ decide to quit basketball

4. What will Robbie probably try in future games?
   Ⓐ to keep the ball inbounds
   Ⓑ to shoot more accurately
   Ⓒ to run faster down the court
   Ⓓ to jump higher when blocking

STRATEGY PRACTICE   Describe a movie, book, or experience that is similar to this story.

_____

_____

READ THE PASSAGE   As you read, think about what modern works of art portray.

Tapestries of the Middle Ages

During the Middle Ages in Europe, people regularly used tapestries for decoration and for warmth. These wall hangings were usually woven from wool by hand on a loom. Many tapestries portrayed detailed scenes from history, religion, and mythology. Unfortunately, most of these works of art from the early Middle Ages have not survived the centuries, and we know of them only through written references from the era.

One of the most famous woven creations from that time is known as the *Bayeux Tapestry.* It shows William the Conqueror's victory in gaining the crown of England. This 230-foot-long (about 70 meters) piece of cloth dates from the eleventh century and gives a unique illustration of medieval clothing and weapons.

Another famous tapestry, *The Lady and the Unicorn,* shows a woman with the mythical horned creature. The tapestry has six different panels, each representing one of the senses—sight, hearing, touch, taste, smell—and one extra panel for love. This creation probably dates from the late 1400s and was most likely woven in Flanders, a region in northern Europe.

While the nature of the designs has changed, tapestries are still made today. Computerized looms create landscapes, floral patterns, animals, and abstract designs. The tapestry fabric can be used as wall hangings, furniture coverings, even clothing. The methods may have changed, but tapestries seem to be here to stay.

SKILL PRACTICE   Read each question. Fill in the bubble next to the correct answer.

1. Current knowledge about tapestries from the Middle Ages comes mostly from writings because _____.

   Ⓐ very few tapestries were made during the Middle Ages

   Ⓑ tapestries from the Middle Ages decayed or were lost over the centuries

   Ⓒ tapestries are kept hidden away from viewers

   Ⓓ modern people do not like tapestries

2. According to the passage, people created tapestries in the Middle Ages to _____.

   Ⓐ portray historical and cultural stories

   Ⓑ teach people how to weave on a loom

   Ⓒ help historians record current events

   Ⓓ display news and weather information

3. What will probably happen to the *Bayeux Tapestry* in the next century?

   Ⓐ It will decay from age.

   Ⓑ It will remain interesting to art lovers.

   Ⓒ It will be replaced by a more recent scene from history.

   Ⓓ It will be remade to show modern clothing and weapons.

4. Tapestries woven in the future will probably _____.

   Ⓐ depict cultural events

   Ⓑ be used to keep houses warm

   Ⓒ hang on museum walls

   Ⓓ be created using modern methods

STRATEGY PRACTICE   Write a question you had at the beginning of the passage. How did your question help you understand the passage?

_____

_____

Nonfiction Text Features

Students practice identifying and comprehending common features of nonfiction text.

Visual Information

Students examine and evaluate information that is depicted visually.

DAY 1

Review the *Nonfiction Text Features* skill. Say: **This is a partial table of contents. A table of contents is located at the beginning of a book or magazine to tell what information is included in the complete work. When reading a table of contents, pay attention to how the text is arranged and what kind of information is included.** Then review the *Determine Important Information* strategy (Week 5). Say: **As you read, think about situations in which this information would be important.** When students have finished reading, direct them to complete the skill and strategy practice activities. Review the answers together.

DAY 2

Remind students of the *Nonfiction Text Features* skill. Say: **Authors add many features to nonfiction, such as captions, labels, headings, illustrations, maps, or different fonts. These features guide readers and help to efficiently organize information.** Review the *Organization* strategy (Week 4). Say: **The author of this passage has organized information into three main paragraphs. As you read, think about why the author organized the passage in this way.** When students have finished reading, direct them to complete the skill and strategy practice activities. Review the answers together.

DAY 3

Review the *Visual Information* skill with students. Say: **Visual information is information that is shown through illustrations, diagrams, graphs, maps, photos, or other graphic-based elements. Often, authors use visual information to enhance or further explain information that is presented in a text.** Remind students of the *Determine Important Information* strategy. Say: **As you study the diagram, think about why the labels are included.** Have students read the passage, study the diagram, and complete the skill practice activity. Review the answers together. Then have partners complete the strategy practice activity.

DAY 4

Remind students of the *Visual Information* skill. Say: **It can be difficult for some people to visualize complicated information in a text. Many authors include visual information to aid comprehension.** Then remind students of the *Organization* strategy. Say: **Authors can organize information by sequence, cause and effect, problem and solution, or main idea and details. As you read the passage, think about which way the information is organized.** When students have finished reading the passage and studying the image, direct them to complete the skill and strategy practice activities. Review the answers together.

DAY 5

Tell students they will practice using both the *Nonfiction Text Features* and *Visual Information* skills to learn how to make a delicious meal. Say: **Notice that there is both text and a picture. Think about what type of information each element includes.** Remind students of the *Determine Important Information* strategy. Say: **Think about the most essential details someone would need to know to make his or her own bento.** When students have finished reading, direct them to complete the skill and strategy practice activities. Review the answers together.

    Daily Reading Comprehension • EMC 3457 • © Evan-Moor Corp.

READ THE TABLE OF CONTENTS   Read the partial table of contents from a book about the human body.

Table of Contents (cont.)

SKILL PRACTICE   Read each question. Fill in the bubble next to the correct answer.

1. The section about the central nervous system is located on _____.
   - Ⓐ pages 112–130
   - Ⓑ page 111
   - Ⓒ pages 112–119
   - Ⓓ page 120

2. The main purpose of this table of contents is to _____.
   - Ⓐ tell about the autonomic nervous system
   - Ⓑ show where information is located
   - Ⓒ explain the definitions of medical terms
   - Ⓓ give information about medical school

3. What information can you learn from reading the text in parentheses?
   - Ⓐ which pages cover the topic
   - Ⓑ antonyms for the section headings
   - Ⓒ other topics covered in the sections
   - Ⓓ explanations of what each system or body part does

4. The two systems dealing with involuntary functions of your organs and glands are the _____.
   - Ⓐ somatic and autonomic systems
   - Ⓑ sympathetic and parasympathetic systems
   - Ⓒ instinct and fight-or-flight systems
   - Ⓓ brain and spinal cord systems

STRATEGY PRACTICE   Would this book help you find out what causes headaches? Why or why not?

_____

_____

READ THE PASSAGE   As you read, think about how the passage is organized.

The Beloved Goat-Hoofed God

An Amusing Musician

In Greek mythology, Pan was the god of shepherds, flocks, and herds. He was noisy, rather immature, and quite silly. Certainly, Pan was one of the most troublesome Greek gods, yet he was a capable musician and is said to be the inventor of panpipes. Pan loved to dance and chase nymphs. In spite of the chaos he caused, the Greeks loved this little goat-hoofed god and sang many hymns to him.

Pan's Name

The Greek word *pan* means "all," and Thomas Bulfinch describes Pan in his famous and colossal volume *Bulfinch's Mythology* as the "Greek god of nature and the universe." The words *panorama, pantheon,* and *pandemic* come from the Greek root *pan.* The words *panic* and *pandemonium* also come from Pan's name. Can you guess why?

Pan is typically shown with goat hoofs and horns, wearing the pelt of a lynx.

Pan's Birth

According to many myths, Pan was born in Arcadia,* but scholars do not agree on his parentage. Some say his parents were Zeus and Hybris. Others say he was the son of Penelope, who was either a nymph or one of Odysseus's wives. Many sources say that Pan's father was Hermes. Whatever his origin, Pan certainly made his mark on history.

*Arcadia: a region in ancient Greece known for its innocence, peaceful beauty, and simple pleasures

SKILL PRACTICE   Read each question. Fill in the bubble next to the correct answer.

1. Information about Pan's parents is located under _____.
   - Ⓐ the illustration
   - Ⓑ An Amusing Musician
   - Ⓒ Pan's Name
   - Ⓓ Pan's Birth

2. The asterisk after "Arcadia" indicates that _____.
   - Ⓐ the word is explained below
   - Ⓑ it is a foreign word
   - Ⓒ everyone agrees on its name
   - Ⓓ it is an imaginary place

3. What information does the caption provide?
   - Ⓐ a definition of the word *pan*
   - Ⓑ a description of what Pan looks like
   - Ⓒ an overview of who Pan is
   - Ⓓ the exact location of Arcadia

4. Which of the following best describes the purpose of the headings?
   - Ⓐ to tell the main idea of the passage
   - Ⓑ to give geographical information about Pan
   - Ⓒ to tell what each section is mostly about
   - Ⓓ to illustrate Pan's characteristics

STRATEGY PRACTICE   Why do you think the passage is divided into three parts?

_____

_____

READ THE PASSAGE   Read the passage and study the water-cycle diagram.

The Water Cycle

Water is considered to be a renewable natural resource. However, Earth's water resources are not constantly refilled. This means that no new water is being made; it is simply recycled. Each drop of rain you feel, each glass of water you drink, every stream of water—whether it is cascading through the Rockies or flowing through San Antonio's canals—represents water that has cycled around Earth billions of times before. The water simply changes from liquid water to water vapor to solid crystals of ice and back to water again.

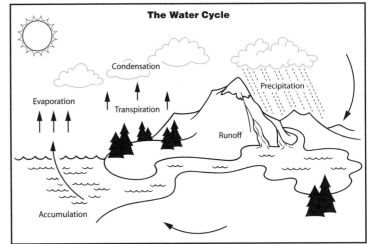

This diagram represents the constant journey of water from land and sea to air and back again.

SKILL PRACTICE   Read each question. Fill in the bubble next to the correct answer.

1. Which information is provided in the diagram?
   Ⓐ how water changes its form
   Ⓑ several ways to save water
   Ⓒ different ways to collect water
   Ⓓ water levels in different places

2. According to the diagram, water comes from the sky to the ground through _____.
   Ⓐ precipitation
   Ⓑ transpiration
   Ⓒ evaporation
   Ⓓ accumulation

3. What is the process of forming clouds called?
   Ⓐ evaporation
   Ⓑ condensation
   Ⓒ precipitation
   Ⓓ accumulation

4. In the diagram, transpiration is _____.
   Ⓐ rainwater that runs into the sea
   Ⓑ rainwater that collects on the ground
   Ⓒ water from trees that enters the atmosphere
   Ⓓ water from the sea that enters the atmosphere

STRATEGY PRACTICE   Explain to a partner what you learned about the water cycle. Use the information you learned from the passage and the diagram.

_____

_____

READ THE PASSAGE   Read the passage and study the map to learn about time zones.

The Land of Many Times

The world is divided into 24 time zones. These zones follow the lines of longitude, beginning at the prime meridian at 0°. There are 12 time zones to the west of the prime meridian and 12 time zones to the east. Each time zone is separated by 15° of longitude and by one hour.

All lines of longitude meet at the poles. There is no land at the North Pole, but it can be very confusing to measure time at research stations near the South Pole. Since the lines of longitude are not spaced apart as widely as they are farther north, someone could run around in a circle and cross all 24 time zones in a few minutes. Because of this and the lack of a large human population, the small groups of people who live in Antarctica can choose any time zone they want. This means that scientists from England might use London time while they work just a few miles away from a team using clocks set 3 hours earlier to a time zone in Argentina!

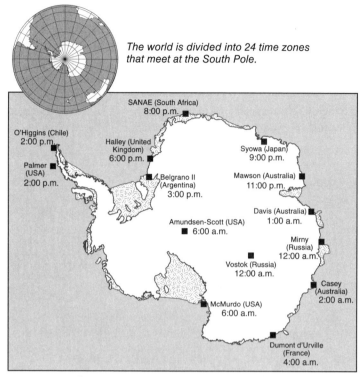

The world is divided into 24 time zones that meet at the South Pole.

A map of Antarctica, prominent research stations, and the time zone each station uses

SKILL PRACTICE   Read each question. Fill in the bubble next to the correct answer.

1. What are the time zone divisions based on?
   Ⓐ the lines of longitude
   Ⓑ the two poles
   Ⓒ research stations
   Ⓓ major countries

2. How many time zones are there at the South Pole?
   Ⓐ 1
   Ⓑ 12
   Ⓒ 15
   Ⓓ 24

3. Which continent is best shown on the maps?
   Ⓐ North America
   Ⓑ South America
   Ⓒ Antarctica
   Ⓓ Asia

4. When it is 3:00 p.m. at the Vostok research station, what time is it at the Amundsen-Scott research station?
   Ⓐ 9:00 p.m.
   Ⓑ 6:00 a.m.
   Ⓒ 4:00 p.m.
   Ⓓ 2:00 a.m.

STRATEGY PRACTICE   How is the text organized? How do the maps support this organization?

_____

_____

READ THE PASSAGE   Think about what information is most important for making your own bento-box lunch.

Bento: A Good Way to Play With Your Food

Packed lunches can be found in almost every country in the world. In Japan, however, the packed meal, or *bento,* is also an art form. Both professional chefs and home cooks put their time, energy, and creativity into forming these tasty—and beautiful—meals.

While there are no hard and fast rules for creating these delightful dishes, if you want to make a traditional bento, there are some things you should know:

Some bentos include foods that look like cartoon characters or animals.

1. A traditional bento has 4 parts rice, 3 parts protein, 2 parts vegetable, and 1 part something either sour or sweet.

2. The food in a bento should not need to be refrigerated or cooked.

3. Messy foods or foods with liquids should be packed in individual containers to keep from ruining the other food in the bento.

4. Perhaps most importantly, the bento should be visually appealing. This means taking some time to arrange the food in the bento in a way that makes it colorful, fun, and inviting. Some bentos are arranged to look like cartoon characters, animals, buildings, or even famous people!

SKILL PRACTICE   Read each question. Fill in the bubble next to the correct answer.

1. The numbered list can best be described as a _____.

   Ⓐ recipe

   Ⓑ how-to

   Ⓒ set of strict rules

   Ⓓ ranking of the best bentos

2. What information does the picture show?

   Ⓐ how to make a bento

   Ⓑ why you should eat a bento

   Ⓒ where to find a bento

   Ⓓ what a bento might look like

3. Why is the word "bento" italicized in the first paragraph of the passage?

   Ⓐ to introduce the word

   Ⓑ to show the word's pronunciation

   Ⓒ to indicate an unusual use of the word

   Ⓓ to show that it is a title

4. Which of the following would make the best traditional bento?

   Ⓐ a bento with more vegetables than protein

   Ⓑ a bento with more than one sweet food

   Ⓒ a bento with equal amounts of rice and vegetables

   Ⓓ a bento with a variety of colorful foods

STRATEGY PRACTICE   Which part of the article would be most useful if you wanted to make your own bento? Explain your answer.

_____

_____

Main Idea and Details

Students look for the central idea or message of a passage or story. They also find details that best support the main idea.

Sequence

Students look for the order of events or steps in a process.

DAY 1

Review the *Main Idea and Details* skill. Say: **Good readers look for main ideas in the entire passage as well as in each individual paragraph. They also look for smaller details that support these main ideas.** Encourage students to look for each paragraph's main idea and details and then use that information to decide on the passage's overall main idea. Remind students of the *Monitor Comprehension* strategy (Week 1). Say: **While you read, pause after each paragraph and review its main idea. Reread any information that you find difficult to comprehend.** Direct students to read the passage and to complete the skill and strategy practice activities. Review the answers together.

DAY 2

Tell students they are going to read about levees. Build background by asking students what they know about Hurricane Katrina and the devastation that occurred when the levees failed. Remind students of the *Main Idea and Details* skill. Say: **Look for details that support a main idea about levees.** Then remind students of the *Visualization* strategy (Week 3). Say: **Even if you have never seen an object or structure in real life, you can create a mental image based on what you read.** Have students read the passage and complete the skill and strategy practice activities. Review the answers together.

DAY 3

Remind students of the *Sequence* skill. Say: **Authors often write about historical events using chronological order. This helps readers to understand the exact sequence in which events occurred. As you read about Mary Shelley, think about where the events in the passage would appear on a timeline.** Then remind students of the *Monitor Comprehension* strategy. Say: **One way to keep track of events in a passage is to mark main events with numbers. As you read, make notes throughout the passage to keep track of the sequence.** When students have finished reading, direct them to complete the skill and strategy practice activities. Review the answers together.

DAY 4

Tell students they are going to read a story set in the future. Then remind students of the *Sequence* skill. Say: **As you read, pause after each paragraph to make mental notes about the sequence. Keep track of the events so you can retell the story if needed.** Then remind students of the *Visualization* strategy. Say: **The passage takes place in the future, but you can still visualize the events. Look for details in the passage that engage the five senses to help you make a mental image.** When students have finished reading, direct them to complete the skill and strategy practice activities. Review the answers together.

DAY 5

Tell students they will practice both the *Main Idea and Details* and *Sequence* skills as they read about radiation. Remind students of the *Monitor Comprehension* strategy. Say: **If there are words or phrases that are not familiar, reread the sentences around them and look for clues to their meaning.** When students have finished reading, direct them to complete the skill and strategy practice activities. Review the answers together.

READ THE PASSAGE   As you read the passage, look for details that support the main idea.

The Elephant's Steward

When many people think of India, they think of elephants. This beautiful ancient country is home to more than 50% of the total wild elephant population in Asia. Elephant sculptures, paintings, and poetry—and even an elephant god—have been an important part of India's culture for centuries. Live Asian elephants can be found at temples, in city parks, and walking in the streets of some towns. It would be difficult to imagine the country without its many elephants.

Long ago, the forests of India were crammed with these dynamic creatures. Although exact numbers are not known, many elephant experts believe that there were easily more than one million wild elephants in the forests and plains of India. Today, fewer than 35,000 Asian elephants remain in the wild in India. Many species around the world are harmed by habitat loss and conflict with humans. Sadly, India's elephants are being negatively affected by these problems as well.

There is hope for the wild elephants, however. Leaders in India have recognized the importance of protecting the species. Large national parks have been established to keep the animals safe, and groups and agencies have formed to monitor elephants and protect them from poaching, or illegal hunting. Given India's massive population and competing human concerns, such as poverty and sanitation, it has been difficult to find the resources to keep the parks and programs running. Fortunately, the deep love that people in India feel toward elephants has helped. Most people in India are ready to do their part to protect the country's most beloved animals.

SKILL PRACTICE   Read each question. Fill in the bubble next to the correct answer.

1. Which of the following best represents the main idea of the passage?
   Ⓐ Wild elephant numbers are declining.
   Ⓑ People in India create elephant art to show they care about elephants.
   Ⓒ India has a long-standing and personal relationship with elephants.
   Ⓓ Protecting elephants in India is a difficult task for many reasons.

2. The passage is mostly about _____.
   Ⓐ the meaningful decorations in India's temples
   Ⓑ why some people choose to poach elephants
   Ⓒ elephant habitats throughout the world
   Ⓓ how the elephant population in India has changed

3. Which detail supports the idea that India used to have a massive elephant population?
   Ⓐ India holds more than 50% of Asia's wild elephant population.
   Ⓑ More than one million wild elephants used to live in India's plains and forests.
   Ⓒ Fewer than 35,000 elephants now live in India.
   Ⓓ India has national parks and agencies to protect elephants.

4. Which word best describes how most people in India probably feel about elephants?
   Ⓐ caring
   Ⓑ annoyed
   Ⓒ fearful
   Ⓓ indifferent

STRATEGY PRACTICE   Did you understand the main point the author is trying to make? Why or why not?

_____

_____

READ THE COLUMN   Look for details about levees in the question-and-answer column.

ASK Mr. Know-It-All

Dear Mr. Know-It-All: I've been reading about the levees in New Orleans. What's a levee?

—*Alan*

Dear Alan: Thank you for your question! A levee is a natural or artificial embankment that runs parallel to a river. A natural levee is made up of ridges that are created when a river floods. As river water rises, it carries sediment with it. After the river level returns to normal, the sediment remains along river banks—and you have levees.

People build artificial levees to prevent flooding near a river or other body of water. The levees in New Orleans were built for two different purposes. Levees that run along the Mississippi River protect that side of the city against flooding from the river; levees on the other side of the city protect against flooding from Lake Pontchartrain. Most of the new levees in New Orleans are between 10 and 20 feet tall.

Artificial levees are usually made of clay, cement, or another material that is less absorbent than soil to keep water from seeping through. Levees are wider at the base and narrower at the top, creating a gradual slope down to the river bed. In addition to controlling flooding, levees also affect the rate of water flow in a river. Because they confine the course of the river, the water flows faster and at a higher level.

—*Mr. Know-It-All*

SKILL PRACTICE   Read each question. Fill in the bubble next to the correct answer.

1. What is the main idea of the column?
   Ⓐ Levees are natural or artificial ridges that help control flooding.
   Ⓑ Artificial levees are more important than natural levees.
   Ⓒ New Orleans has an extensive system of levees that serve two purposes.
   Ⓓ Levees are wider at the base and narrower at the top.

2. Natural levees are made of _____.
   Ⓐ flood water
   Ⓑ cement
   Ⓒ sediment
   Ⓓ clay materials

3. Building a levee next to a river is likely to cause _____.
   Ⓐ an increase in the speed of the river's water flow
   Ⓑ a decrease in the speed of the river's water flow
   Ⓒ an increase in the chance of flooding in the area
   Ⓓ a decrease in the depth of the water in the river

4. Where are levees placed in relation to rivers?
   Ⓐ across them
   Ⓑ parallel to them
   Ⓒ in the middle of them
   Ⓓ 20 feet away from them

STRATEGY PRACTICE   On a separate sheet of paper, sketch a levee as described in the passage.

READ THE PASSAGE   Pay attention to the order of events in the passage.

A Famous Dark and Stormy Night

You might not imagine that sitting around with some friends telling ghost stories could lead to the publication of one of the most popular novels in the world, but that is exactly what happened to Mary Shelley. Little did she know when the evening began that it would eventually lead to *Frankenstein*.

In the summer of 1816, Mary Wollstonecraft Godwin was just 18 years old. She and her soon-to-be husband, Percy Bysshe Shelley, were visiting their friend, Lord Byron, at his home near Lake Geneva in Switzerland. The weather around the world that fateful summer was greatly affected by an Indonesian volcano eruption the year before. The volcano had caused many changes in the weather, and a violent storm took place during Godwin's visit.

Tremendous amounts of rain and lightning kept Godwin and her friends trapped inside, so they passed the hours talking around the fire. One topic was *galvanism,* which is the use of electricity to cause muscles to move. Godwin and her friends discussed the possibility of using electricity to bring organisms back to life. The group then decided to read aloud some German ghost stories. Inspired by a story in which travelers relate their own experiences of the paranormal, Lord Byron challenged everyone to write their own supernatural tales.

The next night, the group shared what they had written, but Godwin was disappointed because she had not been inspired with an idea. Some days later, however, she had an intense nightmare in which "a pale student of the unhallowed arts" created a being from pieces of corpses. When Godwin published her novel (as Mary Shelley) two years later, the pale student of her dreams entered the world as Victor Frankenstein, a scientist who used electricity to investigate the shadowy line between life and death.

SKILL PRACTICE   Read each question. Fill in the bubble next to the correct answer.

1. Which of the following events happened before Mary Wollstonecraft Godwin visited Lord Byron?

   Ⓐ Godwin married Percy Shelley.

   Ⓑ A volcano erupted in Indonesia.

   Ⓒ A heavy storm kept friends indoors.

   Ⓓ Godwin wrote *Frankenstein*.

2. When did Lord Byron challenge his friends to write their own scary stories?

   Ⓐ before Godwin's trip to Switzerland

   Ⓑ before the Indonesian volcano eruption

   Ⓒ after Godwin got married

   Ⓓ after reading ghost stories

3. When did Godwin begin to write *Frankenstein*?

   Ⓐ after she had a nightmare

   Ⓑ during the group's discussion

   Ⓒ before the violent storms began

   Ⓓ the night after Lord Byron's challenge

4. In which year was *Frankenstein* published?

   Ⓐ 1815

   Ⓑ 1816

   Ⓒ 1817

   Ⓓ 1818

STRATEGY PRACTICE   On a separate sheet of paper, draw a timeline of the main events in the passage.

READ THE PASSAGE   Visualize the sequence of events as they happen in the passage.

Eating at Ellie's

I knew I would not see an actual person named Ellie at Ellie's Eatery because, like most new restaurants these days, Ellie's is a robo-restaurant.

When I walked in, a cute little manager robot appeared, looking rather like a toaster with blinking blue eyes. It escorted me to a nice table in the back. The menu monitor popped out of my table and showed me pictures of my dining options. I tapped my choices and clicked OK, and the screen slid back down.

I watched as full platters rode the conveyer belts that zoomed along each aisle of tables. In just a few minutes, my appetizer stopped at my table, and I took it from the belt. Later, I placed my empty plate back on the conveyer belt, and it was whisked off into the kitchen to be cleaned.

I watched the little toaster showing customers to tables while I ate my main course. The food was tasty, but I was starting to feel annoyed because dealing with robots always makes me feel inhuman. Pretty soon, I wanted to talk to someone real, even if it was just a few sentences.

So when my dessert arrived, I took action. I smashed my plate on the floor with a satisfying crash. I was so happy when I saw the manager toaster's eyes blink red—at last, a real live person would arrive!

But instead, a crew of two robots quickly appeared. A robot broom rushed over and started to sweep the pieces of the broken plate into a robot dust tray. They finished and whooshed back into the kitchen.

My plan to get a little reality into Ellie's Eatery failed miserably. I hope the robo-restaurant craze ends soon. I want to deal with people again!

SKILL PRACTICE   Read each question. Fill in the bubble next to the correct answer.

1. Which event happened first in the passage?
   - Ⓐ The narrator ordered from a menu.
   - Ⓑ The manager robot's eyes blinked red.
   - Ⓒ The narrator arrived at Ellie's Eatery.
   - Ⓓ Food arrived on a conveyer belt.

2. What happened after the narrator ate the appetizer?
   - Ⓐ Two robots cleaned up a broken dish.
   - Ⓑ The menu popped out of the table.
   - Ⓒ The narrator put the empty plate back on the conveyer belt.
   - Ⓓ The manager robot showed the narrator to a table at the back.

3. The narrator broke a plate in order to _____.
   - Ⓐ try to get human service
   - Ⓑ get more attention from the robots
   - Ⓒ show that the food did not taste good
   - Ⓓ put an end to the robo-restaurant craze

4. Which word best describes how the narrator felt at the end of the story?
   - Ⓐ satisfied
   - Ⓑ playful
   - Ⓒ hungry
   - Ⓓ disappointed

STRATEGY PRACTICE   Which parts of Ellie's Eatery were you able to visualize easily? Why?

_____

_____

READ THE PASSAGE   Look for details in the passage that tell how Victor Hess proved his scientific ideas.

Discovering Cosmic Radiation

In the early twentieth century, many scientists were investigating radioactivity. The scientists were able to measure levels of radioactivity at different places around the world using special measuring tools. They all agreed that radioactivity existed, but where did it come from? This question led to a fierce scientific debate. Most scientists assumed that all of the radioactivity being measured was produced by minerals in the ground. An Austrian physicist named Victor Hess challenged this idea.

Hess doubted that all radioactivity came from ground minerals and hypothesized that it could come from the sky. To test his theory, Hess decided to conduct several experiments using hot air balloons. He concluded that if the source of radioactivity was the ground, the levels should be far lower up in the air. After designing tools that would give accurate readings at high altitudes, Hess conducted 10 balloon flights from 1911 to 1912. He discovered that the levels of radioactivity did not decrease as he rose higher. In fact, when the balloon was several miles above Earth, the radioactivity level was many times greater than it was on the ground. Hess felt confident in his theory that radiation enters Earth's atmosphere from above.

One possible source of the radiation was the sun, but Hess conducted balloon flights both during the day and at night. In 1912, he conducted a balloon experiment during a total eclipse of the sun. Even though the sun's light was almost completely blocked, the levels of radioactivity were the same. Hess argued that the sun could not be the only source of radiation—there were even more sources beyond that, in outer space.

Scientists gradually acknowledged their mistaken thinking and accepted Hess's theories. In 1925, Robert Millikan named the effect that Hess investigated *cosmic radiation*. In 1936, Hess won the Nobel Prize for his work in discovering this fundamental feature of the universe.

SKILL PRACTICE   Read each question. Fill in the bubble next to the correct answer.

1. Victor Hess's experiments proved that radioactivity _____.
   - Ⓐ is not produced at night
   - Ⓑ is produced by ground minerals
   - Ⓒ decreases at higher altitudes
   - Ⓓ primarily comes from outer space

2. What did Hess have to do before he could conduct in-air experiments to test his theory?
   - Ⓐ study a total eclipse of the sun
   - Ⓑ design tools for use at high altitudes
   - Ⓒ prove that minerals were not radioactive
   - Ⓓ collaborate with other scientists

3. After Hess proved that radiation enters the atmosphere from above, he _____.
   - Ⓐ took his first trip in a hot air balloon
   - Ⓑ developed a theory about ground radiation
   - Ⓒ created the term *cosmic radiation*
   - Ⓓ determined there were other radiation sources

4. What is the main idea of the passage?
   - Ⓐ Scientists often disagree about unproven theories.
   - Ⓑ Victor Hess used hot air balloons in his experiments.
   - Ⓒ Victor Hess discovered cosmic radiation by diligently testing his own theory.
   - Ⓓ The Nobel Prize is an award for people who study radioactivity.

STRATEGY PRACTICE   Write one word you found confusing and describe how you figured out its meaning.

_____

Author's Purpose

Students identify the author's reason for writing about a subject.

Evaluate Evidence

Students practice evaluating evidence by identifying the author's main idea and examining the evidence the author uses to support that idea.

DAY 1

Remind students of the *Author's Purpose* skill. Say: **Authors often write about historic figures to explain why that person was, and still is, considered important. As you read, think about why the author wanted to share details about Abigail Adams's life.** Then remind students of the *Determine Important Information* strategy (Week 5). Say: **As you read, think about how you would summarize the information in the passage in one or two sentences. Ask yourself:** *What made Abigail Adams special?* Then have students read the passage. When they have finished, direct them to complete the skill and strategy practice activities. Review the answers together.

DAY 2

Remind students of the *Author's Purpose* skill. Say: **Authors can write to teach, inform, persuade, or entertain. As you read, think about** *why* **the author wrote the passage.** Then remind students of the *Ask Questions* strategy (Week 6). Say: **Asking questions as you read can help you to better understand the content of a passage. When you think of a question, pause to write it down. Look for the answer as you continue reading.** When students have finished reading, direct them to complete the skill and strategy practice activities. Review the answers together.

DAY 3

Tell students they are going to read about a musical organization called El Sistema. Remind students of the *Evaluate Evidence* skill. Say: **As you read, think about the claims the author makes about El Sistema. Look for evidence that supports these claims or that proves the claims are true.** Then remind students of the *Determine Important Information* strategy. Say: **As you read, think of each claim the author is making, and look for important information that supports the claim.** When students have finished reading, direct them to complete the skill and strategy practice activities. Review the answers together.

DAY 4

Remind students of the *Evaluate Evidence* skill. Say: **Scientific writing often centers on a conclusion that the scientist must support with evidence. As you read, look for claims that are supported with factual information in the passage.** Then remind students of the *Ask Questions* strategy. Say: **You can ask questions before, during, and after reading. Asking questions before and during reading helps you stay focused. Asking questions when you finish reading can help you determine whether you understood the text.** Then have students read the passage. When students have finished reading, direct them to complete the skill and strategy practice activities. Review the answers together.

DAY 5

Tell students they will practice both the *Author's Purpose* and *Evaluate Evidence* skills as they read about probiotics. Remind students of the *Determine Important Information* strategy. Say: **Underline key information as you read. When you have finished, decide which pieces of key information are the most important.** Then have students read the passage. When students have finished, direct them to complete the skill and strategy practice activities. Review the answers together.

READ THE PASSAGE   As you read, think about the author's reasons for writing the passage.

Abigail Adams, America's Founding Mother

Though people often speak of America's many Founding Fathers, such as Thomas Jefferson, George Washington, and Benjamin Franklin, there is only one woman who deserves the title of Founding Mother. Abigail Adams, the wife of President John Adams, was more than just a First Lady. She was a powerful woman who has earned an important place in American history.

Adams held strong views about the equality of the sexes, believing that women should be given the same educational opportunities as men. She also believed in racial equality and thought slavery was evil. Adams shared her then-controversial views on these topics with the press and in letters to many powerful people, but her most famous writing is contained in the personal correspondence she kept with her husband. These letters, published after her death, showcase her remarkable mind and spirit.

Adams wrote her most famous letter regarding women's rights in 1776, when her husband was working hard at the Second Continental Congress to convince other leaders to declare independence from England. Arguing that men should not have too much power over women in the new system of government, Adams wrote: "I long to hear that you have declared an independency. And, by the way, in the new code of laws which I suppose it will be necessary for you to make, I desire you would remember the ladies and be more generous and favorable to them than your ancestors. Do not put such unlimited power into the hands of the husbands. Remember, all men would be tyrants if they could." We would all do well to remember this extraordinary lady, the Founding Mother of equal liberty for all.

SKILL PRACTICE   Read each question. Fill in the bubble next to the correct answer.

1. What is the author's main purpose in the passage?
   A) to entertain readers with a funny story about Abigail Adams
   B) to explain Abigail Adams's importance in history
   C) to teach readers how to think like Abigail Adams
   D) to inform readers about Abigail Adams's early life

2. Why does the author mention Adams's letters?
   A) to explain how she influenced others
   B) to describe how she spent her time
   C) to persuade readers to write letters
   D) to show that she was educated

3. The author most likely includes the quotation in the last paragraph to _____.
   A) show how bitter and angry Adams was
   B) indicate why Adams was less important than her husband
   C) prove that Adams communicated in letters
   D) give an example of Adams's powerful writing and thinking

4. The author calls Adams "the Founding Mother of equal liberty for all" because Adams _____.
   A) participated in the Second Continental Congress
   B) was the wife of a Founding Father
   C) believed in equality and freedom for women and slaves
   D) helped write the Declaration of Independence

STRATEGY PRACTICE   Use information from the passage to write one sentence that describes Abigail Adams.

_____

_____

READ THE PASSAGE   Look for details in the passage that offer clues about the author's purpose.

Lyme Disease and Guinea Fowl

Lyme disease is a dangerous bacterial infection that is spread by deer ticks. People who contract Lyme disease suffer from fevers, fatigue, sore joints, and sore muscles. If the illness is not treated when it first appears, people may develop chronic Lyme disease, which causes long-term fatigue and pain.

The ticks that cause Lyme disease live on deer, and these ticks can come into contact with humans in natural settings. One approach to controlling these infected ticks is to control the deer population, but a better solution may be to control the population of the ticks themselves.

In 1992, model Christie Brinkley worried about her daughter playing outside, since the Brinkley family lived in an area of New York known for having a high number of deer ticks. She helped start a study that looked into whether guinea fowl, a type of bird that originally came from Africa, might help control the number of ticks in the area. Guinea fowl eat insects—especially ticks. The study found that guinea fowl do indeed help control tick populations.

Guinea fowl can be maintained rather easily, but they do have certain requirements. For example, they need to be kept on unforested grounds that are at least three to five acres. Humans raising the fowl need to keep them protected, especially when they are young, because foxes and raccoons prey on the vulnerable birds. Guinea fowl also need to be fed and watered every day during winter when it snows. Nonetheless, the work may well be worth the trouble, especially if the birds can help prevent the spread of this painful disease.

SKILL PRACTICE   Read each question. Fill in the bubble next to the correct answer.

1. The author's main purpose for writing the passage is to _____.
   - Ⓐ persuade readers to raise an unusual animal
   - Ⓑ instruct readers on how to treat a painful infection
   - Ⓒ inform readers about a way to control a harmful insect
   - Ⓓ entertain readers with a story about a celebrity's unusual pets

2. Why does the author mention Christie Brinkley's family?
   - Ⓐ to explain the origin of the study
   - Ⓑ to persuade readers to treat Lyme disease
   - Ⓒ to help readers visualize the problem
   - Ⓓ to give an example of a family affected by ticks

3. The author includes information about the guinea fowl study to show that _____.
   - Ⓐ scientists agree that ticks are a problem
   - Ⓑ research supports the guinea fowl solution
   - Ⓒ research needs to be better funded
   - Ⓓ the deer population needs to be controlled

4. The author most wants readers to understand that _____.
   - Ⓐ it is important to protect the guinea fowl population
   - Ⓑ Christie Brinkley is concerned about her family's health
   - Ⓒ someone affected by Lyme disease must be treated quickly
   - Ⓓ guinea fowl may be the best way to reduce the number of ticks

STRATEGY PRACTICE   What question do you still have about Lyme disease? How can you find the answer?

_____

_____

READ THE PASSAGE   As you read, look for evidence that proves El Sistema has been a success.

El Sistema—Creating Music, Changing the World

Venezuelan José Antonio Abreu was an accomplished musician in the 1970s, but something about his life did not feel right. The gap between rich and poor people in his country was enormous. Abreu felt that all children should have the same chances he had been given. He felt that an orchestra would bring people together. To create music, there must be cooperation and appreciation for one another's talents. Why not use music to build togetherness and bridge the gap between rich and poor?

In 1975, Abreu founded El Sistema to give less-advantaged children in Venezuela the chance to play classical music. At his first rehearsal, he expected around 100 children. Only 11 showed up, but that very night, he promised those 11 children that he would turn their "orchestra" into one of the best orchestras in the world. Abreu was true to his word. Today, El Sistema includes about 200 youth orchestras, 60 children's orchestras, 280 music centers, and more than 310,000 young musicians. Most are from humble backgrounds, and music is changing their lives for the better.

Abreu's program has been wildly successful. Standing ovations after performances have been known to last up to half an hour. And several El Sistema students have gone on to major international careers. At 17, bassist Edicson Ruiz became the youngest musician ever to join the Berlin Philharmonic. Violinist Gustavo Dudamel is now the music director of the Los Angeles Philharmonic.

"To sing and play together means to intimately coexist," says Abreu. "Music transmits the highest values: solidarity, harmony, and mutual compassion." El Sistema has accomplished many things, yet perhaps its greatest triumph is Abreu's message that, whether rich or poor, we can all succeed if we work together.

SKILL PRACTICE   Read each question. Fill in the bubble next to the correct answer.

1. Which best supports the idea that El Sistema is successful at bringing people together?
   - Ⓐ the number of children at the first rehearsal
   - Ⓑ the length of standing ovations at concerts
   - Ⓒ the number of children currently involved in the program
   - Ⓓ the humble backgrounds of the students

2. Which statement shows that José Antonio Abreu was devoted to his philosophy?
   - Ⓐ Abreu was true to his word.
   - Ⓑ He expected around 100 children.
   - Ⓒ The gap between rich and poor was enormous.
   - Ⓓ Abreu was an accomplished musician in the 1970s.

3. Which evidence from the passage proves that some students have gone on to have professional careers?
   - Ⓐ Abreu was a talented musician in the 1970s.
   - Ⓑ Dudamel is the music director of the Los Angeles Philharmonic.
   - Ⓒ Standing ovations for the performances can last half an hour.
   - Ⓓ El Sistema includes 280 music centers.

4. The current number of children involved in El Sistema gives evidence of the program's _____.
   - Ⓐ high cost
   - Ⓑ humble beginnings
   - Ⓒ international fame
   - Ⓓ popularity in Venezuela

STRATEGY PRACTICE   Which information is most important in determining how much El Sistema has grown?

_____

Name: _____

READ THE PASSAGE   As you read, look for evidence of factual information about *archaeopteryx*.

The World's First Bird?

Archaeopteryx was a creature that lived over 150 million years ago, during the time of the dinosaurs. At that time, dinosaurs had already been around for millions of years, and some had started to evolve. Scientific evidence suggests that many species of dinosaurs began becoming more birdlike; they were growing feathers, they had beaks, and they had bones that were light enough for flight. *Archaeopteryx* was one of these evolving curiosities.

First discovered in the 1800s, *archaeopteryx* is still considered to be a dinosaur, but it looked nothing like *brontosaurus* or *tyrannosaurus rex*. It was about the size of a raven, was covered in the kind of feathers needed for flying, and had bones that were light and hollow. However, *archaeopteryx* also had sharp teeth, claws, and a bony tail. Given that it had features of both birds and dinosaurs, *archaeopteryx* is the best proof to support the theory that birds evolved from dinosaurs. But does that mean that all birds evolved from *archaeopteryx*?

Many scientists have doubts about *archaeopteryx* as the world's first bird. This is because there are only 11 known fossils of the creature. That is enough for scientists to learn a lot about the creature, but it does not prove how birds evolved. Also, scientists have found other animals that could have been the direct ancestors of birds. Many now wonder if *archaeopteryx* is a relative of the bird instead of a direct ancestor, similar to how woolly mammoths are related to (but are not the exact ancestors of) elephants. Though scientists may never be able to prove the origins of *archaeopteryx*, one thing is for sure—they are fascinating creatures to study.

SKILL PRACTICE   Read each question. Fill in the bubble next to the correct answer.

1. What evidence supports classifying *archaeopteryx* as a dinosaur?

   Ⓐ It looks nothing like *brontosaurus*.

   Ⓑ Its bones were light and hollow.

   Ⓒ It had sharp teeth, claws, and a bony tail.

   Ⓓ It was the size of a raven.

2. The most reliable factual evidence about *archaeopteryx* would probably come from _____.

   Ⓐ fossils of the creature

   Ⓑ theories from modern scientists

   Ⓒ scientific documents from the 1800s

   Ⓓ comparisons to dinosaurs and birds

3. What can scientists determine from *archaeopteryx*'s light bones?

   Ⓐ It flew as well as modern birds.

   Ⓑ It probably communicated through song.

   Ⓒ It ate the same foods birds eat now.

   Ⓓ It might have been able to fly.

4. Evidence from the passage supports the idea that _____.

   Ⓐ dinosaurs and birds were related

   Ⓑ *archaeopteryx* was the only dinosaur that flew

   Ⓒ *archaeopteryx* was the first true bird

   Ⓓ all dinosaurs once had feathers

STRATEGY PRACTICE   Write one question you had while reading the passage. What is the answer?

_____

_____

READ THE PASSAGE   Look for evidence that supports the use or avoidance of probiotics.

Probiotics: Fad or Fantastic?

Not another food fad! This time, it is probiotics. Is the probiotics movement just another fad, or could it be one of the few popular dietary practices that actually works? Let's take a closer look.

Probiotics are live microorganisms, most of which are bacteria. They can be found in dietary supplements or in actual food, such as yogurt. Whether they are in tablets or foods, probiotics contain friendly bacteria that are similar to those that naturally live inside the human body.

So what do probiotics do? Research is beginning to suggest that, like the helpful bacteria inside us, probiotics can assist with digestion and protect against harmful bacteria. Encouraging evidence suggests that probiotics might help prevent or treat certain infections. They may even prevent or treat a serious inflammation called *pouchitis* that can occur after colon surgery.

Clinical studies from the mid-1990s and later have shown that probiotic therapy can help treat some gastrointestinal problems and delay the development of allergies in children. The best results by far, however, have been in treating diarrhea. Controlled experiments involving a probiotic called *Lactobacillus rhamnosus* GG resulted in shortened attacks of diarrhea in infants and children.

So, are probiotics safe and beneficial? So far, the U.S. Food and Drug Administration is neutral on the topic, and authorities seem to agree that more research is needed. Probiotics are, after all, live bacteria, and when people consume them, they are introducing tiny foreign critters into their bodies.

Over the years, many food fads have come and gone. Only with time, research, and results will we know for sure if probiotics really are the wave of the food future.

SKILL PRACTICE   Read each question. Fill in the bubble next to the correct answer.

1. The author's main purpose for writing the passage is to _____.
   Ⓐ describe popular dietary practices
   Ⓑ explain how human digestion works
   Ⓒ give information about a new diet trend
   Ⓓ persuade readers to avoid food fads

2. The author mentions pouchitis to _____.
   Ⓐ point out a possible danger of probiotics
   Ⓑ give an example of one of the risks of probiotics
   Ⓒ describe a type of probiotic bacteria
   Ⓓ illustrate the potential range of uses of probiotics

3. Why does the author suggest that probiotics could be just another fad?
   Ⓐ The human body already contains helpful bacteria.
   Ⓑ There is not enough evidence to say whether probiotics are always useful.
   Ⓒ The U.S. Food and Drug Administration has not approved the use of probiotics.
   Ⓓ *Lactobacillus rhamnosus* GG has been used in controlled experiments.

4. According to the author, probiotics are questionable because they _____.
   Ⓐ are foreign bacteria
   Ⓑ come in tablet form
   Ⓒ are used for gastrointestinal problems
   Ⓓ appear naturally in some foods

STRATEGY PRACTICE   Which information from the passage best supports the use of probiotics? Why?

_____

_____

Compare and Contrast

Students practice comparing and contrasting by looking at the similarities and differences between two or more people or things.

Make Inferences

Students practice making inferences by using clues in a passage to understand what is being implied.

DAY 1

Remind students of the *Compare and Contrast* skill. Tell students they will practice making comparisons by reading about robots from science fiction and robots from real life. Say: **Look for details that tell how these two types of robots are alike and different.** Remind students of the *Make Connections* strategy (Week 2). Say: **When you make a personal connection with a text, you think about how something from the text relates to something from your own life. Making text-to-self connections can help you better understand a passage.** When students have finished reading, direct them to complete the skill and strategy practice activities. Review the answers together.

DAY 2

Remind students of the *Compare and Contrast* skill. Say: **To make comparisons, think about all of the ways two or more subjects are alike. To find contrasts, think about how two or more subjects are different.** Then remind students of the *Organization* strategy (Week 4). Say: **Sometimes there are several characters or situations to compare. Think about how the author organizes these comparisons in the passage.** When students have finished reading, direct them to complete the skill and strategy practice activities. Review the answers together.

DAY 3

Remind students of the *Make Inferences* skill. Say: **You are going to read about emotional intelligence. While you read, think about what you already know and the new information you learn. Together, these things will help you to make inferences.** Then remind students of the *Make Connections* strategy. Say: **When you have something in common with a friend, you can better understand him or her. In the same way, making a connection to something you read will help you to better understand the text.** When students have finished reading, direct them to complete the skill and strategy practice activities. Review the answers together.

DAY 4

Review the *Make Inferences* skill with students. Say: **Think about information that is not directly stated in the passage. Use your own background knowledge to help you "read between the lines."** Then review the *Organization* strategy. Say: **Authors organize their stories in many ways. Some authors begin at the end of a story and then tell you what happened leading up to it. Others begin with the main problem a character faces and show how the problem is resolved. By understanding how the story is told, we can make sense of what we are reading.** When students have finished reading, direct them to complete the skill and strategy practice activities. Review the answers together.

DAY 5

Tell students they will practice both the *Compare and Contrast* and *Make Inferences* skills by reading about two distinct types of dancing. Say: **As you read, look for similarities and differences between the two dancing styles. Use your own knowledge or dancing experience to make inferences.** When students have finished reading, direct them to complete the skill practice activity. Review the answers together. Then remind students of the *Make Connections* strategy. Have students complete the strategy practice activity and share their answers with the group.

READ THE PASSAGE   Think about how fictional and real-life robots are alike and different.

Robots: Imagined and Real

Robots have been a staple of science fiction since the early days of the genre. Generally, robots have been portrayed as mechanical beings that are shaped roughly like humans and have the ability to speak. Robots have often been included in cautionary tales about science, where rogue robots escape the control of their human designers and take over civilization. In real life, this has never happened, but that does not stop people from considering the possibility.

The word "robot" was first used in the 1920 play *R.U.R.,* which stood for "Rossum's Universal Robots." In the play, a group of robots is created to serve humans but instead rises up against them. After that first appearance on the stage, robots continued to appear in books, movies, and television programs. More often than not, they have been portrayed as having evil intentions.

Today, robots have stepped off the science fiction pages and into our world. Though these robots do not look like mechanical people, they do work that has traditionally been done by their human counterparts, such as vacuuming or cleaning floors, gutters, and even swimming pools.

Other robots have been designed for industrial work, doing repetitive or dangerous jobs that are required for manufacturing goods. Robots put together cars, work with extremely hot or toxic materials, and mine resources from remote or dangerous locations.

While robots have never rebelled against their makers, ethical questions can come into play. Some robots used by the military have been designed to have decision-making capabilities. Although there are a few people who are wary of the robots' increasing power, most of society realizes that their value is much greater than the risk they pose.

SKILL PRACTICE   Read each question. Fill in the bubble next to the correct answer.

1. Robots in real life are different from science-fiction robots because real-life robots _____.
   Ⓐ have the ability to speak
   Ⓑ do not usually have human shape
   Ⓒ rarely do human work
   Ⓓ appear in television shows and movies

2. How are real-life and fictional robots similar?
   Ⓐ They both perform jobs for humans.
   Ⓑ They both try to control their masters.
   Ⓒ They both look like people.
   Ⓓ They both have evil intentions.

3. What do all real-life robots do?
   Ⓐ clean up dirty areas
   Ⓑ work with dangerous materials
   Ⓒ perform programmed tasks
   Ⓓ work in industrial settings

4. How does society's current view of robots compare to the 1920 view?
   Ⓐ People are more afraid than ever that robots will take over.
   Ⓑ People want robots to make decisions for them.
   Ⓒ People are struggling to stay ahead of robots' growing capabilities.
   Ⓓ People appreciate the help that robots offer.

STRATEGY PRACTICE   Describe a robot that could help you in your everyday life. Why would it be useful?

_____

_____

Look for details that tell about the real King Richard the Lionheart.

King Richard the Lionheart: Fact and Fiction

Robin Hood, the legendary character in English folklore, is known for stealing from the rich and giving to the poor. Robin set out to serve his ruler, King Richard the Lionheart of England. In the legend, King Richard is portrayed as a wise king who is generous to his subjects as well as to Robin.

The main action in Robin Hood's story takes place while the brave King Richard is in Jerusalem, fighting a series of religious battles known as the Crusades. During this time, Richard's brother John steals the throne. John is a selfish leader and taxes the poor relentlessly, causing great suffering. Robin, of course, is his archenemy, and the tale follows Robin as he fights to make things right again.

According to history books, the real King Richard had some similarities to his fictional counterpart. Like the fictional King Richard, he was brave and prone to fighting his enemies at home and in neighboring countries. He also fought early on against his own father, King Henry II. When King Henry II stopped Richard's rebellion against him, all was forgiven. Later on, however, when Richard feared that his older brother would inherit the crown, he went to war against him, and his brother died.

However, the real King Richard differed from the legend regarding his goodwill. When fighting in the Crusades, King Richard needlessly insulted other rulers. On his way home, he was captured by a man he had insulted. England had to pay a huge ransom for the king's release, and the people of England were taxed to pay for the expense. King Richard spent very little time in England. He was more interested in holding on to land that the French king, Philip II, wanted to rule. Despite any questionable real-life behavior, King Richard lives on as a fictional hero.

Read each question. Fill in the bubble next to the correct answer.

1. In the legend, how is Robin Hood different from King Richard?
   - Ⓐ Robin Hood works to help people.
   - Ⓑ Robin Hood is not in power.
   - Ⓒ Robin Hood is an enemy of John.
   - Ⓓ Robin Hood is considered a hero.

2. The real-life King Richard and his fictional counterpart both _____.
   - Ⓐ fought in the Crusades
   - Ⓑ rebelled against King Henry II
   - Ⓒ respected Robin Hood
   - Ⓓ kept land out of French rule

3. Which important issue is a concern of both the real and fictional King Richard?
   - Ⓐ Robin Hood's thievery
   - Ⓑ disputed land
   - Ⓒ being on the throne
   - Ⓓ unfair taxation

4. While King Richard from *Robin Hood* is known as a hero, King Richard of history can be described as _____.
   - Ⓐ wise
   - Ⓑ cowardly
   - Ⓒ greedy
   - Ⓓ focused

Describe the organization of each paragraph.

_____

_____

READ THE PASSAGE   Use clues from the passage to make inferences about emotional intelligence.

Emotional Intelligence

Since early in the twentieth century, there have been tests to measure an individual's intelligence quotient, or IQ. Generally, having a higher IQ is associated with getting a better education and having a successful career. There seems to be another important factor in achieving success, however. Since the 1990s, psychologists have been using the term "emotional intelligence" to describe the kinds of emotional and social skills that play a part in an individual's success.

According to psychologists John D. Mayer and Peter Salovey, emotional intelligence involves specific skills. These include the ability to:

- identify our own emotional states and the emotional states of others with whom we are interacting
- generate the appropriate emotions ourselves
- understand why we are feeling a certain way and why others are feeling the way they do
- control our own emotional responses

While some have claimed that emotional intelligence is much more important than IQ, Mayer and Salovey dispute that claim. They do believe, however, that emotional intelligence is fundamentally important to relationships such as marriage and friendship, and for those holding jobs that require strong "people skills," such as social workers, business managers, and sales people.

SKILL PRACTICE   Read each question. Fill in the bubble next to the correct answer.

1. Which of these people probably has high emotional intelligence?

   Ⓐ someone who cries easily

   Ⓑ an honor student

   Ⓒ a police detective

   Ⓓ someone who likes to talk a lot

2. Identifying personal emotions can help people _____.

   Ⓐ predict their future successes

   Ⓑ protect themselves from bad experiences

   Ⓒ act out in emotionally unhealthy ways

   Ⓓ determine if an emotion is appropriate to the situation

3. Understanding why others feel the way they do can help you _____.

   Ⓐ improve your IQ

   Ⓑ respond with sensitivity

   Ⓒ tell them how you feel

   Ⓓ control their feelings

4. Why is it important for social workers to have high emotional intelligence?

   Ⓐ They are often lonely.

   Ⓑ They frequently interact with others.

   Ⓒ They need to have good memories.

   Ⓓ They work for marriage counselors.

STRATEGY PRACTICE   Describe someone you know who has high emotional intelligence. What abilities does this person have?

_____

_____

READ THE FOLK TALE Use clues from the passage and your own experiences to make inferences as you read.

Keeping the Cuckoo

A long time ago, in a small village in Wales called Risca, a young man noticed something interesting about the spring weather. "My friends, have you noticed that it's usually sunny and mild when the cuckoo bird is here?" The other people in the village thought about it and found they had to agree.

The townsfolk wished the weather could be nice year-round. It was often cold and rainy in Risca, so the townsfolk hatched a plan for keeping the cuckoo bird with them for good. They would be ready the next time the bird flew in for spring.

In preparation for the cuckoo bird's next visit, the villagers started to build a high wall around the town. They built the wall out of slate. At first, it was as high as the rooftops. That way, it would also protect against thieves. Then they remembered that birds live in trees, so they kept building until it was higher than even the tallest tree.

When spring came, the cuckoo bird arrived as usual. The bird stayed all summer long, and the sun shone until fall. Then, as usual, the bird flew away. This time, it flew out of the town above the high wall that the townspeople had built.

"The bird is gone!" cried the man who had first noticed the connection between the cuckoo and the sunny weather. "If only we had built the wall higher!" His friends mournfully agreed, and ever since, the people in the village have suffered through winter and enjoyed the cuckoo's spring return.

SKILL PRACTICE Read each question. Fill in the bubble next to the correct answer.

1. What did the young man realize about the cuckoo bird at the beginning of the passage?
   Ⓐ The bird brings the village good weather.
   Ⓑ The bird likes the sun as much as the villagers do.
   Ⓒ The bird likes to travel to different villages.
   Ⓓ The bird would like to spend more time in the village.

2. The villagers made a plan to keep the cuckoo bird because they thought the bird _____.
   Ⓐ was getting too old to fly
   Ⓑ was in danger of being stolen
   Ⓒ needed a permanent home
   Ⓓ made spring happen

3. The villagers built a wall because they thought it would _____.
   Ⓐ block out the cold rain
   Ⓑ trap the cuckoo bird
   Ⓒ attract more cuckoo birds
   Ⓓ protect the town from thieves

4. What can you infer from the man's statements at the end of the passage?
   Ⓐ The cuckoo bird has learned to fly even higher.
   Ⓑ Someone robbed the town of its cuckoo bird.
   Ⓒ The man does not understand the mistakes he made.
   Ⓓ The man is afraid the town will never have a mild spring.

STRATEGY PRACTICE How is the folk tale organized?

_____

_____

READ THE PASSAGE Use your background knowledge and information from the passage to compare ballet and hip-hop and to make inferences about dance.

Hip-Hop and Ballet

Two of the most popular types of dance for young dancers are hip-hop and ballet. The beats and rhythms of hip-hop are quite different from the classical sounds that usually accompany ballet, but the differences between the two styles extend beyond the type of music involved.

Ballet began in France during the late sixteenth century, so the art form has been studied and mastered for hundreds of years. When students of ballet refine their techniques, they are able to do incredible things with their bodies. For example, women in ballet corps often dance on the tips of their toes, a technique known as dancing *sur le pointe,* or "on pointe." Both men and women are able to perform graceful, high leaps through the air—moves that are virtually impossible for non-dancers to accomplish.

Hip-hop dancing began with the popularity of hip-hop music during the last quarter of the twentieth century. Hip-hop dancers often learn new moves from each other informally. In the 1970s, dancers in New York, Fresno, and Los Angeles started to dance in competitive teams. They developed new styles, such as popping, locking, and the robot, which spread through the pop culture world. Break dancers, who do flips and shoulder spins and can dance on their hands and head, are some of the most athletic hip-hop dancers.

Ballet takes great discipline and years of dedication, even with prior experience in some other form of dance. Some ballet dancers can learn many hip-hop moves in under a year, although they may have more trouble capturing the style. While ballet dancers learn specific, choreographed dances, hip-hop dancers generally improvise, choosing their moves to suit the moment. Whether it is through ballet or hip-hop, both forms of dance are a great way for people to show personal expression and artistic flair.

SKILL PRACTICE Read each question. Fill in the bubble next to the correct answer.

1. Ballet dancing is different from hip-hop dancing because ballet _____.
   - Ⓐ includes graceful moves and high leaps
   - Ⓑ requires strength and control
   - Ⓒ is still danced today
   - Ⓓ allows dancers to express themselves

2. Compared to ballet dancing, hip-hop dancing is _____.
   - Ⓐ less physical
   - Ⓑ more delicate
   - Ⓒ more improvised
   - Ⓓ harder on the feet

3. How are ballet dancers and hip-hop dancers alike?
   - Ⓐ They both study in formal classes.
   - Ⓑ They both use their bodies for artistic expression.
   - Ⓒ They both learn new moves from each other.
   - Ⓓ They both dance on pointe.

4. What can you infer from the passage?
   - Ⓐ Musicians are likely to be good dancers.
   - Ⓑ Only the best dancers can choreograph dances.
   - Ⓒ It is easier for children to learn to dance than adults.
   - Ⓓ Knowing one kind of dance can help you learn another.

STRATEGY PRACTICE Which style of dance most appeals to you? Why?

_____

_____

Character and Setting

Students practice analyzing character and setting by looking at the traits and motivations of a character and where and when a passage's events take place.

Theme

Students practice identifying the theme by looking for the central message or lesson in a passage.

DAY 1

Tell students they will practice the *Character and Setting* skill by reading about the first woman to drive across the country in a car. Say: **You are going to read a nonfiction passage, so the character is a person from real life. Look for where and when the events took place to understand the setting.** Then remind students of the *Visualization* strategy (Week 3). Say: **If you have difficulty visualizing something, close your eyes. Then think about what you have read and create a detailed mental picture.** When students have finished reading, direct them to complete the skill and strategy practice activities. Review the answers together.

DAY 2

Review the *Character and Setting* skill with students. Say: **You can learn a lot about a character by thinking about the setting. As you read, ask yourself:** *How would these events be different if they happened in a different country or at a different time in history?* Then remind students of the *Monitor Comprehension* strategy (Week 1). Say: **A good way to ensure that you understand the biographical details of someone's life is to make a timeline of events. When making a timeline, put dates or events in chronological order.** When students have finished reading, direct them to complete the skill and strategy practice activities. Review the answers together.

DAY 3

Review the *Theme* skill with students. Say: **Authors often do not directly state themes in their works. To find the theme, read the entire passage. Then pause briefly to think about the lesson that is being taught.** Remind students of the *Monitor Comprehension* strategy. Read aloud the strategy practice activity to students. Say: **Complete this section of the page as you read.** When students have finished reading, direct them to complete the skill practice activity. Review the answers together.

DAY 4

Remind students of the *Theme* skill. Say: **Not all themes are heavy, serious life lessons. Sometimes, a theme is a gentle reminder or a simple suggestion.** Tell students they will practice finding the theme of a passage by reading about a family picnic. Say: **Think about how you could summarize the theme of the passage in one simple sentence.** Then remind students of the *Visualization* strategy. Say: **When you visualize, think of more than just people and objects. Challenge yourself to also see color and movement, taste flavors, hear sounds, smell odors, and feel textures. Visualizing in this way will help you to create a complete mental image.** When students finish reading, direct them to complete the skill and strategy practice activities. Review the answers together.

DAY 5

Tell students they will practice evaluating character and setting and finding the theme. Say: **As you read about Aung San Suu Kyi, a woman involved in political action, think about the setting and its effect on her.** Remind students to monitor their comprehension by making notes next to sentences that give good details and help students visualize Aung San Suu Kyi and where she lives. Then have students read the passage. When students have finished, direct them to complete the skill and strategy practice activities. Review the answers together.

READ THE PASSAGE Think about the characteristics needed to succeed at new and complicated tasks.

Alice Ramsey: Driving Phenomenon

In 1909, 22-year-old Alice Ramsey was one of the few women who not only knew how to drive a car but loved it. Soon, she began competing in meets, which were contests that tested how well drivers could handle their cars. In those days, driving required not only skill but physical strength, and Ramsey, who had both, quickly distinguished herself as a top-notch driver.

At one of Ramsey's driving meets, she caught the attention of Cadwallader Kelsey, a charming and creative sales manager for the Maxwell-Briscoe Car Company. Kelsey had an idea for a brilliant publicity stunt guaranteed to generate huge sales for Maxwell-Briscoe. Kelsey challenged Ramsey to drive across the country in a specially equipped Maxwell-Briscoe touring car, with all expenses paid by the company. Ramsey did not care about car sales, but she welcomed the challenge and the chance for the adventure of a lifetime. Ramsey accepted Kelsey's offer. For the trip, she would bring along three female companions. Ramsey was the only one in the group who knew how to drive.

The trip began on June 9, 1909, just outside of the Maxwell-Briscoe salesroom in New York City. Of the 3,800 miles the group would travel, only 152 miles were on paved roads. In addition to rough terrain, Ramsey had to deal with 11 flat tires, flooding, heavy rains, hailstorms, and broken wheel axles. With practically no service stations along the way, Ramsey and her companions had to handle any needed repairs alone.

Finally, 59 days later, on August 7, 1909, Alice Ramsey arrived in San Francisco to a cheering crowd. She had done it. Ramsey was the first woman to drive straight across the country, and she had completed the trip in less time than any of the 24 men who made the trip before her.

SKILL PRACTICE Read each question. Fill in the bubble next to the correct answer.

1. According to the passage, in 1909, most women _____.
   - Ⓐ did not drive cars
   - Ⓑ had many travel opportunities
   - Ⓒ knew a lot about car repair
   - Ⓓ were excellent drivers

2. What weather difficulties did Alice Ramsey face on her road trip?
   - Ⓐ strong winds
   - Ⓑ extreme heat
   - Ⓒ snowstorms
   - Ⓓ floods and rain

3. What convinced Ramsey to make the trip?
   - Ⓐ the opportunity to show off her skill
   - Ⓑ the challenge of doing something difficult
   - Ⓒ the chance to teach her friends how to drive
   - Ⓓ the opportunity to drive a Maxwell-Briscoe car

4. Which adjective best describes Ramsey as she is presented in the passage?
   - Ⓐ young
   - Ⓑ reckless
   - Ⓒ creative
   - Ⓓ adventurous

STRATEGY PRACTICE Visualize one of the obstacles Ramsey faced on her trip. On a separate sheet of paper, sketch the scene.

Look for details that explain why Judit Polgar is a leading chess player.

Judit Polgar: Grandmaster Chess Player

Chess is one of the oldest board games in the world. A version of the game was first played in India in the sixth century. Throughout time, the game has been played by kings, knights, and generals who wanted to prove their military skills and practice war strategies. Today, the game is played by millions of ordinary people as well. Most play for fun, but there are players who compete seriously and have gone on to gain the rank of grandmaster—the highest rank a player can achieve.

In 1991, when Hungarian Judit Polgar achieved the rank of grandmaster, it caused quite an uproar. First of all, Polgar was a female playing in a sport traditionally dominated by men. Also, Polgar was only 15 years old, making her the youngest grandmaster in history at the time. In 1993, she defeated former world champion Boris Spassky in Budapest, Hungary. In 1998, she became the first woman in history to win the U.S. Open Chess Championship, which was held in Kailua-Kona, Hawaii.

Like her two older sisters, Polgar was rigorously trained to be a master chess player as a young girl. She was homeschooled in all her subjects and played chess several hours every day. At the age of five, she was beating her father at the game. At eight years old, she was competing internationally. At the age of nine, she competed in and won the New York Open Chess Tournament, placing first among unranked players. The young Polgar was just getting started.

Known for her fiercely competitive nature and ability to understand her opponent's strategy early in a game, Polgar quickly won the respect of both fans and fellow chess players. Despite her achievements and clear talent, she often had trouble getting into top competitive situations because many of them excluded women. Polgar wanted to compete with the best—to be a world champion and not just a female champion. For this reason, she absolutely refused to play in women-only competitions. Her refusal helped demolish gender stereotypes and paved the way for the next generation of female chess players.

SKILL PRACTICE   Read each question. Fill in the bubble next to the correct answer.

1. What led Judit Polgar to master chess at such a young age?
   - Ⓐ international travel
   - Ⓑ rigorous chess training
   - Ⓒ being homeschooled
   - Ⓓ having sisters who played chess

2. Why did Polgar have trouble entering competitions as a child?
   - Ⓐ She was too young to enter tournaments.
   - Ⓑ She could beat only her father.
   - Ⓒ Many tournaments did not allow female players.
   - Ⓓ There were no tournaments in her country.

3. Why did Polgar refuse to compete in women-only tournaments?
   - Ⓐ She wanted to compete with the world's best players.
   - Ⓑ She did not like playing against women.
   - Ⓒ She disapproved of the tournaments' locations.
   - Ⓓ She found it easier to beat male players.

4. Which ability makes Polgar such a successful chess player?
   - Ⓐ the ability to travel easily
   - Ⓑ the ability to beat female players
   - Ⓒ the ability to see her opponent's strategy early
   - Ⓓ the ability to win respect

STRATEGY PRACTICE   On a separate sheet of paper, draw a timeline that shows Polgar's major achievements.

READ THE PASSAGE   As you read, think about what each character in the story values.

The Scholar and the Boatman

A scholar, a man who had many degrees and was well respected in his town, asked a boatman to row him across a river. It would be a long and slow journey.

Once they got started, the scholar became incredibly bored. What was there to do? So, to pass the time, he said to the boatman, "Let's engage in conversation!"

The scholar, impressed with his own accomplishments, suggested a topic that would showcase his achievements. "Let's talk about poetry, phonetics, or grammar," the scholar suggested. The boatman, who was concentrating on getting the scholar across the river, said nothing.

After sitting in silence for a while, the boatman said bluntly, "I have no use for poetry and grammar and have nothing to say about them."

"Oh, that's too bad," said the scholar with a clear air of superiority. "My dear man, you've wasted most of your life. You have no idea how important it is to learn such things."

Ignoring the scholar, the boatman remained silent. Then, suddenly, the flimsy boat crashed into a rock. The boatman said, "Pardon my uneducated mind, sir, but have you ever learned to swim?"

"Oh, no," the scholar said. "I have been far too busy studying more important things like poetry."

"In that case," the boatman said, "I have to tell you that it is *you* who has wasted his life. The boat is sinking in the deepest part of the river, and you can't swim. Tell me, will your poetry save you now?"

SKILL PRACTICE   Read each question. Fill in the bubble next to the correct answer.

1. **Which of these best describes the theme, or moral, of the story?**
   - Ⓐ Don't travel in a boat across a river.
   - Ⓑ Don't assume that poetry is useless.
   - Ⓒ Don't make people talk when they do not want to.
   - Ⓓ Don't think your skills are more important than others' skills.

2. **What does the author probably believe?**
   - Ⓐ People don't realize that they need grammar.
   - Ⓑ Practical knowledge can be useful.
   - Ⓒ Academic achievement is important only for some people.
   - Ⓓ There is a time to learn skills, and there is a time to use them.

3. **What does the scholar value?**
   - Ⓐ ideas
   - Ⓑ time
   - Ⓒ nature
   - Ⓓ patience

4. **What can be learned from this story?**
   - Ⓐ It is better to be a boatman than a scholar.
   - Ⓑ First impressions are usually correct.
   - Ⓒ Not every important lesson is learned from books.
   - Ⓓ It is wasteful to spend one's time boating.

STRATEGY PRACTICE   As you read, write notes that help you understand the character, setting, and theme of the story.

_____

_____

READ THE PASSAGE   As you read, visualize the events as they unfold in the story.

Bug Attack!

They all came. Aunt Thelma with her big, sloppy kisses plopped herself into the only lawn chair. Uncle Frank, who loves talking about politics, sat himself on the blanket right next to the cooler. My cousin, Mario, did what he always does—told jokes and teased me. It was going to be a typical Saturday.

The picnic was all my mother's idea. She thought it would be great fun if we all got together by the lake for some good food. She carefully organized the whole event.

It all started off fine. We had watermelon, fruit salad, fried chicken, iced tea, and chips and salsa. All the food was spread out on a blanket, and I was laughing at Mario trying to sneak a chip from his father's plate. Just as I was about to take a sip of my iced tea, I suddenly shrieked. Some flying thing had gotten into my iced tea, and when I went to take a sip, it tried to fly into my mouth! I was horrified!

I flung my iced tea onto the grass and looked over to the blanket where all the food was located. The watermelon and fruit salad were covered with black creepy-crawlies, and the bugs were scurrying straight toward the fried chicken. Aunt Thelma, feeling something crawling up her leg, let out a bloodcurdling scream, jumped up, ran, tripped over the cooler, and landed headfirst in the grass. Uncle Frank raced over to help her, but he went flying as he slipped on the ice from my tea. The only happy person during all that time was Mario—he had a good laugh while everyone else panicked.

My mother knew she was defeated. The bugs had won, and we had lost. As my mother shouted orders, everyone quickly gathered the food and blankets. The picnic would resume, but this time it would be inside and far, far away from bugs.

SKILL PRACTICE   Read each question. Fill in the bubble next to the correct answer.

1. What lesson can be learned about handling problems?
   Ⓐ Choose your words carefully.
   Ⓑ Stay calm in a commotion.
   Ⓒ Wait for the problem to go away.
   Ⓓ Make use of everyone's talents.

2. What would be another good title for the passage?
   Ⓐ "The Exterminator!"
   Ⓑ "The Big Family Fight"
   Ⓒ "Picnic Disaster!"
   Ⓓ "Planning a Picnic "

3. Which best states the theme of the story?
   Ⓐ It is important to protect food from bugs.
   Ⓑ Even the best plans can easily go wrong.
   Ⓒ Relatives need to spend less time together.
   Ⓓ People react differently to the same joke.

4. From their actions, you can tell that the narrator's family members most value _____.
   Ⓐ spending time together
   Ⓑ eating outdoors only
   Ⓒ having chaos at their gatherings
   Ⓓ laughing at each other

STRATEGY PRACTICE   Visualize your favorite moment from the story. Describe your visualization.

_____

_____

READ THE PASSAGE   As you read, think about the character and personality of Aung San Suu Kyi.

Burma's Iron Woman

No one might guess that Aung San Suu Kyi is an international symbol of peaceful resistance to brutal oppression, but that is exactly what she is. This petite, slender, soft-spoken woman is a force to be reckoned with. Born in 1945, Aung San Suu Kyi was the daughter of the Burmese nationalist leader, General Aung San. The general resisted British colonial rule, which ended in 1948 when Burma, also known as Myanmar, became independent. Then, when Aung San Suu Kyi was only two years old, her father was assassinated. She moved to India with her mother, then studied at universities in Oxford and New York.

In 1988, Aung San Suu Kyi returned to Burma to care for her sick mother. When she arrived, a national rebellion aimed at removing the oppressive military regime, or government, from power and securing democracy for the country was in full force. Students had taken to the streets to fight for their cause.

Aung San Suu Kyi quickly became involved. She joined the newly formed National League for Democracy (NLD) and began giving speeches calling for democracy in Burma. The military regime responded viciously to the rebellion, killing up to 10,000 demonstrators and children in a matter of months.

When Aung San Suu Kyi actively campaigned for the NLD, she and other campaigners were arrested and detained by the military regime. Despite its brutal show of force, however, the military regime was unable to maintain power. In 1990, the regime was forced to hold a general election. Even though the NLD went on to win a stunning 82% of the seats in the legislature, the military regime refused to recognize the results. Aung San Suu Kyi has been in and out of the military's custody ever since. In 1991, she won the Nobel Peace Prize but was unable to travel to accept it for 21 years. Finally being allowed to run for and win a legislative seat herself in 2012, she continues to work toward democracy in her country.

SKILL PRACTICE   Read each question. Fill in the bubble next to the correct answer.

1. Where did most of the events in the passage take place?
   Ⓐ England
   Ⓑ the United States
   Ⓒ India
   Ⓓ Burma

2. What was happening in Burma when Aung San Suu Kyi returned there to care for her mother?
   Ⓐ Burma was resisting British rule.
   Ⓑ Burma had just won its independence.
   Ⓒ The NLD won a majority of legislative seats.
   Ⓓ There was a rebellion against military rule.

3. Which best describes the character of Aung San Suu Kyi as she is presented in the passage?
   Ⓐ unhappy
   Ⓑ anxious
   Ⓒ unselfish
   Ⓓ mischievous

4. Which best describes the theme of the passage?
   Ⓐ Most governments are corrupt.
   Ⓑ Fighting for causes requires a firm belief.
   Ⓒ Returning to a troubled country is too dangerous to consider.
   Ⓓ Brutal force is very effective.

STRATEGY PRACTICE   Write two sentences from the passage that helped you understand Aung San Suu Kyi's character.

_____

_____

Cause and Effect
Students practice identifying cause-and-effect relationships by looking for what happens (the effect) and why it happens (the cause).

Prediction
Students practice using clues from a passage to predict what will happen next.

DAY 1

Review the *Cause and Effect* skill with students. Say: **Authors can alert us about problems that may happen in the future based on events that are happening today.** Tell students they are going to read about the future of plastics. Say: **Look for cause-and-effect relationships between plastics and human life in the future.** Then remind students of the *Ask Questions* strategy (Week 6). Say: **Asking questions when you have finished reading can help you remember what you have read or remind you what you still want to learn. You can search for more information about a topic based on any remaining questions you have.** When students have finished reading the passage, direct them to complete the skill and strategy practice activities. Review the answers together.

DAY 2

Review the *Cause and Effect* skill with students. Tell students they will practice finding causes and effects by reading about the history of soda bottles. Remind students that an effect is what happened; the cause is why that event happened. Then remind students of the *Make Connections* strategy (Week 2). Say: **As you read, think about the various liquid containers that you are familiar with. Think about how they open.** When students have finished reading, direct them to complete the skill and strategy practice activities. Review the answers together.

DAY 3

Tell students they will practice the *Prediction* skill by reading about zebra mussels. Say: **As you read, think about how zebra mussels are affecting the environment today. Use what you learn to make predictions about how zebra mussels might affect people or places in the future.** Remind students to ask questions before, during, and after reading to aid comprehension. When students have finished reading, direct them to complete the skill and strategy practice activities. Review the answers together.

DAY 4

Tell students they will practice making predictions by reading about honeybees. Say: **When you read a fiction story, you can predict what will happen next in the plot. When you read nonfiction, you can make predictions about what will happen in the future based on the information presented in the text.** Tell students they are going to read a nonfiction passage about honeybees. Remind students of the *Make Connections* strategy. Say: **As you read, think about how problems with the honeybee population could affect people all across the world.** When students have finished reading, direct them to complete the skill and strategy practice activities. Review the answers together.

DAY 5

Tell students they will practice the *Cause and Effect* and *Prediction* skills by reading about urban legends. Say: **When you make predictions about what might happen in the future, base them on information you learned in the passage. You can use causes and effects from the passage to help you make these predictions.** Remind students of the *Ask Questions* strategy. Say: **Asking and answering questions about a text helps you retain the information for future use.** When students have finished reading, direct them to complete the skill practice activity. Review the answers together. Then have partners complete the strategy practice activity.

READ THE PASSAGE   Think about the effects of the limited amount of petroleum in the world.

A Life Without Plastics

You may have heard that one day there will be no more petroleum in the world—and it is true. Most experts believe that the world's petroleum could be exhausted between 50 and 200 years from now, depending on how well people manage the existing supplies. The most obvious impact of running out of petroleum will be the end of gasoline. But many people do not realize that there will be a much bigger impact—no more plastics.

Most commercial plastics today are made from petroleum. Almost every product, from food containers to clothing, contains a certain amount of the fossil fuel. Plastics have been practical because they have always been cheap to produce. As petroleum becomes more expensive, however, so will plastics. Eventually, petroleum will become too expensive for companies to use in order to make plastics. So what happens then?

Fortunately, scientists are already working with new forms of plastics that are not made from petroleum. Because petroleum started out as plant and animal parts millions of years ago, scientists are looking at using plant parts to make new kinds of plastics. These new plastics are less toxic than traditional plastics. Some of them even biodegrade, or break down, which will reduce the impact on landfills.

As the world's fossil fuel supply slowly runs out, people will need to make big changes in how they live, work, and play. Plastics is just one of the industries that will look much different in the decades to come.

SKILL PRACTICE   Read each question. Fill in the bubble next to the correct answer.

1. The world will eventually run out of petroleum because _____.
   Ⓐ food containers and clothes contain petroleum
   Ⓑ it is very costly and difficult to produce
   Ⓒ people are not managing existing supplies well
   Ⓓ there is a limited supply of petroleum on Earth

2. Why have plastics been so widely used?
   Ⓐ They are less toxic than metals.
   Ⓑ They are inexpensive to make.
   Ⓒ They come from plants that are in great supply.
   Ⓓ They are left over after producing gasoline.

3. Running out of petroleum will cause the end of plastics and the _____.
   Ⓐ end of gasoline
   Ⓑ development of new plant species
   Ⓒ increase of landfill use
   Ⓓ end of plant life

4. According to the passage, scientists made new plastics from plant parts because _____.
   Ⓐ plant parts are cheap
   Ⓑ plant parts contain petroleum
   Ⓒ petroleum came from plant parts
   Ⓓ petroleum is more toxic than plastic

STRATEGY PRACTICE   Write a question you thought of while reading the passage. How can you find the answer?

_____

_____

Name: _____

READ THE PASSAGE   Look for cause-and-effect relationships as you read the passage.

The History of Soda Bottles

If you walked outside right now, chances are you would see at least one plastic soda bottle. Soda manufacturers produce over one billion bottles of soda every year, so it is not surprising to see bottles everywhere. However, there was a time when seeing a soda bottle was an uncommon occurrence.

For hundreds of years, drink bottles were made by hand from blown glass. As a result, drinks in glass bottles were expensive. The bottles were called "blob tops" because each bottle had a small blob of glass at the top where it had been attached to the glassblowing tools. The work was hot, dirty, and hard, and not every glassblower created high-quality bottles. The bottles often broke, leaked, or ruined the drink inside by letting in dirt and outside air. Bottle makers also made many different styles and sizes of bottles, so they rarely looked alike. They were sealed with stoppers made of cork, rubber, glass, or metal.

Between 1880 and 1910, however, everything in the soda bottle industry changed. First, an inventor named William Painter patented a new type of bottle stopper called the "crown cap." If you have ever twisted or pried a metal top off of a bottle of soda, you have used Painter's invention. The crown cap was the best and cheapest way to seal a bottle, so it became the industry standard. Then, in 1903, Michael Owens invented a machine that could blow bottles automatically. Instead of making around 1,500 bottles a day, bottle makers could suddenly make tens of thousands.

Bottled drinks became even more popular as their prices decreased and quality levels increased. Later in the twentieth century, aluminum cans and plastic bottles replaced glass as the most common way of storing drinks. You can still find glass bottles today, but they are a far cry from the bottles of the past.

SKILL PRACTICE   Read each question. Fill in the bubble next to the correct answer.

1. Why weren't all blob-top bottles the same shape?
   (A) They were made from plastic.
   (B) Glassblowers made them individually.
   (C) Bottle makers wanted each one to look unique.
   (D) Machines made them in different sizes.

2. Since glassblowers varied in ability, early glass bottles were often _____.
   (A) dirty
   (B) heavy
   (C) expensive
   (D) leaky

3. The crown-cap bottle stopper probably got its name because it _____.
   (A) is shaped like a crown
   (B) was made for royalty
   (C) is made from gold
   (D) was patented

4. What effect did inventions between 1880 and 1910 have on bottled drinks?
   (A) They cost less than before.
   (B) They became less popular than cans.
   (C) Their quality decreased.
   (D) The variety of bottle types increased.

STRATEGY PRACTICE   Write a sentence about what you like or dislike about beverage containers you have used.

_____

_____

READ THE PASSAGE Think about the problems in the passage and what the results will be.

The Zebra Mussel Invasion

Zebra mussels are small, striped, freshwater mollusks that live in eastern Europe. In 1988, however, zebra mussels were sighted far from home. They had suddenly appeared in the United States. It is believed that the mollusks were brought over on a ship from the Black Sea. Once they were in the United States, they rapidly took over. By 1990, they had spread throughout the Great Lakes, and by 2008, they were in bodies of water in at least 24 of the 50 states. In only 20 years, these tiny creatures had made their way halfway across the country.

Zebra mussels have wreaked havoc in every ecosystem they have encountered in their new home. They take over the habitats of native mollusks and fish and eat their food. They affect humans by attaching themselves to boats and structures in the water. Zebra mussels can destroy wood, concrete, and even steel. They sink buoys and slow down ships by attaching to the vessels in enormous numbers. They are numerous enough to clog water pipes leading to and from power and water plants. Zebra mussels also foul beaches, and their sharp shells are a hazard to swimmers.

There is no single effective way to deal with zebra mussels. They can be removed with scrapers, hot water, and air pressure. They can also be prevented from attaching by using chemicals, barriers, and coatings. Power stations and water treatment plants spend hundreds of thousands of dollars a year to deal with them, but the zebra mussels can always return. Unfortunately, zebra mussels are here to stay. Hopefully, one day researchers will find a way to truly combat this bewildering invasion.

SKILL PRACTICE Read each question. Fill in the bubble next to the correct answer.

1. If the ship from eastern Europe had gone to Brazil instead of the United States in 1988, the zebra mussels would have probably _____.
   Ⓐ disappeared from the Black Sea
   Ⓑ invaded Brazilian waterways
   Ⓒ struggled to compete with Brazilian mollusks
   Ⓓ made their way to the United States

2. What will probably happen to zebra mussels in the future?
   Ⓐ They will continue to thrive.
   Ⓑ They will be stopped by native fish.
   Ⓒ They will run out of food.
   Ⓓ They will all die off.

3. What will probably happen to native mollusks in the future?
   Ⓐ They will change what they eat.
   Ⓑ They will move to other countries.
   Ⓒ They will decrease in number.
   Ⓓ They will clog water treatment plants.

4. How can we prevent an invasion from another marine species in the future?
   Ⓐ Don't let ships travel to the Black Sea.
   Ⓑ Get rid of the invasive species' food supply.
   Ⓒ Bring in a predator species to keep the population down.
   Ⓓ Inspect all docking ships and their contents.

STRATEGY PRACTICE Write a question you thought of while you read the passage.

_____

_____

READ THE PASSAGE   As you read each paragraph, make predictions about what you will learn next.

What Happened to the Bees?

In 2006, beekeepers around the country began to notice that their honeybee colonies were disappearing. Some colonies collapsed completely; others had only the queen and a few young workers remaining. By 2007, over 30% of all honeybee colonies in the United States had died out, and similar losses had occurred around the world.

Scientists began working frantically to find the cause of the honeybee losses. Speed was essential, because one-third of the world's agriculture depends on pollination by honeybees. Bees are also an important part of the balance of many ecosystems. Throughout their research, scientists identified many possible causes for loss: parasites, diseases, poison by pesticides, or a combination of factors. Even though different bee colonies seemed to have different problems, the result—death—was the same.

Scientists determined that something was affecting the bees' immune systems, which left them open to numerous other problems. Researchers and regular citizens alike began developing theories about the possible causes of the bees' problems. Some people believed the bees were being affected by radiation from cellphones. One rather unconventional theorist stated that bees were being taken away from Earth by aliens. There has been no agreement on the exact source, but the problem was given an official name that was adopted by all concerned: colony collapse disorder, or CCD.

In 2009, Spanish scientists found a parasite in some colonies and treated those bees with an antibiotic. Thankfully, the colonies recovered completely. Whether this solution will work for all affected colonies is not yet clear, but one fact is evident: a cure must be found, and quickly.

SKILL PRACTICE   Read each question. Fill in the bubble next to the correct answer.

1. What will most likely happen if a cure for CCD is not found?
   Ⓐ Scientists will stop studying bees.
   Ⓑ Crop levels will decrease greatly.
   Ⓒ People will use more cellphones.
   Ⓓ The number of colonies will increase.

2. The people most directly affected by CCD will probably be _____.
   Ⓐ beekeepers
   Ⓑ scientists
   Ⓒ theorists
   Ⓓ students

3. What would probably happen to bee colonies without the parasite if scientists treated them?
   Ⓐ The colonies would start to grow.
   Ⓑ The parasite would infect the colonies.
   Ⓒ The bees would join a different colony.
   Ⓓ The bees' death rates would not change.

4. What will farmers most likely do if the antibiotic does not treat all affected colonies?
   Ⓐ plant crops that do not rely on bees for pollination
   Ⓑ stop farming and find new businesses
   Ⓒ become beekeepers to try to help the bees
   Ⓓ harvest plants before pollination

STRATEGY PRACTICE   Describe how CCD might affect your community if a cure is not found.

_____

_____

READ THE PASSAGE   Before you begin reading, predict what you will learn about the causes and effects of urban legends.

Urban Legends

Have you heard the story about finding a million-dollar painting at a garage sale? Or the one about the kid who ate fizzy candy, drank soda, and then exploded? These are just two of the hundreds of urban legends that are passed around by people every year. Almost always, these types of stories turn out to be false. Nevertheless, these stories are shared between friends and spread like wildfire on the Internet. People seem to love the attention they get retelling a captivating, bizarre tale, but where do these stories come from?

Some urban legends are inspired by real events that are often surprising or gross. For example, some stories about people finding live bugs in their food are true. The legends, however, will often change details of the original stories, such as how big the bug was or where the meal was served.

Other urban legends are the results of popular beliefs or fears in a society. Alligators in the sewers, strange things happening at night, and people mysteriously disappearing—these stories are usually just created around issues or events that scare people the most. Luckily, the more ridiculous or scary a story seems, the less likely it is to be true.

Some urban legends involve common science misconceptions, such as a penny on a railroad track derailing a train. Some put forth predictions that a natural event, such as an eclipse, will cause a natural disaster. People have acted on these predictions, making permanent, life-altering decisions for no good reason. While the majority of these stories are just stories, it is always best to check out any possible urban legend with a reliable source before acting on it.

SKILL PRACTICE   Read each question. Fill in the bubble next to the correct answer.

1. A small news event would mostly likely become an urban legend if it _____.
   Ⓐ did not really happen
   Ⓑ included a strange or scary detail
   Ⓒ contained regular, everyday matters
   Ⓓ happened in the United States

2. Why do people spread urban legends?
   Ⓐ They believe they are true.
   Ⓑ They want to warn their friends.
   Ⓒ They are trying to verify the information.
   Ⓓ They like the attention they get.

3. Which of the following will probably be true about urban legends in the future?
   Ⓐ They will all be proven true.
   Ⓑ They will travel more slowly.
   Ⓒ They will be based on current fears.
   Ⓓ They will all sound more believable.

4. Which of these could be caused by believing a false urban legend?
   Ⓐ science discoveries
   Ⓑ natural disasters
   Ⓒ a bad decision
   Ⓓ a train accident

STRATEGY PRACTICE   Write a question that can be answered with information from the passage. Ask a partner to answer it.

_____

_____

Nonfiction Text Features

Students practice identifying and comprehending common features of nonfiction text.

Visual Information

Students examine and evaluate information that is depicted visually.

DAY 1

Review the *Nonfiction Text Features* skill with students. Say: **Nonfiction text features highlight or help organize factual information.** Tell students they are going to read a table of contents for a book about the Olympics. Say: **Pay attention to the features of the table of contents, and think about how they would aid readers of the book.** Then remind students of the *Determine Important Information* strategy (Week 5). Say: **As you study the table of contents, think about which information would be the most useful to readers.** When students have finished reading, direct them to complete the skill and strategy practice activities. Review the answers together.

DAY 2

Tell students they will study the nonfiction text features of a science experiment. Say: **Nonfiction text features can include lists, headings, and charts. These features can help authors divide experiments into different parts or steps.** Remind students of the *Organization* strategy (Week 4). Say: **This experiment has been organized into separate sections. As you read, think about how the experiment would be difficult to understand if it had been written as a simple passage.** When students have finished reading, direct them to complete the skill and strategy practice activities. Review the answers together.

DAY 3

Review the *Visual Information* skill with students. Say: **Sometimes, it can be difficult to describe an object or area using words alone. Authors can add visuals to help readers understand the information in a text.** Challenge students to read the passage while covering the image of Skylab with one hand. Then have them reread the passage and study the visual. Ask: **How did the visual help you better understand the passage?** Then remind students of the *Determine Important Information* strategy. Say: **Think about how you would describe Skylab to someone based only on the visual information. Which important details would you share?** When students have finished, have them complete the skill and strategy practice activities. Review the answers together.

DAY 4

Remind students of the *Visual Information* skill. Say: **Sometimes, authors give information in a visual that is not included in the text. It is important to combine visual and written information to fully understand the topic being presented.** Then remind students of the *Organization* strategy. Say: **This author put some information in a passage, some in a list, and some in a map. Think about why the author organized the information this way.** Then have students read the passage. When students have finished, direct them to complete the skill and strategy practice activities. Review the answers together.

DAY 5

Tell students they will practice using the *Nonfiction Text Features* and *Visual Information* skills as they read about the ways dogs communicate. Say: **As you read the passage and study the visual, think about dogs you have encountered before. Did they look or act like the dogs you read about or see here?** Remind students of the *Determine Important Information* strategy. Say: **Which information would be the most helpful to keep people safe around unknown dogs?** When students have finished reading, direct them to complete the skill and strategy practice activities. Review the answers together.

READ THE TABLE OF CONTENTS   Pay attention to how the table of contents is organized.

The Olympic Games: Basic to Bizarre Facts
Table of Contents

SKILL PRACTICE   Read each question. Fill in the bubble next to the correct answer.

1. On page 34, you can probably find _____.
   - Ⓐ a list of gold medal winners
   - Ⓑ a description of the Olympic Games
   - Ⓒ a list of significant Olympic dates and events
   - Ⓓ a comparison of ancient and modern Olympics

2. In which section would you likely read about Mukmuk, the Vancouver Island Marmot?
   - Ⓐ chapter 3
   - Ⓑ chapter 4
   - Ⓒ chapter 7
   - Ⓓ chapter 10

3. In chapter 7, you can probably learn about _____.
   - Ⓐ the fastest marathon winner
   - Ⓑ the equipment used in luge
   - Ⓒ which countries compete in weightlifting
   - Ⓓ when volleyball became an Olympic sport

4. Which section would describe the 1980 U.S. men's ice hockey team's unexpected, last-minute defeat of the legendary Soviet team?
   - Ⓐ chapter 1
   - Ⓑ chapter 5
   - Ⓒ chapter 8
   - Ⓓ chapter 12

STRATEGY PRACTICE   Why do you think this book is divided into four parts?

_____

_____

As you read the experiment, think about the type of information found in each part.

Experimenting with Blubber

Introduction:

Find out what it is like to be a penguin! In this experiment, you will make a "blubber glove" and learn how blubber is useful for animals.

Materials:

- 4 quart-size freezer bags
- 3 cups of solid vegetable shortening
- a large serving spoon
- duct tape
- a bucket of ice water
- a clock with a second hand

Directions:

1. With the spoon, put all the shortening into one freezer bag.

2. Turn a second bag inside out and place it inside the bag with the shortening. Seal the edges of the two bags together. The pocket that is formed will be your "blubber glove." Gently knead the shortening to distribute it all the way around the inner bag.

3. Take the remaining two bags and place one inside the other. This is your empty glove.

4. Put the blubber glove on one hand. Put your other hand in the empty glove. Have someone tape the bags around your wrists. Dip both gloved hands in the ice water for as long as you can stand it. Record in the table below the length of time each hand stayed in the water.

Results:

Glove	Time
blubber	
empty	

Read each question. Fill in the bubble next to the correct answer.

1. How is the introduction to the experiment helpful?
   - Ⓐ It gives you the expected results.
   - Ⓑ It provides a list of the needed materials.
   - Ⓒ It explains what you will investigate.
   - Ⓓ It tells you how to make a blubber glove.

2. The items you need to conduct the experiment are included in the _____.
   - Ⓐ bulleted list
   - Ⓑ introduction
   - Ⓒ table
   - Ⓓ numbered list

3. Which section tells you what to do with the shortening?
   - Ⓐ Introduction
   - Ⓑ Materials
   - Ⓒ Directions
   - Ⓓ Results

4. Where would you look to find out what should be recorded in the table?
   - Ⓐ in the introduction
   - Ⓑ in the "Results" section
   - Ⓒ in the last bullet under "Materials"
   - Ⓓ in step 4 of the directions

Why are the directions for the experiment written in steps?

_____

_____

READ THE PASSAGE Read the passage carefully. Then study the diagram.

Skylab: America's First Space Station

For over 200 years, American scientists have dreamed of people living in space. In the 1960s, the United States began sending rocket flights into space. In 1973, the United States launched a space station called Skylab that orbited Earth until 1979. As its name suggests, Skylab was used primarily to conduct experiments and gather data about space.

In the early 1970s, people did not have cellphones, hybrid cars, or Internet service. There was no satellite television or Wi-Fi, and people took pictures on film. While a space station might seem ordinary today, Skylab was the stuff of science fiction during the time it was built and used.

❶ Airlock module
❷ Command and service module
❸ Docking adapter
❹ Micrometeroid shield
❺ Solar observatory
❻ Solar panels
❼ Workshop (living and working area)

Length: 117 feet   Width: 90 feet

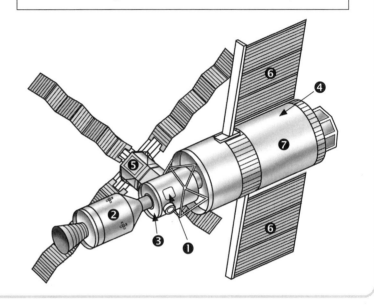

SKILL PRACTICE Read each question. Fill in the bubble next to the correct answer.

1. Which information is provided only in the diagram?
   Ⓐ when Skylab was built
   Ⓑ what Skylab was used for
   Ⓒ why Skylab seemed advanced
   Ⓓ what Skylab looked like

2. According to the diagram, where was the solar observatory?
   Ⓐ It was near the docking adapter.
   Ⓑ It was connected to the command module.
   Ⓒ It was part of the airlock module.
   Ⓓ It was at the front of the workshop.

3. What detail can you learn from the diagram?
   Ⓐ how the crew communicated
   Ⓑ where the crew slept in Skylab
   Ⓒ how much Skylab weighed
   Ⓓ what life was like in 1970s

4. According to the diagram, Skylab received some power from _____.
   Ⓐ other space stations
   Ⓑ the sun
   Ⓒ wind
   Ⓓ meteorites

STRATEGY PRACTICE What information from the diagram is most important for describing Skylab?

_____

_____

READ THE PASSAGE   Think about how the passage and map both give information about the library.

Maple Knoll High School Library

Welcome, new students, to the Maple Knoll High School library! Our goal is to make sure you find everything you need to succeed in high school, read for fun, and become a lifelong learner. Use the map below to help you become familiar with the library's resources:

- Fiction and nonfiction titles for all subjects
- Up-to-date reference books
- Current newspapers and magazines
- Study carrels for working on reports and projects
- Computers accessible with your student ID number
- Helpful library staff

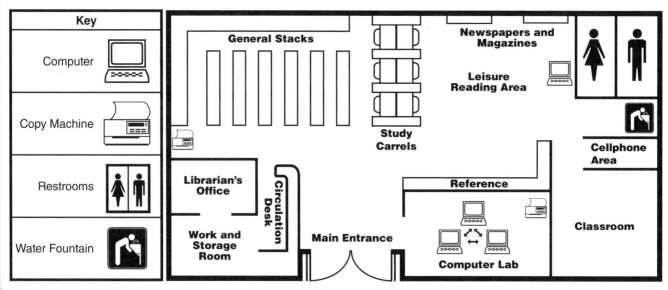

SKILL PRACTICE   Read each question. Fill in the bubble next to the correct answer.

1. Which part of the map can help you best understand the map's contents?
   Ⓐ the key
   Ⓑ the computers
   Ⓒ the circulation desk
   Ⓓ the reference section

2. Which information is included on the map but not in the passage?
   Ⓐ that there are computers for student use
   Ⓑ that the reference materials are current
   Ⓒ that there are places to write reports
   Ⓓ that the library has a place to talk on the phone

3. According to the map, where could you find a water fountain?
   Ⓐ by the stacks
   Ⓑ in the leisure reading area
   Ⓒ by the restrooms
   Ⓓ near the study carrels

4. How many copy machines are there?
   Ⓐ one
   Ⓑ two
   Ⓒ three
   Ⓓ four

STRATEGY PRACTICE   Why did the author include some information in text, some in a list, and some in a map?

_____

_____

READ THE PASSAGE   Use information in the diagram to help you understand the passage.

Do You Speak Dog?

Some dog trainers seem to have supernatural powers when it comes to communicating with dogs, so they are known as "dog whisperers." Actually, these trainers have learned to observe a dog closely and figure out how it is feeling based on its appearance and behavior.

Ears
Friendly: relaxed ears
Warning: ears that are turned forward or "perked up"
Threatening: ears that are flattened back

Tail
Friendly: a relaxed tail or a tail wagging quickly
Warning: a tail that is down but not tucked or is wagging slowly
Threatening: a tail high and rigid

Mouth
Friendly: a relaxed mouth or panting
Warning: a tightly closed mouth
Threatening: lips pulled back and teeth showing

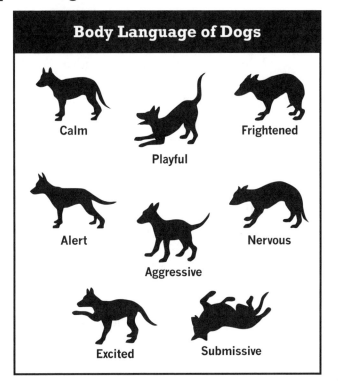

Body Language of Dogs

Calm • Playful • Frightened • Alert • Aggressive • Nervous • Excited • Submissive

SKILL PRACTICE   Read each question. Fill in the bubble next to the correct answer.

1. How do a friendly dog's ears look?
   Ⓐ relaxed
   Ⓑ flopped down
   Ⓒ perked up
   Ⓓ flattened back

2. Which signs does an alert dog display?
   Ⓐ a relaxed tail and ears flattened back
   Ⓑ a tail that is down and ears turned forward
   Ⓒ a tightly closed mouth and a tucked tail
   Ⓓ ears flattened back and a relaxed mouth

3. Which of these types of dog is probably the most safe to pet?
   Ⓐ alert
   Ⓑ nervous
   Ⓒ aggressive
   Ⓓ submissive

4. What is the trick to being a "dog whisperer"?
   Ⓐ petting and playing with many dogs
   Ⓑ having supernatural powers
   Ⓒ watching dogs carefully
   Ⓓ giving dogs orders quietly

STRATEGY PRACTICE   What part of the passage contains the most important information? Why is it the most important?

_____

_____

Main Idea and Details

Students look for the central idea or message of a passage or story. They also find details that best support the main idea.

Sequence

Students look for the order of events or steps in a process.

DAY 1

Review the *Main Idea and Details* skill with students. Say: **Studying the details of a passage can help you figure out the main idea. Think about how the details relate to each other. Then consider them together to figure out the main idea.** Tell students they are going to read about South American gauchos. Then remind students of the *Monitor Comprehension* strategy (Week 1). Say: **Use context clues to figure out the meanings of words you do not recognize.** Have students read the passage. When students have finished, direct them to complete the skill and strategy practice activities. Review the answers together.

DAY 2

Tell students they will practice the *Main Idea and Details* skill by reading about an unusual gathering of snakes. Say: **Look for at least three details that support the main idea.** Then remind students of the *Visualization* strategy (Week 3). Say: **Visualizing what you read can help you remember important details from the passage.** When students have finished reading, direct them to complete the skill and strategy practice activities. Review the answers together.

DAY 3

Review the *Sequence* skill with students. Say: **The author of this passage is going to share information about how to become a meteorologist. Pay attention to the order of steps a person would need to take to achieve this goal.** Then remind students of the *Monitor Comprehension* strategy. Say: **Taking notes or underlining information you did not already know will help you remember the new information.** When students have finished reading, direct them to complete the skill and strategy practice activities. Review the answers together.

DAY 4

Inform students they will practice the *Sequence* skill as they read about how to make custom T-shirts. Then remind students of the *Visualization* strategy. Say: **As you read, create images in your mind to accompany each step of the process. This will help you better understand the instructions.** When students have finished reading, direct them to complete the skill and strategy practice activities. Review the answers together.

DAY 5

Tell students they will practice both the *Main Idea and Details* and *Sequence* skills by reading about medieval jousting. Say: **Think about the most important idea in the passage and how the smaller details support that main idea. Also look for the sequence of events that took place during a jousting match.** Remind students of the *Monitor Comprehension* strategy. Say: **When you have finished reading the passage, go back and read it again. This will help you to retain the information so you can share it with others.** When students have finished reading, direct them to complete the skill and strategy practice activities. Review the answers together.

READ THE PASSAGE   Think about the main idea of each paragraph in the passage.

The Gaucho: A South American Legend

In the United States, cowboys have a special place in folklore as free-spirited, adventurous, and noble men. In Argentina and Uruguay, people have a similar larger-than-life historical hero: the gaucho.

Like the North American cowboy, the gaucho was generally regarded as a strong, tough man who worked hard. Gauchos were nomadic, preferring to camp on prairies rather than in towns or on farm settlements. Above all, they were skilled riders, hunters, and cow herders, quite capable of living completely off the land. Often, a gaucho's horse was his only worldly possession.

For more than 400 years, gauchos roamed the Pampas, an immense grassy expanse of land covering about 800,000 square miles of Argentina, Uruguay, Chile, and Brazil. In the beginning, gauchos were widely regarded as little more than savages who stole or hunted free-roaming cattle. But in time, as their legend grew, they became known for their fierce independence, fiery tempers, and unparalleled horsemanship.

The gaucho's attire was quite different from that of the North American cowboy. A typical gaucho outfit included a *chambergo* (a flat, wide-brimmed hat tied under the gaucho's chin with a leather cord), a large knife, and a leather whip. Gauchos wore trousers that were baggy around the thighs and tapered at the ankles to fit into their boots. They also wore ponchos, which could also be used as saddle blankets or sleeping gear. Whereas the cowboy always started his day with strong black coffee, the gaucho's preferred drink was *yerba mate,* a hot, bitter herbal drink.

Today, very few true gauchos remain. But, much like the old-fashioned cowboys in North America, their exciting and inspiring legends continue to entertain people throughout South America.

SKILL PRACTICE   Read each question. Fill in the bubble next to the correct answer.

1. **What is the passage mostly about?**
   - Ⓐ the history and description of gauchos
   - Ⓑ how gauchos and cowboys made a living
   - Ⓒ what gauchos traditionally wore
   - Ⓓ where gauchos are living today

2. **How did gauchos support themselves?**
   - Ⓐ They farmed cattle.
   - Ⓑ They competed in rodeos.
   - Ⓒ They developed special clothing.
   - Ⓓ They lived off the land.

3. **Which phrase best describes the trousers worn by gauchos?**
   - Ⓐ attached to a poncho
   - Ⓑ loose around the ankles
   - Ⓒ tied on with a leather cord
   - Ⓓ baggy around the thighs

4. **What are the Pampas?**
   - Ⓐ farm settlements
   - Ⓑ open grassland
   - Ⓒ free-roaming cattle
   - Ⓓ historical cowboys

STRATEGY PRACTICE   List two words you found confusing and how you figured out their meanings.

_____

_____

As you read, look for details that support the main idea.

The Snake Dens of Manitoba

Do you love snakes? Are you fascinated by these thin, legless reptiles as they slither along the ground, eyes wide open, forked tongues flicking to catch scents? If so, the Interlake region of Manitoba, Canada, is where you want to be during April and May. For snake enthusiasts, it is a feast for the eyes as tens of thousands of red-sided garter snakes emerge from the depths of the earth onto the plains to mate. It is the largest gathering of snakes on the planet.

As Canada's harsh winter approaches, the red-sided garter snakes slip underground to nest in roomy limestone dens, or caverns. Like all snakes, garter snakes are cold-blooded. They would die in Manitoba's winter temperatures, which can drop to -34°C (-30°F). However, both the snakes' body temperature and the air temperature in the caverns stay just above freezing, around 4°C (39°F). The snakes spend this time underground in a limited-activity state similar to hibernation.

Male snakes emerge first. Warming themselves up in the sunlight, they wait patiently for the females. The snakes mate and then head for the swamps and marshes. Each snake has lost approximately 10% of its body weight over the winter and continues to lose weight once it emerges from its den. For this reason, after mating, eating is an absolute priority. Fortunately, the numerous lakes in Manitoba have an abundance of frogs and rodents for the snakes to feed on.

For snakes and snake fans alike, in late spring, Manitoba is the place to be!

Read each question. Fill in the bubble next to the correct answer.

1. Which statement best summarizes the main idea of the passage?
   - Ⓐ Male garter snakes come out of the ground first.
   - Ⓑ Manitoba's garter snakes spend the winter in underground dens.
   - Ⓒ Snakes are legless reptiles that smell with their tongues.
   - Ⓓ Manitoba is a popular place for snakes and snake enthusiasts.

2. Why are garter snakes in a hurry to eat in the spring?
   - Ⓐ Food is scarce in spring.
   - Ⓑ They have lost weight over the winter.
   - Ⓒ Garter snakes are always hungry.
   - Ⓓ The males and females compete for food.

3. Which detail best supports the idea that snake lovers would enjoy Manitoba in the spring?
   - Ⓐ Visitors can see thousands of snakes at a time.
   - Ⓑ The snakes warm themselves in the sunlight.
   - Ⓒ The snakes are thinner in the spring.
   - Ⓓ Visitors can see the snakes eat frogs.

4. Which word best describes the snake dens in the winter?
   - Ⓐ bright
   - Ⓑ cramped
   - Ⓒ cold
   - Ⓓ wet

Which details from the passage helped you visualize the Manitoba snakes?

_____

_____

READ THE PASSAGE   As you read, pay attention to the order of the steps needed to become a meteorologist.

Becoming a Meteorologist

What do you think of when you hear the word *meteorologist*? Most likely, it is the person on TV who presents the weather forecast each day. However, many of these TV personalities are not meteorologists at all but are simply people who report the forecasts made by actual meteorologists.

Meteorology is the study of the atmosphere. Meteorologists investigate the forces that shape the weather and the effects human activity can have on the climate. Very few meteorologists work for TV or radio stations. Most work for the government at the National Weather Service or at NASA, but many have careers in private companies. These companies may do weather research, provide weather information to other companies, or develop atmospheric measurement technologies.

If you think you might want to become a meteorologist, begin by asking yourself a few questions. Do you have a deep curiosity about the physical world around you? Have you always watched the sky, read articles about weather, or found yourself fascinated by storms? Are you already keeping your own weather diary? Do you enjoy and do well in math, science, and computer courses?

Next, take physics, chemistry, math, computer science, and environmental science courses in high school. Also, develop your written and spoken skills, as you will need these to explain scientific concepts.

After high school, plan on four years of college to earn a degree in meteorology. Talk to your high school guidance counselor for help choosing the right college for you. After you have gotten basic college classes out of the way, your college advisor can steer you toward more specialized classes for the type of meteorology career you choose.

SKILL PRACTICE   Read each question. Fill in the bubble next to the correct answer.

1. What is the first thing you should do to become a meteorologist?
   Ⓐ Ask yourself questions.
   Ⓑ Watch TV weather forecasts.
   Ⓒ Take a computer course.
   Ⓓ Talk with a meteorologist.

2. What should you do second?
   Ⓐ Apply at the National Weather Service.
   Ⓑ Study science and math in college.
   Ⓒ Choose your high school classes carefully.
   Ⓓ Develop a fascination with storms.

3. What step does the author suggest if you need help choosing a college?
   Ⓐ Consult your weather diary.
   Ⓑ Talk with your guidance counselor.
   Ⓒ Talk with a college advisor.
   Ⓓ Read articles about weather.

4. According to the passage, when should you decide on a specific career within meteorology?
   Ⓐ after you have earned your degree
   Ⓑ when you first decide to study science
   Ⓒ before you begin high school
   Ⓓ after you start college

STRATEGY PRACTICE   Write two facts you did not already know before reading the passage.

_____

_____

READ THE PASSAGE Pay attention to the sequence of steps needed to customize a T-shirt.

Print Your Own T-Shirts

How many times have you seen a T-shirt with a design on it that made you think that you could produce something better? Here is a simple way to bring your personal design from idea to shirt:

1. First, get your supplies ready. You will need a T-shirt, a design to trace, an embroidery hoop, nylon pantyhose, water-resistant glue, fabric paint, a large piece of cardboard, a paintbrush, and a pencil.

2. Stretch the pantyhose over the embroidery hoop as tightly as possible without causing tears. Lay the hoop over the design and trace its outline with a pencil.

3. Spread the water-resistant glue over the pantyhose, but fill in only the negative space. This means putting the glue along the parts of the pantyhose where you do not want paint to seep through onto the T-shirt.

4. Once the glue has dried, place the hoop on top of the T-shirt facing down, with the nylon touching the shirt. Also place the piece of cardboard inside the T-shirt, between the front and back. This will prevent the paint from bleeding through.

5. Add enough fabric paint to cover the design. Use a paintbrush to spread the paint gently and evenly. Be careful not to move the hoop. (You may wish to weigh down the hoop so that it does not move.) Let the paint sit for a few minutes and then slowly peel the hoop away from the T-shirt.

6. Let the T-shirt sit for a few hours until the paint is completely dry. Then put a piece of paper over the design and iron the T-shirt slowly for a few minutes to help the design set. Now it is ready to wear!

SKILL PRACTICE Read each question. Fill in the bubble next to the correct answer.

1. **What should you do right before adding fabric paint to the pantyhose?**
   Ⓐ trace a design on the pantyhose with a pencil
   Ⓑ place cardboard between the T-shirt layers
   Ⓒ gather together all of the supplies
   Ⓓ iron the T-shirt to help the design set

2. **When do you trace the design in pencil on the pantyhose?**
   Ⓐ after you stretch the pantyhose over the hoop
   Ⓑ after peeling the hoop from the shirt
   Ⓒ after adding glue to the pantyhose
   Ⓓ after you let the paint design dry

3. **Which pair of supplies do you use first?**
   Ⓐ a T-shirt and a design
   Ⓑ fabric paint and glue
   Ⓒ an embroidery hoop and pantyhose
   Ⓓ a design and a pencil

4. **What would happen if someone forgot to do step 3?**
   Ⓐ The pantyhose would tear.
   Ⓑ The design would not show up.
   Ⓒ The paint would not dry on the shirt.
   Ⓓ The T-shirt would stick to the pantyhose.

STRATEGY PRACTICE On a separate sheet of paper, sketch illustrations to accompany steps 2 through 5.

READ THE PASSAGE   Pay attention to the details and to the order of the steps in the jousting process.

Medieval Jousting: An Extreme Sport

Are you an extreme sports enthusiast? Do you live for motocross, ice climbing, or windsurfing? If so, chances are that if had you lived around the fifteenth century, you might have loved jousting.

Jousting was a sport played in the Middle Ages by two armored knights mounted on horses. The sport took place at tournaments—a series of contests that continued until one contestant won the final round. Tournaments also had the advantage of keeping knights in excellent physical and mental condition in case they were called upon to fight in a war.

Jousting knights rode for a local noble, a respected leader from a higher class. Often, their horses were decorated with emblems representing those nobles. Sometimes, knights also carried hair ribbons or handkerchiefs representing women who were married and from a higher class than the knights.

To start a jousting match, the knights mounted their horses and set their lances, or wooden spears, in the resting position. Then they waited for the herald, the official who made announcements at the tournaments, to give the signal to charge. Upon hearing the signal, the knights galloped straight toward each other. The object of the joust was to knock the opponent off his horse using a lance. If both knights remained seated and unhurt, they wheeled their horses around and began the charge again. Charging continued until one of the knights—and often his horse, as well—was knocked to the ground.

Jousting offered participating knights substantial prize money, as well as the adoration of the crowd. However, it was an extremely dangerous sport that could be bloody and brutal. Knights often broke bones as they fell from their horses or were injured when hit by their opponent's lance. At least in motocross, no one is trying to make you fall!

SKILL PRACTICE   Read each question. Fill in the bubble next to the correct answer.

1. **What is the main idea of the passage?**
   Ⓐ Knights used jousting to fight wars.
   Ⓑ Knights jousted for the respect of local nobles and the crowd.
   Ⓒ Jousting was an exciting and dangerous sport.
   Ⓓ Jousting kept knights in top physical and mental condition.

2. **When did a contest between two knights end?**
   Ⓐ when the herald said it was over
   Ⓑ after the first charge was completed
   Ⓒ when the herald signaled the charge
   Ⓓ when one of the knights was knocked off his horse

3. **Which detail best supports the idea that jousting was a dangerous sport?**
   Ⓐ Knights usually rode for a local noble.
   Ⓑ Knights often broke bones.
   Ⓒ Knights were ready to go to war.
   Ⓓ Knights competed for prize money.

4. **What happened if the knights remained seated after the first charge?**
   Ⓐ The knights mounted their horses.
   Ⓑ The knights set their lances in a resting position.
   Ⓒ The knights charged each other again.
   Ⓓ The knights waited for the herald's signal.

STRATEGY PRACTICE   How did rereading the passage help you better understand what jousting was like?

_____

Author's Purpose

Students identify the author's reasons for writing about a subject.

Evaluate Evidence

Students practice evaluating evidence by identifying the author's main idea and examining the evidence the author uses to support that idea.

DAY 1

Review the *Author's Purpose* skill with students. Say: **As you read, try to make a personal connection with the author. Think about what message the author is trying to convey.** Tell students they are going to read about table manners. Then remind students of the *Determine Important Information* strategy (Week 5). Say: **Look for the most important information the author has included to help you use good table manners.** When students have finished reading, direct them to complete the skill and strategy practice activities. Review the answers together.

DAY 2

Remind students of the *Author's Purpose* skill. Say: **Authors can write to inform, entertain, persuade, or teach. As you read, think about which of these categories the passage best matches.** Then remind students of the *Ask Questions* strategy (Week 6). Say: **You might still have questions when you finish a passage. You can find the answers by reading more articles, asking a friend, looking on the Internet, or speaking with someone who is an expert on the topic.** When students have finished reading, direct them to complete the skill and strategy practice activities. Review the answers together.

DAY 3

Review the *Evaluate Evidence* skill with students. Say: **Good authors support the claims they make with factual evidence. Good readers search for this evidence to determine whether or not an author's information can be trusted.** Tell students they will read about giant squids. Then remind students of the *Determine Important Information* strategy. Say: **The author describes giant squids. As you read, look for the most important information about these amazing creatures.** When students have finished reading, direct them to complete the skill and strategy practice activities. Review the answers together.

DAY 4

Tell students they will practice the *Evaluate Evidence* skill as they read about cougar sightings. Say: **Some people believe cougars, or mountain lions, live in New York. Others believe these animals are not in the New York area at all. Pay attention to the evidence the author gives to support both of these theories.** Then remind students of the *Ask Questions* strategy. Say: **As you read, think about any questions you have about the topic.** Direct students to the strategy practice activity section. Say: **Write down any questions you have while reading.** When students have finished reading the passage, direct them to complete the skill practice activity. Review the answers together. Then have partners take turns asking and answering the questions they wrote for the strategy practice activity.

DAY 5

Tell students they will practice finding an author's purpose and evaluating evidence as they read about the Trojan Horse. Say: **Think about why the author wrote the passage. Also look for evidence that supports the author's claims.** Remind students of the *Determine Important Information* strategy. Say: **As you read, think about what information would make good topic sentences for a report.** When students have finished reading, direct them to complete the skill and strategy practice activities. Review the answers together.

As you read, think about why the author wrote the passage.

Basic Table Manners: A Short Guide

Do you want to make a great impression at a meal? Want your dining companions to focus on you instead of your eating habits? Whether you are at a family holiday get-together, trying to impress someone on a first date, or going out with your colleagues for a business lunch, you will feel more comfortable if you have mastered good table manners.

When you first sit down, spread your napkin out on your lap. Before you begin to eat, make sure that everyone has been served and that the host is eating, too. If you are in a large group and the host says to start eating, go ahead, as long as you are not the only one to do so.

If you need something you cannot reach, such as the water pitcher or butter, ask someone to pass it to you; do not reach across anyone else's space. If you are passing a serving dish to someone who requested it, do not help yourself first. If those rolls look tasty, ask for the basket back afterward. If you change your mind after you have touched the roll, take it anyway.

Before you start a conversation, ask yourself if the topic is appropriate to discuss while eating. Try to keep things positive, and definitely avoid anything gross! Do not text or talk on your cellphone at the table. If you must take a call, politely excuse yourself.

Toward the end of the meal, compliment the host. If you keep all of these directions in mind, you should make a fine impression in any setting. Happy dining!

Read each question. Fill in the bubble next to the correct answer.

1. What was the author's purpose for writing the passage?
   - Ⓐ to inform readers about the history of table manners
   - Ⓑ to entertain readers with a funny story about table manners
   - Ⓒ to instruct readers on proper table manners
   - Ⓓ to persuade readers to buy a guide to good manners

2. The author asks questions of the reader to _____.
   - Ⓐ find out what the reader already knows
   - Ⓑ help the reader connect to the topic
   - Ⓒ see if the reader is paying attention
   - Ⓓ ask for advice about dining in a group

3. The author talks about making a good impression to _____.
   - Ⓐ explain why good table manners are important
   - Ⓑ describe a good impression
   - Ⓒ give examples of good manners
   - Ⓓ persuade readers not to judge others by their first impressions

4. The author believes that table manners _____.
   - Ⓐ are the most important part of human behavior
   - Ⓑ are an amusing, old-fashioned idea
   - Ⓒ can solve problems in relationships
   - Ⓓ help make a meal pleasant for everyone

Which information from the passage would you share with a friend?

_____

_____

READ THE PASSAGE   Look for clues in the passage that hint at the author's purpose.

Run for Your Life

For people who wonder which type of exercise they should try, I have a one-word answer: running! While I am not a fitness trainer or medical doctor, I am able to assess the facts, and the facts favor running. Running is a great form of exercise because you do not need a gym membership in order to run. You also do not need a bunch of fancy equipment (a pair of basic running shoes should do). Finally, you do not need to rely on other people, as you do when playing team sports. That means you can easily fit exercise into your schedule.

When you run, you build stamina and endurance. You give your heart a great workout, too. On top of these benefits, you also build bone density, which has long-term benefits. Many runners use the time on the track or road to think through problems, so running can have mental health benefits, as well. In fact, the expression "runner's high" exists because running helps increase your level of endorphins, which are chemicals that relieve pain and make you more relaxed. When these endorphins reach the brain, they can make the runner feel a kind of elation. And, beyond the temporary runner's high, running regularly helps people with depression improve their moods.

Some people may argue that swimming and biking are easier on the joints than running, but swimming requires a pool, and biking requires a bicycle and a helmet. Additionally, no one has ever proven that the average runner's routine leads to joint problems. So grab a pair of running shoes and start your new life as a runner!

SKILL PRACTICE   Read each question. Fill in the bubble next to the correct answer.

1. The author feels that running is _____.
   Ⓐ the only way to treat depression
   Ⓑ a great way to improve your life
   Ⓒ designed for wealthy people
   Ⓓ a fun activity instead of exercise

2. The author wrote the passage to _____.
   Ⓐ describe how running helps you lose weight
   Ⓑ tell a personal story about running
   Ⓒ explain how running is safer than other sports
   Ⓓ persuade readers to take up running

3. Which of the following provides the strongest support for the author's argument?
   Ⓐ Running does not cause joint problems.
   Ⓑ You do not need to rely on other people in order to run.
   Ⓒ Running is good for the heart, bones, and mental health.
   Ⓓ You can run outside a gym.

4. In the author's opinion, running is better than bicycling or swimming because _____.
   Ⓐ you do not need extra equipment or facilities
   Ⓑ you can do it by yourself
   Ⓒ it is easier on the joints
   Ⓓ it is a routine form of exercise

STRATEGY PRACTICE   Write a question you still have about running. Where can you find the answer?

_____

_____

READ THE PASSAGE   As you read, look for evidence that supports the author's claims.

The Real Sea Monster

In November of 1861, a French ship called the *Alecton* was off the coast of Africa when the sailors aboard spotted a sea monster. It was a giant squid that had numerous arms and an immensely long tail. The sailors tried to capture the squid but succeeded only in cutting off its tail, which they sent back to France.

Despite the evidence of the tail, scientists did not believe in the existence of the giant squid for many years. However, over time, giant squid bodies washed up on shore and were found in the stomachs of whales. The scientific community had to accept that these sea creatures, up to 60 feet in length, were real.

The squids were not just enormous; they were also fierce fighters. In 1965, whalers saw a giant squid and a sperm whale fight, and the battle killed them both. In 1966, lighthouse keepers watched a giant squid attack and drown a baby whale.

Scientists could not study the squids in their natural habitat because they live so deep in the ocean— between 600 and 2,300 feet under the surface. Then, in 2004, Japanese scientist Tsunemi Kubodera and his team used a remote control camera to take the first photographs of the giant squid deep below the ocean's surface. Two years later, Kubodera's team captured and photographed a small (24-foot) giant squid, though it was killed in the capture. Scientists hope to see and safely study this great creature of the deep in the near future.

SKILL PRACTICE   Read each question. Fill in the bubble next to the correct answer.

1. Which evidence from the passage best supports the idea that giant squids are fierce fighters?

   Ⓐ their great size and length

   Ⓑ their attacks on other sea animals

   Ⓒ how deep they live in the ocean

   Ⓓ the large number of arms

2. Why didn't French scientists believe the giant squid existed after receiving the tail in 1861?

   Ⓐ They thought the sailors were trying to trick them.

   Ⓑ They were sure they already knew about every animal on earth.

   Ⓒ They did not believe there could be marine animals near Africa.

   Ⓓ They needed an entire giant squid as proof.

3. The author's information can be trusted because it includes _____.

   Ⓐ factual information

   Ⓑ personal opinions

   Ⓒ long-held beliefs

   Ⓓ scientists' hopes

4. Which of these statements is best supported by evidence from the passage?

   Ⓐ Giant squids are a threat to humans.

   Ⓑ Giant squids are seriously endangered.

   Ⓒ Giant squids are difficult to observe.

   Ⓓ Giant squids do not really exist.

STRATEGY PRACTICE   What information is most important for explaining why giant squids are hard to study?

_____

_____

READ THE PASSAGE   Think about the evidence the author includes to support both sides of the cougar debate.

Cougars . . . or Not?

When Carol Wilbur's horse was found dead on her farm in rural New York, she was certain it had been killed by an eastern cougar, or mountain lion. The problem with this theory is that there have been no confirmed sightings of wild cougars in New York for over 100 years. The Department of Environmental Conservation (DEC) claims that cougars have been eliminated from New York. In fact, they claim mountain lions do not live anywhere east of the Mississippi River, except for a small population in Florida.

Many upstate New York residents disagree with the statement that mountain lions do not live in the state. Dozens of people claim to have sighted the large, dangerous, long-tailed cats. Reports have come in from the Hudson Valley, northern New York, and the western part of the state. Some people have taken photographs of what they saw. The DEC responded by stating that the sightings and photos are of bobcats, dogs, large cats, or coyotes.

One resident of Cooperstown says he saw a cougar in a cornfield. He points out that, as a hunter, he is very familiar with the differences between cougars and other animals. But DEC officials insist they need hard evidence: the body of a wild cougar. Still, despite the lack of absolute proof, it seems unlikely that so many people could be wrong about seeing these stealthy, solitary animals.

SKILL PRACTICE   Read each question. Fill in the bubble next to the correct answer.

1. What does the author refer to in order to support the DEC's claim that cougars no longer live in New York?
   A statements from eyewitnesses who have seen cougars
   B statistics about the cougar population
   C lack of a confirmed cougar
   D facts about cougars' lives and habits

2. What leads many New Yorkers to believe cougars still live in the state?
   A claims from eyewitnesses
   B descriptions of photographs
   C reports of confirmed sightings
   D information about cougars from the DEC

3. Which evidence from the passage best supports the claim that cougars still live in New York?
   A the horse that was killed
   B the list of animals that look like cougars
   C the hunter's experience with animals
   D the number of people who say they have seen cougars

4. According to the passage, some people have taken photos of cougars. These photos are not considered evidence because they were not _____.
   A taken in New York
   B clear enough to prove they were cougars
   C taken by the DEC
   D of animals that looked dangerous

STRATEGY PRACTICE   Write a question you had while reading about cougar sightings in New York. Have a partner answer it.

_____

_____

READ THE PASSAGE   As you read, think about why the author wrote the passage.

The Trojan Horse

The story of the Trojan Horse from Greek mythology has appeared in several classic works of Greek literature. In the story, the war between the ancient Greeks and Trojans had gone on for a decade. Few even remembered its origin—the abduction from Greece of the beautiful (and married) Helen by the prince of Troy. Many great warriors had died in the countless battles, but neither side could claim victory. The Greeks, camped outside the walls of Troy, were on the verge of giving up.

"I have an idea," declared Odysseus, known for his courage and cleverness. He consulted with his generals. For a time, the hostilities between the Greeks and the Trojans stopped, and the sounds of hammers rang throughout the Greek camp. A few days later, the Greeks sailed off in their ships. After ten long years, the area fell silent.

The Greeks left behind a city of puzzled Trojans—and a gigantic wooden horse, obviously left as a gift or tribute from the Greeks, that sat outside the city's gate. The Trojans marveled at the beauty of the horse, pushed the enormous statue into their city, and began a large, joyful celebration.

Later that very night, the story goes, a hatch in the belly of the horse slowly opened, and out crept the best of the Greek soldiers, led by Odysseus. With surprise on their side, the Greeks were able to ransack the city of Troy, rescue Helen, and finally win the war.

SKILL PRACTICE   Read each question. Fill in the bubble next to the correct answer.

1. The author wrote this passage to _____.
   Ⓐ tell readers a cautionary tale
   Ⓑ give a biography of a creative soldier
   Ⓒ compare ancient war strategies
   Ⓓ inform readers about a historic event

2. Why does the author mention the sounds of hammers?
   Ⓐ to describe the setting of the conflict
   Ⓑ to give an example of how Greeks fought
   Ⓒ to show that a plan was being carried out
   Ⓓ to provide more details about life in ancient Greece

3. Which statement is the best evidence that Odysseus is clever?
   Ⓐ Odysseus consulted with his generals.
   Ⓑ Odysseus led the soldiers out of the horse's belly.
   Ⓒ The Greeks were on the verge of giving up.
   Ⓓ The Greeks were fighting over a woman.

4. What evidence led the Trojans to think they had won the war?
   Ⓐ The war continued for a decade.
   Ⓑ The Greeks sailed off in their ships.
   Ⓒ The Trojans celebrated joyfully.
   Ⓓ The Greeks hid inside the horse.

STRATEGY PRACTICE   Which information from the passage would be the most useful in writing a report about the Trojan Horse?

_____

_____

_____

Compare and Contrast

Students practice comparing and contrasting by looking at the similarities and differences between two or more people or things.

Make Inferences

Students practice making inferences by using clues in a passage to understand what is being implied.

DAY 1

Review the *Compare and Contrast* skill with students. Say: **To compare two or more things, look for how they are alike or different.** Tell students they are going to read an article about four popular beaches where people go surfing. Then remind students of the *Make Connections* strategy (Week 2). Say: **Even if you have never been surfing, you can still make connections with the passage. As you read, ask yourself:** *What does this remind me of from my own life?* When students have finished reading, direct them to complete the skill and strategy practice activities. Review the answers together.

DAY 2

Tell students they will practice the *Compare and Contrast* skill as they read about mythological fairies. Say: **Compare the descriptions of the fairies in the books that are mentioned in the passage. Also look for similarities and differences between male and female fairies.** Then remind students of the *Organization* strategy (Week 4). Say: **The author has organized the passage into basic paragraphs. As you read, think about why the author organized the passage this way.** When students have finished reading, direct them to complete the skill and strategy practice activities. Review the answers together.

DAY 3

Remind students of the *Make Inferences* skill. Say: **You can make inferences by looking for information that is not directly stated. As you read, think about what you already know. Use your background knowledge and details from the text to infer additional information about the story or characters.** Then remind students of the *Make Connections* strategy. Say: **You can make a text-to-self connection as you read. Think about who or what the passage reminds you of from your own life.** When students have finished reading, direct them to complete the skill and strategy practice activities. Review the answers together.

DAY 4

Tell students they will practice making inferences as they read a piece of historical fiction about China's navy. Say: **Think about what the author is *not* saying. Is there "hidden information" included in the passage?** Then remind students of the *Organization* strategy. Say: **Authors can organize information in a passage by making comparisons and finding contrasts, giving the main idea and details, stating facts and opinions, or explaining causes and effects. As you read, think about which way the author organized the information in the passage.** When students have finished reading, direct them to complete the skill and strategy practice activities. Review the answers together.

DAY 5

Inform students they will practice both the *Compare and Contrast* and *Make Inferences* skills as they read about one of the world's oldest and most mysterious civilizations—the Maya. Remind students of the *Make Connections* strategy. Say: **Think about how what you read in the passage relates to the world today.** When students have finished reading, direct them to complete the skill and strategy practice activities.

READ THE ARTICLE   As you read the surfing article, think about how the locations are alike and different.

Surfing: Famous Beaches, Famous Waves

North Shore, Oahu, Hawaii: Famous for being the birthplace of surfing

Wide, sandy beaches stretch nearly 20 miles along the Pacific Ocean. Between October and February, this surfing destination is suitable only for experienced surfers, as its monstrous waves can reach 30 feet. In summer, the ocean can be almost completely flat, making it perfect for swimming or snorkeling.

Huntington Beach, California: Famous for the US Open of Surfing competition

This busy 8.5-mile-long beach attracts 8 million visitors a year for bodysurfing, boogie boarding, and board surfing at every level, beginner to expert. At night, the beach's fire pits draw families as much as the waves do during the day. The best time for surfers is winter, when the swells can hit 15 feet.

Jeffreys Bay, South Africa: Famous for being the setting of the classic movie *The Endless Summer*

This area of the ocean may contain the most consistent waves on the planet, with some up to 10 feet. The best waves are between late May and late August. The beach sometimes closes because of sharks, but at other times, surfers are lucky enough to surf alongside dolphins. Expect a lot of Aussies and events from barefoot to black-tie in the bustling nearby town.

Tamarindo, Costa Rica: Famous for being featured in the movie *The Endless Summer II*

This beach has waves up to 12 feet high, which are good for longboarders or shortboarders, beginners or experts, with the best waves from April to July. Bodysurfing is not recommended because of offshore rocks. The laid-back atmosphere and nearly perfect year-round weather make it feel like the California beaches of the 1950s.

SKILL PRACTICE   Read each question. Fill in the bubble next to the correct answer.

1. The beach with the biggest waves is _____.
   Ⓐ Oahu's North Shore
   Ⓑ Huntington Beach
   Ⓒ Jeffreys Bay
   Ⓓ Tamarindo

2. Jeffreys Bay and Tamarindo are both known for _____.
   Ⓐ offshore rocks
   Ⓑ competitions
   Ⓒ movies
   Ⓓ dolphins

3. How are North Shore and Huntington Beach similar?
   Ⓐ The waves reach the same height.
   Ⓑ Both are suitable for all surfing levels.
   Ⓒ Winter is the best time to surf at both beaches.
   Ⓓ Both beaches are the same length.

4. The Huntington Beach information is different from the others because it includes _____.
   Ⓐ the height of the waves
   Ⓑ the number of visitors each year
   Ⓒ the best time to visit
   Ⓓ the levels of surfers who would enjoy it

STRATEGY PRACTICE   How do these beaches compare with beaches you have seen or read about?

_____

_____

READ THE PASSAGE   As you read, think about how the descriptions of fairies are alike and different.

Fairies: From Peter Pan to Harry Potter

For centuries, writers of classic literature have included fairies and other fantastical creatures in stories for both children and adults. While fairies are especially common in the folklore of Ireland and Scotland, they appear in fairy tales and stories throughout most of Europe and in legends from around the globe.

According to *Encyclopædia Britannica,* fairies are mythical beings who typically have magic powers and dwell on Earth in close relationship with humans. *Encyclopædia Britannica* also says that they vary in size from three inches tall to the height of a human. In contrast, *The Encyclopedia of Things That Never Were* says that fairies are usually "as high as a small man's knee." However, they can change their size at will, shrinking to the size of an acorn or growing to the size of a full-grown human.

According to fairy experts, there are different kinds of fairies. For instance, Shakespeare's powerful and sassy Titania in *A Midsummer Night's Dream* is very different from J.M. Barrie's jealous but kind Tinker Bell in *Peter Pan.* And some experts consider elves, such as the house elves described by J.K. Rowling in the *Harry Potter* novels and those from J.R.R. Tolkien's *Lord of the Rings* series, to be fairies as well.

In a variety of tales, female fairies are depicted with sheer, fragile wings and are considered insubstantial creatures, yet male fairies are often portrayed as heroic warriors—and a battalion of fairy soldiers can be a fearsome sight. According to some writers, fairies are neither naturally good nor bad. Instead, like humans, they act with kindness or wickedness as a result of how they have been treated. Although their actions range from mischievous to helpful, fairies are often portrayed as good-natured, festive creatures who just want to be left alone. Their greatest joy is living free in the secretive, hidden glades and woodlands in which they have always lived.

SKILL PRACTICE   Read each question. Fill in the bubble next to the correct answer.

1. *Encyclopædia Britannica* and *The Encyclopedia of Things That Never Were* disagree about _____.
   Ⓐ where fairies come from
   Ⓑ whether elves are considered fairies
   Ⓒ the usual height of fairies
   Ⓓ which powers fairies have

2. Male fairies are often depicted differently from female fairies because the male fairies _____.
   Ⓐ have delicate wings
   Ⓑ can be heroic
   Ⓒ are much taller
   Ⓓ live in woodlands

3. Where are all fairies found?
   Ⓐ in fiction stories and myths
   Ⓑ in Ireland and Scotland
   Ⓒ in people's houses
   Ⓓ in battle

4. Which word best describes all the fairies in the passage?
   Ⓐ mischievous
   Ⓑ helpful
   Ⓒ kind
   Ⓓ magical

STRATEGY PRACTICE   Why do you think the author chose this way to organize the passage?

_____

_____

READ THE PASSAGE   Use information from the passage and what you already know to make inferences.

Weekends at the Flea Market

It was Sunday, so Dad and I were at the flea market, scouting out tools, silverware, appliances, and other things that needed sprucing up. Some were broken; others, like copper pots and silver trays, just needed to be cleaned and polished. It was 1974, and the recession was in full swing. Dad worked full-time at a factory, but the money wasn't enough. Dad had tried a second job for a while, but he found it was too hard on the family. One day, he had a crackerjack idea that set me on a lifelong course of self-sufficiency.

Standing beside a crowded table at the flea market, I looked over an ancient manual sewing machine. Someone had converted it to run on electric power. It was way older than Mom's machine, but it looked like it had quality and longevity built into it. "Dad!" I called. "This is a beaut!"

Dad strode over, pulling a cart full of audio equipment, tools, worn-out appliances, and what appeared to be a block of dull kitchen knives. "Whatcha got, Son?" I described what I saw and what I figured I could do to fix the beauty up. Dad paid for my discovery, and we headed home.

Every day after school I worked on the ancient contraption, and every night Dad and I sharpened tools and knives, sanded off rust, polished metal, and replaced missing screws from various items. The next Saturday we headed off, as we did every weekend, to that same flea market, where we sold the treasures we'd purchased the week before—at a tidy profit. My antique beauty brought in more money than anything else, and Dad let me keep every penny.

Dad's gone now, but I can never thank him enough. Even if we hadn't needed the extra funds Dad and I brought in, I wouldn't have traded those weekends for all the picnics or Little League games in St. Louis—not in a million years.

SKILL PRACTICE   Read each question. Fill in the bubble next to the correct answer.

1. Dad's crackerjack idea was _____.
   Ⓐ getting a second job for a while
   Ⓑ having his son get an after-school job
   Ⓒ buying things and fixing them up for resale
   Ⓓ saving money by buying only used items

2. The narrator wanted to buy the sewing machine to _____.
   Ⓐ sew his own clothes to save money
   Ⓑ replace his mother's machine
   Ⓒ fix it up and sell it for a profit
   Ⓓ spend more time with his father

3. You can infer that the narrator thanks his father the most for _____.
   Ⓐ letting him shop at flea markets
   Ⓑ taking a second job to feed the family
   Ⓒ working full-time at a factory
   Ⓓ teaching him how to restore old objects

4. As an adult, the narrator most likely _____.
   Ⓐ repairs sewing machines professionally
   Ⓑ fixes his own broken items
   Ⓒ buys only secondhand goods
   Ⓓ works at several jobs

STRATEGY PRACTICE   Who are you thankful for in your life? What did that person teach you?

_____

_____

READ THE PASSAGE   Look for clues in the passage that you can use to make inferences.

A New Journey

Yuen was standing on the deck of a large Chinese junk at twilight. Although his ship was quick and easy to navigate, Yuen was more impressed by the 300 ships around him. Yuen had recognized supply ships, battleships, horse transports, and some other ships at the launch. Yuen's junk was near the beginning of the fleet. He had watched while Admiral Zheng He sailed into the Yellow Sea. Now Yuen was out there in the open water as well. Thousands of Chinese citizens had stood along the Yangtze River to see the armada off that morning in July of 1405. A young deckhand with limited experience, Yuen was to be part of an event unlike anything that had come before it.

Yuen did not know exactly what he was doing on this new journey. He had been told that the armada was going on a simple trading mission. He had heard that the emperor had directed Admiral Zheng He to make new alliances, find and bring back exotic animals, and get the rulers of other countries to pay tribute to China. Some people secretly believed that the admiral's real job entailed much more. They told Yuen he would probably be sailing much farther than was stated. It was rumored that the great ships would sail all the way across the world—to places that Yuen could not even imagine in his mind.

The sky grew dark. As stars began to appear, Yuen watched a man on his boat take out an unfamiliar instrument. The man pointed the object at the heavens and looked through it to take measurements. Yuen was finally on his way. He had a lot of work ahead of him, so he reached for the nearest sail and listened for his instructions.

SKILL PRACTICE   Read each question. Fill in the bubble next to the correct answer.

1. What was Yuen's job?
   - (A) junk collector
   - (B) admiral's advisor
   - (C) reporter
   - (D) sailor

2. How did Yuen probably feel?
   - (A) nervous but excited
   - (B) disappointed but willing
   - (C) jealous but understanding
   - (D) happy but bored

3. Yuen could not imagine where they were going because he had _____.
   - (A) never been sailing before
   - (B) never been far away from China
   - (C) no interest in seeing new things
   - (D) been told not to waste time daydreaming

4. What object is the man near the end of the passage using?
   - (A) binoculars
   - (B) glasses
   - (C) a ruler
   - (D) a navigation tool

STRATEGY PRACTICE   How did the author organize information about ancient China in the passage?

_____

_____

READ THE PASSAGE   Use what you know and what you read to make inferences.

The Codices of the Maya

The Maya have been justly called "the Greeks of America." Hundreds of years before the Spanish Conquest, they created a civilization on the Yucatán Peninsula of North America that surpassed most other cultures worldwide. They were scientists, mathematicians, artists, and astronomers, and they had the most advanced system of writing in the Americas, dating back to 200 or even 300 BC. Their writings have been found on standing stone slabs (also known as *stelae*), sculpture, pottery, and in books called *codices*.

Mayan codices were printed on fig-bark paper and folded like an accordion, and had a cover often made of jaguar skin. While hundreds of codices existed when the Spanish arrived, only three or four remain today. Believing the texts to be in conflict with the Catholic religion, a Spanish priest burned most of them in the 1500s. Ironically, he included in his journal about the Maya a few notes about their writing, which helped modern scholars decipher the surviving codices.

Like the Egyptians, the Maya wrote in hieroglyphs. Each glyph consists of one or more signs. While some signs, called *logograms,* stand for entire words such as a noun, a verb, or the name of a month, others represent a syllable. Each glyph appears in a block on a grid; the glyphs are read in pairs of columns.

Few people understood Mayan writing at all until the early 1950s, when a Russian linguist named Yury Knorozov figured out that some signs represented specific sound combinations. Then Tatiana Proskouriakoff linked the stelae with important events in history, which led to unlocking the meaning of many glyphs. Scholars have identified the pronunciation of about 80% of the glyphs and the meaning of about 60% and are now on their way to uncovering more factual information about this mysterious culture.

SKILL PRACTICE   Read each question. Fill in the bubble next to the correct answer.

1. **Mayan writing is the most similar to _____.**
   Ⓐ Egyptian hieroglyphs
   Ⓑ English writing
   Ⓒ Spanish numbers
   Ⓓ scientific symbols

2. **The burned Mayan codices were likely _____.**
   Ⓐ additional copies of the ones scholars now have
   Ⓑ written in a form of writing different from hieroglyphs
   Ⓒ filled with valuable information about the Maya
   Ⓓ representative of Catholic beliefs

3. **What can you infer about Spanish priests in the 1500s?**
   Ⓐ They admired the Mayan culture.
   Ⓑ They taught the Maya how to write.
   Ⓒ They were able to read Mayan codices.
   Ⓓ They did not respect the Mayan civilization.

4. **How were the Maya different from most other cultures of the same time period?**
   Ⓐ They were more advanced.
   Ⓑ They were the oldest civilization.
   Ⓒ They wrote in hieroglyphs.
   Ⓓ They recorded important events.

STRATEGY PRACTICE   Why do some groups want to suppress or silence other cultures today?

_____

_____

Character and Setting

Students practice analyzing character and setting by looking at the traits and motivations of a character and where and when a passage's events take place.

Theme

Students practice identifying the theme by looking for the central message or lesson in a passage.

DAY 1

Remind students of the *Character and Setting* skill. Say: **You can learn a lot about historical figures by thinking about the time period in which they lived. You are going to read about William Harvey, who was a doctor in the 1500s and 1600s. As you read, think about how Harvey's time period affected his work.** Then remind students of the *Monitor Comprehension* strategy (Week 1). Say: **Pause briefly after each paragraph to ask yourself:** *Do I understand what I just read?* **If needed, reread the paragraph.** When students have finished reading, direct them to complete the skill and strategy practice activities. Review the answers as a group.

DAY 2

Tell students they will practice studying character and setting as they read a journal entry. Say: **Pay attention to the journal writer's descriptions. Which events does the writer include? What do these details tell you about the writer?** Then remind students of the *Visualization* strategy (Week 3). Say: **The journal entries describe an art project. As you read, make a mental picture of what the project looks like in each state of completion.** When students have finished reading, direct them to complete the skill and strategy practice activities. Review the answers together.

DAY 3

Review the definition of *Theme* with students. Say: **A theme in fiction is sometimes called "the moral of the story" and is the central message. The theme in nonfiction is also the central message. Look for the underlying central message the author is sharing.** Then remind students of the *Monitor Comprehension* strategy. Say: **You are going to read about a charitable organization. Look for details that tell about the main mission of the group.** When students have finished reading, direct them to complete the skill and strategy practice activities. Review the answers together.

DAY 4

Remind students of the *Theme* skill. Say: **The theme is a lesson the author wants you to "take away" from the passage when you have finished reading. Good authors present themes that you can apply to your own life.** Then remind students of the *Visualization* strategy. Say: **This passage gives information about a race between a turtle and a man. It is *not* an ordinary race. Pay attention to the details the author gives to help you make an accurate visualization.** When students have finished reading, direct them to complete the skill and strategy practice activities. Review the answers together.

DAY 5

Tell students they will practice studying characters, setting, and theme as they read a Native American folk tale. Say: **Think about how the author conveys the theme through the characters' actions and words.** Remind students of the *Monitor Comprehension* strategy. Say: **Even if you feel you completely understand a passage, it still helps to read it again. Each time you reread a story or nonfiction passage, you will be able to gather more information about the characters or topic.** When students have finished reading, direct them to complete the skill and strategy practice activities. Review the answers together.

READ THE PASSAGE   Think about William Harvey and the time period in which he lived.

William Harvey (1578–1657)

William Harvey was a doctor in Elizabethan England during the same period that the playwright William Shakespeare lived. Just as Shakespeare expanded literature's scope, Harvey's sharp observations and careful conclusions brought landmark changes to the world of biology.

Scientific knowledge in the seventeenth century was often based on theories that had never been tested. Harvey's main area of research was blood circulation. He did not agree with the scientific beliefs of the time. Most European doctors thought that blood was pushed through the body by a pulsing movement in the arteries. They also thought that the liver converted food into blood.

Harvey studied the flow of blood in animals, identifying the crucial role played by the heart. In 1628, he published *An Anatomical Study of the Motion of the Heart and of the Blood in Animals*. In the text, Harvey explained that the heart pumps blood throughout the body—blood leaves the heart, travels through blood vessels, and then returns to the heart. It is not created in the liver; it circulates again and again.

Although Harvey supported his model with careful observations and analyses, people were reluctant to accept his radical new ideas. Many of Harvey's patients were horrified and left him for doctors who held more conventional beliefs.

Today, medical science recognizes that Harvey was correct, and his theories are the core of the modern understanding of blood circulation. By testing and retesting his hypothesis, Harvey also helped develop the modern scientific method, which helps all scientists separate true findings from superstition.

SKILL PRACTICE   Read each question. Fill in the bubble next to the correct answer.

1. William Harvey was notable for being _____.
   Ⓐ an accomplished playwright
   Ⓑ Shakespeare's doctor
   Ⓒ the first heart surgeon
   Ⓓ a science innovator

2. In seventeenth-century medicine, _____.
   Ⓐ biology was not well understood
   Ⓑ beliefs were confirmed with the scientific method
   Ⓒ theories were based on careful research
   Ⓓ doctors did not treat patients

3. Which words best describe Harvey?
   Ⓐ extreme and superstitious
   Ⓑ logical and precise
   Ⓒ curious and conventional
   Ⓓ arrogant and stubborn

4. Most biologists today probably _____.
   Ⓐ agree with Harvey's model of blood circulation
   Ⓑ use the modern scientific method reluctantly
   Ⓒ have replaced Harvey's key theories
   Ⓓ find the subject of circulation unimportant

STRATEGY PRACTICE   Did you understand the main points the author tried to make? Why or why not?

_____

_____

As you read, think about the journal writer's characteristics.

One Wall, One Week

Monday, July 12

This year's World Wide Wall project is off and running! I met the students and staff at Richmond Vocational High School this morning and was extremely impressed with the preparations the students had made for my arrival. They had already selected the wall, cleaned it, and primed it with paint donated by local merchants. We spent the day brainstorming ideas and creating preliminary sketches.

Tuesday, July 13

We finalized the design for the mural and created the sketch. Alicia and Jaipal volunteered to pencil in the grid lines so that we can transfer the sketch to the wall. The airbrush master class was a big success, though Maya lost control and ended up with most of her hair green.

Wednesday, July 14

The transformation is underway, and almost all of the background elements are in place in shades of blue, green, and purple. The theme of undersea exploration is highlighted by the giant octopus that Raimundo spent all day airbrushing. Each of its arms is almost 12 feet long!

Thursday, July 15

Will wonders never cease? Paula had been reluctant to paint all week, but today she dove in with a black marker and added incredibly beautiful, intricate details to the coral reef.

Friday, July 16

Kyle is the mathematician of the group, and he assures us that there are 247 fish in the mural, which is exactly 324 square feet in size. I don't know if he's right, but I do know it looks spectacular! I hope the mural at next week's school turns out this well.

SKILL PRACTICE Read each question. Fill in the bubble next to the correct answer.

1. Which words best describe the journal writer?
   - Ⓐ ambitious and judgmental
   - Ⓑ powerful and strong
   - Ⓒ dedicated and enthusiastic
   - Ⓓ shy and bored

2. Where was the journal writer working?
   - Ⓐ at a church
   - Ⓑ at a city pool
   - Ⓒ at a hospital
   - Ⓓ at a school

3. The journal writer asked "Will wonders never cease?" because Paula _____.
   - Ⓐ does not like to paint or draw
   - Ⓑ was the most talented artist of all
   - Ⓒ showed a surprising change in attitude
   - Ⓓ covered the mural with black marks

4. The journal writer is probably _____.
   - Ⓐ a Richmond Vocational staff member
   - Ⓑ a visiting project leader
   - Ⓒ a marine biologist
   - Ⓓ an art critic

STRATEGY PRACTICE On a separate sheet of paper, sketch what you visualize the completed mural looks like. Compare your visualization with a partner's.

READ THE PASSAGE   As you read, think about what Nora Gross is like and what the theme of the passage is.

A Penny Saved

When Nora Gross was just four years old, she and her father passed a homeless man. Concerned about the cold winter weather, Gross asked, "Can we take him home?" Her innocent question became the starting point of a project that has become one of the largest youth philanthropy programs in the world.

Gross's big idea was small coins. She knew that pennies often seem like worthless clutter. But she thought that if she and other students could gather enough of them, the money could really make a difference. This was the beginning of the Penny Harvest. Today, more than half a million students take part in the program. In its first 20 years, the Penny Harvest has collected $8.1 million in pennies!

Gross and her father founded Common Cents, a not-for-profit organization, to manage their fundraising efforts. They believe the penny drives can help develop young people's generosity and moral character. After the pennies are collected, students form philanthropy roundtables to evaluate community problems and to decide where to donate the collected funds. Many students become inspired by the process and go on to become volunteers at the organizations they support, which include animal care facilities, community gardens, senior centers, and homeless shelters.

Teddy Gross explains: "We at Common Cents regard America's billion-dollar resource of idle pennies—found in startling quantities in the homes of both the rich and poor—as the philanthropic property of young people. For this reason, every penny the children collect is theirs to give away in an educational group process." The students involved with the Penny Harvest have changed the world for the better, and they have learned valuable lessons about caring for others in their communities.

SKILL PRACTICE   Read each question. Fill in the bubble next to the correct answer.

1. **What was the basis of Nora Gross's idea?**
   Ⓐ We should prepare for harsh weather.
   Ⓑ We should take care of people in need.
   Ⓒ We should clean up city streets.
   Ⓓ We should be more careful with money.

2. **The Penny Harvest was created to help young people _____.**
   Ⓐ save money for college
   Ⓑ get rid of worthless pocket change
   Ⓒ contribute to their communities
   Ⓓ learn about how people become homeless

3. **Teddy Gross would most likely agree that young people _____.**
   Ⓐ can be trusted to make smart giving decisions
   Ⓑ must be taught to be generous
   Ⓒ can run businesses more efficiently than adults
   Ⓓ are too idealistic to be practical

4. **Which of these best describes Common Cents?**
   Ⓐ a critical voice against poverty
   Ⓑ a positive force for social change
   Ⓒ a logical response to monetary waste
   Ⓓ a group effort to solve housing problems

STRATEGY PRACTICE   What is the difference between the Penny Harvest and Common Cents? How did you figure it out?

_____

_____

READ THE PASSAGE   Think about the lesson Zeno was trying to teach.

Can a Tortoise Be Outrun?

A Greek philosopher named Zeno created many paradoxes that still puzzle readers today. A paradox is a situation in which two opposing ideas both appear to be true. In his famous paradox called "Achilles and the Tortoise," Zeno suggested that, in a race, a runner can never catch up to a competitor who was given a head start.

In Zeno's story, a tortoise challenges Achilles to a race. Knowing that he is far faster than the tortoise, Achilles not only accepts the challenge but agrees to give the tortoise a big head start. The race begins, and the tortoise starts running before Achilles.

Eventually, Achilles catches up to the place where the tortoise was when Achilles began, but by then the tortoise has run a little bit farther. When Achilles reaches that new spot, the tortoise has run a bit farther still. Achilles must always reach the spot where the tortoise was, and during that time, the tortoise can always run a little bit farther. Achilles can never overtake the tortoise, so there is no way he can win.

Zeno did not really believe that the tortoise would always win, of course. This story, like all of his paradoxes, challenges people to find a logical explanation for what they think. The paradox is based on the false assumption that you can continue to divide distance and time by half indefinitely. Zeno turns the race into an infinite series of steps that can never end—when Achilles reaches where the tortoise was, the tortoise has always moved ahead slightly. Even though the distances decrease, there are an infinite number of distances. Zeno's paradox proves that this assumption is wrong because space and time are not infinitely divisible, and Achilles would, in fact, beat the tortoise.

SKILL PRACTICE   Read each question. Fill in the bubble next to the correct answer.

1. In the "Achilles and the Tortoise" paradox, Zeno _____.
   Ⓐ helps people improve their physical abilities
   Ⓑ proves that forward motion is impossible
   Ⓒ shows underdogs that they can win
   Ⓓ challenges the way people think

2. Which best represents the theme of the passage?
   Ⓐ You should always follow your instinct.
   Ⓑ He who runs slowly but steadily will always win.
   Ⓒ People should challenge assumptions as well as explanations.
   Ⓓ Philosophy and mathematics do not mix.

3. A paradox is something that _____.
   Ⓐ proves an assumption is correct
   Ⓑ is true in every situation
   Ⓒ is based on emotion rather than logic
   Ⓓ seems to contradict reality

4. "Achilles and the Tortoise" is based around a false assumption about _____.
   Ⓐ space and time
   Ⓑ determination and speed
   Ⓒ men and tortoises
   Ⓓ races and distance

STRATEGY PRACTICE   How did visualizing help you to better understand the passage?

_____

_____

READ THE FOLK TALE   As you read, think about Redfeather and the main lesson he learns.

The Story of Redfeather: An Ojibwe Tale

There once was a little boy called Redfeather who lived with Grandfather in a village near a large meadow and a pond that was filled with frogs. Grandfather taught Redfeather to shoot a bow and arrow and told him stories about the different creatures that lived in their area.

Springtime came, and in the evenings, Redfeather would take his bow and arrow to the pond and shoot all the frogs he could find. One evening, Heron came along and told Redfeather that she would give him her best feather if he would leave the frogs alone.

"I have babies to feed," she said. "You are wasting all of the food." But Redfeather laughed at her and continued to shoot the frogs.

When Redfeather had finished at the pond, he returned home. Instead of going to bed, Redfeather ran around making noise until Crane came by.

"Redfeather, you must be quiet," Crane said. "You are scaring away the animals that I eat for dinner." Again, Redfeather laughed at the bird and continued his behavior.

Finally, the birds went to wise Owl who lived near Redfeather's village. Owl became angry when he heard of Redfeather's misbehavior and swooped down into the village and carried Redfeather away as his prisoner.

Owl would have fed Redfeather to his babies if not for Grandfather, who held a feast for all the birds. Grandfather hunted for three days and nights until he had enough food for the feast. Owl agreed to release Redfeather, and Redfeather promised never again to misuse the food that the birds need.

SKILL PRACTICE   Read each question. Fill in the bubble next to the correct answer.

1. Which feature of the setting makes it clear the passage is a folk tale?
   Ⓐ There is a meadow with talking animals.
   Ⓑ There is a pond with frogs.
   Ⓒ The season is springtime.
   Ⓓ It is evening in a village.

2. Throughout most of the folk tale, Redfeather can best be described as _____.
   Ⓐ humorous and mischievous
   Ⓑ disrespectful and selfish
   Ⓒ skillful and lucky
   Ⓓ helpful and silly

3. What lesson does Grandfather teach Redfeather at the end of the folk tale?
   Ⓐ how to hunt frogs in ponds
   Ⓑ how to shoot a bow and arrow
   Ⓒ how to honor other creatures
   Ⓓ how to escape from mean owls

4. From the folk tale, you can infer that the Ojibwe believe that _____.
   Ⓐ the young are more important than adults
   Ⓑ animals and people both have rights
   Ⓒ hunting animals for sport is a valuable skill
   Ⓓ elders should excuse young people who make mistakes

STRATEGY PRACTICE   How does rereading help you better understand the folk tale?

_____

Cause and Effect

Students practice identifying cause-and-effect relationships by looking for what happens (the effect) and why it happens (the cause).

Prediction

Students practice using clues from a passage to predict what will happen next.

DAY 1

Review the *Cause and Effect* skill with students. Say: **Causes lead to effects. Think about an event and go backward to look for its cause. Last night, you got tired and went to sleep. You slept—this was the effect. To find the cause, think about** *why* **you slept. The cause was that you were tired. You slept** *because* **you were tired.** Then tell students they are going to read an essay about a robot named ASIMO. Review the *Ask Questions* strategy (Week 6). Say: **Asking and answering questions about a passage will help you stay focused on the topic and gather the most information.** When students have finished reading, direct them to complete the skill practice activity. Review the answers together. Then have partners complete the strategy practice activity.

DAY 2

Tell students they will practice finding causes and effects as they read about brain-controlled devices. Remind students that some causes can have multiple effects. Then remind students of the *Make Connections* strategy (Week 2). Say: **You can make a text-to-text connection by thinking about articles or books you have read that include information about this technology. You can also think about movies, songs, or other pop culture references related to this topic to make a connection to the passage.** When students have finished reading, direct them to complete the skill and strategy practice activities. Review the answers together.

DAY 3

Review the *Prediction* skill with students. Say: **You can make predictions by thinking about what has already happened in the passage along with experiences from your own life.** Tell students they are going read a story about two sets of campers. Say: **When you have finished reading the story, predict what could happen next.** Remind students of the *Ask Questions* strategy. Say: **To continue the story in your mind, ask:** *What would this character do or say next? How would I react in that situation?* When students have finished reading, direct them to complete the skill and strategy practice activities. Review the answers together.

DAY 4

Tell students they will practice making predictions as they read one of Aesop's classic fables. Say: **As you read, predict how the characters in this fable might act differently in the future.** Then remind students of the *Make Connections* strategy. Say: **Think about the characters in the story. How are they the same as or different from people you know?** When students have finished reading, direct them to complete the skill and strategy practice activities. Review the answers together.

DAY 5

Tell students they will practice both the *Cause and Effect* and *Prediction* skills as they read about soccer in the United States. Remind students of the *Ask Questions* strategy. Say: **Authors do not include every single detail about a topic in their writing. As you read, think about additional things you would like to learn about soccer. What questions do you still have?** When students have finished reading, direct them to complete the skill and strategy practice activities. Review the answers together.

Daily Reading Comprehension • EMC 3457 • © Evan-Moor Corp.

READ THE PASSAGE   Think about why engineers would want to build a robot like ASIMO.

ASIMO

In 1986, engineers at Honda, the car and motorcycle company, wanted to create a robot that could walk like a person. This might sound like a strange goal, but building a robot that walks like a person has been one of the most difficult challenges for robot designers and builders. If you think about it, most robots invented today have wheels or do not have movement at all. The first walking robot that the Honda team built was just a pair of legs. It took teams of workers almost 15 years (and several generations of robots) before they finally created a true humanoid robot called ASIMO, which stands for Advanced Step in Innovative Mobility.

ASIMO looks like a small astronaut. The robot stands at 4 feet 3 inches tall and weighs 119 pounds. ASIMO has motors and joints that allow it to move its head, arms, hands, legs, and feet much like humans do. ASIMO has danced, jogged, and conducted orchestras at public demonstrations in order to help inspire kids to stay interested in science, as well as to show off some of the new inventions and discoveries that scientists have made while creating ASIMO. ASIMO is even a featured attraction at Disneyland in California.

Can you imagine a team of firefighting robots rushing into a burning building or clean-up robots responding to a chemical spill? Some people are hoping that human-like robots such as ASIMO will one day be able to perform dangerous jobs so that humans will not have to. In the meantime, scientists have invented new devices based on Honda's ASIMO to help people walk, stand, and work with less back and leg strain. Scientists hope these devices can help disabled people move and work more easily.

SKILL PRACTICE   Read each question. Fill in the bubble next to the correct answer.

1. Why did it take scientists almost 15 years to build ASIMO?
   - Ⓐ People were not interested in a walking robot.
   - Ⓑ Building a walking robot was very difficult.
   - Ⓒ Honda did not assign many workers to the ASIMO project.
   - Ⓓ The engineers could not agree on the design of the robot.

2. Why has ASIMO conducted orchestras?
   - Ⓐ to replace human orchestra conductors
   - Ⓑ to encourage children to join orchestras
   - Ⓒ to keep humans from doing a dangerous job
   - Ⓓ to show one of the surprising things the robot can do

3. One reason ASIMO performs at public demonstrations is to _____.
   - Ⓐ inspire students to study science
   - Ⓑ make other companies jealous
   - Ⓒ sell robots made by Honda
   - Ⓓ generate interest in Disneyland

4. What has ASIMO development research already led to?
   - Ⓐ the elimination of dangerous jobs
   - Ⓑ devices to help people move
   - Ⓒ increased space exploration
   - Ⓓ improved fire safety

STRATEGY PRACTICE   Write a question that can be answered with information from the passage. Ask a partner to answer it.

_____

_____

READ THE PASSAGE   Think about the effects of using your mind to perform everyday tasks.

New Ways to Use Your Brain

Comic books and movies have plots involving mind reading, lifting objects by thinking about them, and even flying by simply concentrating. While most of the things superheroes do in stories will forever remain only in science fiction, inspired scientists are now creating toys, medical devices, and electronic gadgets that are controlled directly by the brain.

Every time you think about something, whether it is noticing that your nose is itchy or thinking about what you want for dinner, a part of your brain becomes active. It receives more oxygen, blood flow, and electrical impulses from the rest of your body. Electronic sensors can detect these changes in the brain, and scientists can program machinery and software to respond to these signals.

The most obvious, and perhaps most important, use of this new technology is to help people who are paralyzed or severely disabled. For many people with diseases that affect the brain, muscles, or nervous system, it is difficult or impossible to do things that most people take for granted, such as smiling, speaking, or moving their arms or legs. With brain-controlled devices, people who cannot move or speak on their own may still be able to communicate or perform tasks that were previously impossible.

Of course, there are fun uses of this technology, too. Several toy companies around the world have released games that rely on people concentrating, doing things such as making a ball levitate with their mind. While the technology is still limited, scientists are hoping that one day we will not need to use our hands to turn on an oven or our voices to talk on the phone—it will all happen by just using our brains!

SKILL PRACTICE   Read each question. Fill in the bubble next to the correct answer.

1. **How has science fiction affected the development of brain-controlled devices?**
   Ⓐ Scientists worked from book and movie plots.
   Ⓑ Scientists were motivated to be superheroes.
   Ⓒ Scientists were inspired by ideas and possibilities.
   Ⓓ Scientists used these devices to do their work.

2. **Hearing a familiar song causes an increase in _____.**
   Ⓐ oxygen to part of the brain
   Ⓑ volume on a music player
   Ⓒ software to detect brain signals
   Ⓓ development of helpful technology

3. **How do brain-controlled devices work?**
   Ⓐ Devices send electrical impulses.
   Ⓑ Machines are implanted in people's brains.
   Ⓒ Scientists mimic the movements of machines.
   Ⓓ Sensors record activity in the brain.

4. **What effect could a brain-controlled device have on the life of someone with a disability?**
   Ⓐ It could cure the disability.
   Ⓑ It could help the person communicate or perform tasks.
   Ⓒ It could control the person.
   Ⓓ It could prevent someone from using his or her hands.

STRATEGY PRACTICE   Name a movie, television show, book, or toy you are familiar with that includes a brain-controlled device. How does the device work?

_____

_____

READ THE PASSAGE   Pause briefly after you read each paragraph to predict what will happen next.

A Camping Excursion

Elena and Liza were ready to camp. The secondhand tent they borrowed was already loaded in the car. Elena helped Liza carry the big cooler full of food. "Are you planning to feed an army? Bread, peanut butter, dried fruit, canned stew, beef jerky, corn chips, bottled water, ice. You packed enough trail mix to pave our own trail!" Elena remarked. The girls were set for a weekend of hiking around the serene lake.

Theodore and Enrique were excited about their weekend plans. "I hope the fish are biting! I haven't had a good salmon steak in ages," Enrique said. Theodore paused to examine the back of his pickup truck. Fishing poles, check. Tackle box, check. Hip boots, check. Sleeping bags, check. The boys were ready to rough it under a glorious blanket of stars.

When the girls arrived at the campsite, they set up their tent and loaded their day packs with water bottles, a bag of jerky, and some trail mix and set off. A couple of hours later, they came across an open tackle box, a pail with one small fish, and two boys hip-deep in the lake. "Catching anything?" Liza called out.

"Just one little guy too young to know any better," answered Enrique. "It's like they knew we were coming and vanished." Suddenly the sky turned gray, and within a minute it cracked open and the storm poured out. The boys headed for the shore and ran to scoop up the pail, now blown over and rolling away.

"So much for the sunny forecast," Theodore grumbled. "I'll never get a campfire started in this mess."

"We've got food, but we're miles from our tent. We'll share if you drive us back," Liza offered.

As the crowded truck pulled up and they saw that their tent was ripped, Elena shrieked, "Oh, no! It's about to go!"

SKILL PRACTICE   Read each question. Fill in the bubble next to the correct answer.

1. **What will the campers probably do with the tent?**
   Ⓐ repair it with fishing hooks
   Ⓑ use it to cover the sleeping bags
   Ⓒ weigh down the edges with the food
   Ⓓ sleep on top of it instead of on the wet ground

2. **What will the campers most likely do with the fish in the pail?**
   Ⓐ eat it raw
   Ⓑ cook it inside the tent
   Ⓒ leave it on the shore
   Ⓓ put it on ice in the cooler

3. **What will the girls probably do the next time they go hiking?**
   Ⓐ stay close to the campsite
   Ⓑ bring more trail mix
   Ⓒ get a sturdier tent
   Ⓓ bring along umbrellas

4. **How will the boys probably prepare for their next fishing trip?**
   Ⓐ bring extra food
   Ⓑ pack wood for a fire
   Ⓒ go to a lake with more fish
   Ⓓ check the weather forecast

STRATEGY PRACTICE   Write a question about something that might happen as the story continues.

_____

_____

READ THE FABLE As you read this twist on one of Aesop's fables, make a prediction about how it will end.

The Grasshopper, the Ants, and the Squirrels

One lovely summer morning, a grasshopper jumped and played and danced and sang. All around him, he noticed that ants were busy carrying corn kernels and other bits of food up their steep anthills.

"Why work so hard?" said the grasshopper to one of the ants who passed by. "Come dance with me, and you'll have a much more delightful time today."

"I must prepare for the winter," said the ant smugly. "When are you going to start gathering food?"

"Why should I bother?" responded the grasshopper, looking around. "There is plenty of food, and working would waste a beautiful summer's day."

As the ant and grasshopper parted company, they saw a family of squirrels frolicking around an oak. They were laughing and chasing and racing to snatch up acorns from the ground. Every so often, they would dash up into a hole in the tree and deposit their load of acorns, then pop out and resume their game.

On a not-so-lovely morning in winter, the starving grasshopper was huddled in the snow in the same field where he had once danced and played. He noticed the ants in their anthills only nibbling on their feast. The miserable grasshopper approached the ant. "I have no food. Please give me just a morsel."

The bitter ant replied, "So, you can't live on dancing and playing after all! At least you had fun this summer. We ants are too exhausted to enjoy our bounty."

Just then, the ant and the grasshopper heard a giggle from above as one of the squirrels ran out on a tree limb to catch a snowflake on its tongue while the others cracked open some acorns.

SKILL PRACTICE Read each question. Fill in the bubble next to the correct answer.

1. What will the squirrels probably do next?
   Ⓐ eat breakfast
   Ⓑ play with the acorns
   Ⓒ look for food in the snow
   Ⓓ tell the grasshopper to get to work

2. What will the squirrels probably tell the grasshopper and the ant?
   Ⓐ Acorns are the most delicious food.
   Ⓑ The snow is just right for eating.
   Ⓒ Animals each have their own habits.
   Ⓓ Work and play are equally important.

3. What will the grasshopper most likely do next?
   Ⓐ dance among the snowflakes
   Ⓑ ask the squirrels for some food
   Ⓒ help the ant carry food to the anthill
   Ⓓ find another grasshopper to talk to

4. What will the ant probably do next summer?
   Ⓐ work harder to collect more food
   Ⓑ share his food with the grasshopper
   Ⓒ rest for a few moments each day
   Ⓓ spend all his time with the grasshopper

STRATEGY PRACTICE Describe someone you know who acts like the grasshopper, the ants, or the squirrels.

_____

_____

READ THE PASSAGE   As you read, think about why soccer has been unpopular or popular in the United States.

Soccer in the United States

While soccer is the most popular sport in the world, people in the United States watch far more baseball, basketball, and football games on television. Still, as soccer becomes more and more popular as a recreational sport in the United States, the audience for soccer is sure to grow. In fact, soccer's fan base in the United States has already increased due to changing population patterns.

Some soccer experts trace the popularity of the sport in the United States back to 1975. That year, a Brazilian player known as Pelé came to play professional soccer for the New York Cosmos, a team in the North American Soccer League. Pelé, many agree, was the best player in the history of the game. Soon after he joined the team, professional soccer stars from Great Britain and Germany also joined the Cosmos. The Cosmos and Pelé turned many Americans into soccer fans. Unfortunately, once Pelé retired, the team lost much of its following, and the league shut down in 1984.

Nonetheless, interest in soccer has begun to take hold once again in the United States. Attention increased during the early 2000s when women's teams from the United States had great success in international competitions—including winning Olympic and World Cup championships. Now that a women's professional soccer league has been formed and men's teams in Major League Soccer have once again had success in building an audience, soccer's popularity seems likely to build—if not explode.

SKILL PRACTICE   Read each question. Fill in the bubble next to the correct answer.

1. Which best explains why soccer players came from Europe to the United States in the 1970s?
   Ⓐ enthusiastic fans
   Ⓑ Pelé's success and popularity
   Ⓒ interest in other sports
   Ⓓ problems in other countries

2. How has soccer in the United States benefited from changing population patterns?
   Ⓐ The United States is winning more championships.
   Ⓑ Fans of other sports are moving away.
   Ⓒ The number of soccer viewers has risen.
   Ⓓ The United States is recruiting more international soccer stars.

3. From the current number of soccer leagues in the United States, you can predict that _____.
   Ⓐ more fans will want to watch professional soccer matches
   Ⓑ the leagues will shut down, as they did before
   Ⓒ the majority of Brazilian soccer players will play professionally in the United States
   Ⓓ immigrants will watch only teams from their homelands

4. Because Pelé helped to build soccer's fan base in the United States, you can predict that local teams will most likely _____.
   Ⓐ focus mainly on coaching
   Ⓑ try to get Pelé to play again
   Ⓒ recruit only players who look like Pelé
   Ⓓ try to recruit international soccer stars

STRATEGY PRACTICE   What is a question you still have about soccer? Where can you find the answer?

_____

_____

Nonfiction Text Features
Students practice identifying and comprehending common features of nonfiction text.

Visual Information
Students examine and evaluate information that is depicted visually.

DAY 1

Review the *Nonfiction Text Features* skill with students. Say: **When you read nonfiction, look for special features that are included to help you better understand the information. Authors can group information into lists, boxes, or numbered steps to aid readers.** Then remind students of the *Determine Important Information* strategy (Week 5). Say: **As you read about how to make a survival kit, think about what information would be the most important for you and your family.** Have students read the passage. When students have finished, direct them to complete the skill and strategy practice activities. Review the answers together.

DAY 2

Tell students they are going to practice identifying nonfiction text features by reading and studying a partial glossary from a book about the history of clothing. Say: **A glossary appears at the end of a book. It defines words or phrases that may be unfamiliar to readers. Usually, a word that appears in the glossary will appear in boldface type the first time it is mentioned in the book. The boldface type alerts readers to look in the glossary for the word's definition.** Remind students of the *Organization* strategy (Week 4). Say: **Glossary entries are usually in alphabetical order. As you read the glossary, think about why this organization is better than organizing by country or clothing type.** When students have finished reading, direct them to complete the skill and strategy practice activities. Review the answers together.

DAY 3

Remind students of the *Visual Information* skill. Say: **Authors can use visual information to help readers better understand complex ideas. This passage includes a chart. Think about how the chart and passage relate to each other.** Remind students of the *Organization* strategy. Say: **The author organized part of the information about greenhouse gases into a table. Ask you read, ask yourself:** *How does the organization of the table help readers?* When students have finished reading, direct them to complete the skill and strategy practice activities. Review the answers together.

DAY 4

Tell students they will practice using visual information as they read about different models of skateboards. Say: **Think about why the author included information in a chart.** Then remind students of the *Determine Important Information* strategy. Say: **As you read the chart, think about how it could be useful.** When students have finished reading, direct them to complete the skill and strategy practice activities. Review the answers together.

DAY 5

Tell students they will practice the *Nonfiction Text Features* and *Visual Information* skills as they read about four different types of wrenches. Say: **The author has included a table that has both visual information and captions. Think about how the illustrations and captions work together.** Remind students of the *Determine Important Information* strategy. Say: **Think about the information presented in the introduction and in the chart. What do you learn from each one?** When students have finished reading, direct them to complete the skill and strategy practice activities. Review the answers together.

READ THE PASSAGE   Think about how the text features help you understand the passage.

Be Prepared When Disaster Strikes

Is your family prepared for a natural disaster, an outbreak of a deadly disease, or an accident that could cause a long-term power outage? Building a survival kit is an easy way to make sure you have what you need in case of an emergency.

Basic Supplies:

- Water*
- Food**
- Diapers and formula for infants
- Portable radio (with extra batteries)
- Flashlight (with extra batteries)
- First-aid kit
- Whistle to signal for help
- Sanitary wipes, garbage bags, and plastic ties
- Manual can opener for food
- Solar cellphone charger

* Provide a minimum of one gallon per person per day for drinking and sanitation.

** Buy food that keeps for a long time, does not require cooking or refrigeration, has a high liquid content, and is something your family will eat.

If you are injured during an emergency, find shelter and dial 9-1-1.

Optional Items

Once you have everything you need for your basic kit, you may want to consider adding **sleeping bags** if you live in an area that gets cold indoors at night. You might also have **books**, **toys**, or **games** in your kit to keep children entertained. If you have pets, include **pet food** and extra water.

SKILL PRACTICE   Read each question. Fill in the bubble next to the correct answer.

1. Where can you find the main materials you should include in a survival kit?

   Ⓐ in the gray box

   Ⓑ in the bold type

   Ⓒ in the introduction

   Ⓓ in the bulleted list

2. Why does the author put additional materials in the "Optional Items" box?

   Ⓐ to discourage people from storing those items

   Ⓑ to indicate items that may not apply to everyone

   Ⓒ to raise awareness about disasters

   Ⓓ to give information about emergency numbers

3. The asterisks alert the reader to information that _____.

   Ⓐ explains why food and water are important

   Ⓑ tells what to do if food and water are unavailable

   Ⓒ suggests where to find food and water

   Ⓓ clarifies what kind of food and how much water to store

4. What information does the introduction provide?

   Ⓐ why to build a survival kit

   Ⓑ what to include in a survival kit

   Ⓒ how to put together a survival kit

   Ⓓ when to build a survival kit

STRATEGY PRACTICE   Which information would be the most important for a person who has lost power? Why?

_____

_____

READ THE GLOSSARY   Pay attention to how the glossary is organized.

Glossary (cont.)

kente cloth	a fine grade of brightly-colored cloth made in West Africa
kimono	traditional dress worn in Japan with wide sleeves and a sash called an **obi**; literally, a "piece of clothing"
kosode	an old style of **kimono** clothing in Japan
kurta	a loose, collarless muslin shirt usually worn in the northern parts of India
lungi	a colored loincloth that is worn in India by males and females
manta	(1) the name given by the Spanish to the simple cloaks worn by indigenous Mexican people (2) Guatemalan white cloth woven on a broad loom (3) a short poncho worn by Chilean cowboys
obi	the sash used on a Japanese **kimono**
odhani	a woman's scarf or stole worn in India
opanky	(1) Eastern European broad-soled sandals wrapped around the bottom of a foot and over the toes, tied with long leather straps around one's feet and legs (2) Eastern European shoe with a buckled strap and leather strips woven across the top
parka	a jacket of the Arctic regions that has a closed front and fur-lined hood and is usually made of hide
quillwork	a North American technique of cutting feather quills for use on clothing; cut quills are stitched together or applied to fabric to create vests or decorative panels

SKILL PRACTICE   Read each question. Fill in the bubble next to the correct answer.

1. The entry words in the glossary are organized _____.

   Ⓐ by their first appearance in the book

   Ⓑ in order of popularity

   Ⓒ in alphabetical order

   Ⓓ by where they come from in the world

2. In the definition for *kimono,* the word *obi* is in boldface type because _____.

   Ⓐ the author wants to show its pronunciation

   Ⓑ it means the same thing as the entry word

   Ⓒ it is a seldom-used word

   Ⓓ it is defined in another part of the glossary

3. In the glossary, quotation marks are used to _____.

   Ⓐ provide English translations of the words

   Ⓑ offer antonyms

   Ⓒ enclose slang words or phrases

   Ⓓ set off direct quotations

4. Some entry words have numbered definitions after them because _____.

   Ⓐ they break up the text for easier reading

   Ⓑ there are multiple meanings for the words

   Ⓒ the numbers refer to pages where the entry word appears

   Ⓓ they may be difficult to pronounce in English

STRATEGY PRACTICE   How does the organization of the glossary make it easy to use?

_____

_____

READ THE PASSAGE   Think about how the information in the table supports the passage.

Greenhouse Gases

The greenhouse effect is the natural trapping of the sun's energy by gases in Earth's lower atmosphere. It is what makes most of Earth a comfortable place to live. Without the gases of the greenhouse effect, the planet would be colder than humans would prefer—roughly 60°F colder! The industrial era has added new gases to the mix, however. When added to the natural water vapor, ozone, and carbon dioxide in the atmosphere, the gases hold too much of the sun's heat, causing rapid climate change. While Earth's climate has changed many times throughout its 4.5-billion-year history, the speed at which climate change is occurring today is causing problems. Climate change may alter rainfall patterns and cause a rise in sea level that could cover some islands and coastal areas. Changes in Earth's climate are already negatively affecting plants, wildlife, and humans.

Greenhouse Gases in the Atmosphere at the End of the Twentieth Century			
Gas	**Chemical Formula**	**Main Sources**	**Contribution to Global Warming**
Carbon dioxide	CO_2	fossil fuel combustion, land-use conversion, production of cement	26%
Methane	CH_4	fossil fuels, rice paddies, waste dumps, livestock	4.4%
Nitrous oxide	N_2O	fertilizer, industrial processes, combustion	1.5%
CFC-12	CCl_2F_2	liquid coolants, foams	still being determined

American Meteorological Society, February 1997

SKILL PRACTICE   Read each question. Fill in the bubble next to the correct answer.

1. The third column in the table shows the _____.
   - Ⓐ specific uses of greenhouse gases
   - Ⓑ main effects of greenhouse gases
   - Ⓒ common names of greenhouse gases
   - Ⓓ primary causes of greenhouse gases

2. The table indicates that methane _____.
   - Ⓐ has a chemical formula of CO_2
   - Ⓑ causes 1.5% of global warming
   - Ⓒ is given off by waste dumps
   - Ⓓ has an unknown effect on global warming

3. According to the passage and the table, carbon dioxide comes from _____.
   - Ⓐ fertilizers that are used on farms
   - Ⓑ the atmosphere and industrial activities
   - Ⓒ the process of making liquid coolants
   - Ⓓ natural rainfall on the Earth

4. The main purpose of the table is to _____.
   - Ⓐ explain why greenhouse gases are a problem
   - Ⓑ list the effects of greenhouse gases
   - Ⓒ show what to do about greenhouse gases
   - Ⓓ give details about the main greenhouse gases

STRATEGY PRACTICE   How does the organization of the table help readers?

_____

_____

READ THE PASSAGE   Take time to study the chart before you answer the questions.

Selecting a Skateboard

Are you ready to ride the rolling landscapes of your urban or suburban environment? First, get your parents' permission. (Good luck on that one!) Next, purchase your first skateboard. The chart provides information about four models available at a local sporting goods store. Finally, get your safety gear on and go!

Skateboards at Ozzie's Outdoor Sports			
Model	**Wheels***	**Deck**	**Cost**
DownX-7	90 mm, rubber	7-ply maple	$55.00
KoastKool	65 mm, plastic	plastic	$22.95
Slammin' Slalom	73 mm, polyurethane	9-ply maple	$89.99
Tommy Trickster	52 mm, polyurethane	aluminum	$62.50

*diameter in millimeters

SKILL PRACTICE   Read each question. Fill in the bubble next to the correct answer.

1. Which model is the least expensive?
   Ⓐ DownX-7
   Ⓑ KoastKool
   Ⓒ Slammin' Slalom
   Ⓓ Tommy Trickster

2. How much does the skateboard with rubber wheels cost?
   Ⓐ $55.00
   Ⓑ $22.95
   Ⓒ $89.99
   Ⓓ $62.50

3. What kind of deck does the most expensive skateboard have?
   Ⓐ 7-ply maple
   Ⓑ plastic
   Ⓒ 9-ply maple
   Ⓓ aluminum

4. Larger wheels are better for faster speeds. Which model would be best if you wanted to race?
   Ⓐ DownX-7
   Ⓑ KoastKool
   Ⓒ Slammin' Slalom
   Ⓓ Tommy Trickster

STRATEGY PRACTICE   What information would be most important to you if you were choosing a skateboard? Why?

_____

_____

READ THE PASSAGE   Read the passage and study the drawings.

What's in Your Toolbox?

Wrenches. Who knew there were so many different kinds? Wrenches are tools used for gripping and turning nuts, bolts, pipes, and other things. They come in many different sizes and configurations, and each one has been carefully designed for specific purposes. Here are just a few of the most common wrenches that carpenters, plumbers, mechanics, and do-it-yourselfers all over the world use.

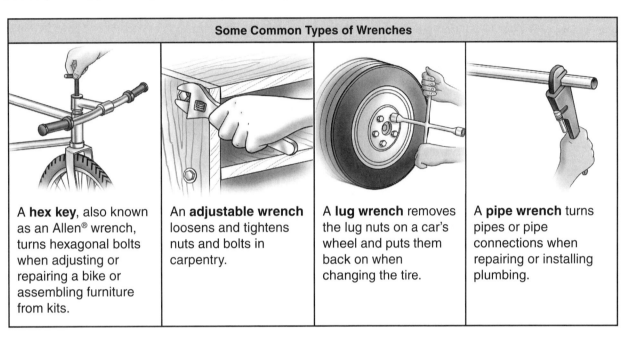

Some Common Types of Wrenches

A **hex key**, also known as an Allen® wrench, turns hexagonal bolts when adjusting or repairing a bike or assembling furniture from kits.

An **adjustable wrench** loosens and tightens nuts and bolts in carpentry.

A **lug wrench** removes the lug nuts on a car's wheel and puts them back on when changing the tire.

A **pipe wrench** turns pipes or pipe connections when repairing or installing plumbing.

SKILL PRACTICE   Read each question. Fill in the bubble next to the correct answer.

1. How can you find out what each tool does?
   Ⓐ look at the bold text
   Ⓑ read the captions
   Ⓒ read the introduction
   Ⓓ look at the table title

2. Which two wrenches could be used to build a bookcase?
   Ⓐ a pipe wrench or a hex key
   Ⓑ an adjustable wrench or a lug wrench
   Ⓒ a lug wrench or a pipe wrench
   Ⓓ a hex key or an adjustable wrench

3. What do the adjustable and pipe wrenches have in common?
   Ⓐ Both clamp onto the thing they are turning.
   Ⓑ Both are used to repair broken vehicles.
   Ⓒ Both work on nuts and bolts.
   Ⓓ Both are used by carpenters.

4. The drawings give information about _____.
   Ⓐ how wrenches are made
   Ⓑ which wrenches are most popular
   Ⓒ what the wrenches look like
   Ⓓ how much the wrenches usually cost

STRATEGY PRACTICE   Which would be most useful to someone learning carpentry—the passage or the chart? Why?

_____

_____

Answer Key

DAY 1
Sample answer: I didn't know what a skydiving photographer did, but I reread the last paragraph and understood that they take photos while they are falling out of a plane.
1. D   2. A   3. D   4. C

DAY 2
Sample answer: I didn't understand why Kim thought the house was creepy, but I reread looking for creepy-sounding details.
1. C   2. D   3. B   4. A

DAY 3
Sample answer: I read what algae and fungi do for the lichens, so I figured out the difference between them.
1. A   2. C   3. B   4. C

DAY 4
Sample answer: The second footnote made me aware of just how big a problem spam is.
1. A   2. B   3. B   4. D

DAY 5
Sample answer: It describes what we might see in an ad or commercial and how it is misleading.
1. B   2. A   3. C   4. B

WEEK 2

DAY 1
Answers will vary but should describe a leader who is creative.
1. A   2. C   3. C   4. D

DAY 2
Answers will vary but should reference a scary story.
1. C   2. D   3. A   4. B

DAY 3
Sample answer: Investigators would use scientific methods to collect evidence and electronic records to check alibis.
1. C   2. A   3. D   4. B

DAY 4
Answers will vary but should have a thematic connection to the passage, such as moving, going to a new school, learning a skill, or joining a group or team.
1. B   2. D   3. C   4. C

DAY 5
Answers will vary but should connect to themes or situations from the passage, such as having stage fright or being nervous before a competition.
1. B   2. C   3. A   4. B

WEEK 3

DAY 1
Sketch should include: darkness and faint light showing only paintings, feet, and/or other people.
1. C   2. A   3. B   4. B

DAY 2
Answers will vary but should include underlined words or phrases that are descriptive.
1. D   2. A   3. A   4. D

DAY 3
Answers will vary but should include descriptive nouns from the passage.
1. B   2. D   3. A   4. C

DAY 4
Sample answer: I visualized getting the "thumbs up" sign with the thumb in the air, the other fingers curled in.
1. A   2. C   3. B   4. D

DAY 5
Sketch should include: looking down on a big city, parks, and/or a river.
1. B   2. C   3. A   4. D

WEEK 4

DAY 1
Sample answer: The reader can easily find each type of diet.
1. B   2. C   3. D   4. C

DAY 2
Sample answer: Each paragraph contains a point addressing the question.
1. D   2. C   3. B   4. A

DAY 3
Sample answer: The information is in chronological order. It is helpful to see how the different types of mills improved production. (Problem and solution is another valid organization.)
1. A   2. D   3. C   4. A

DAY 4
The timeline should include: at least four major events from the passage.
1. C   2. A   3. C   4. D

DAY 5
Sample answer: The author can elaborate and provide much more detail on each category of event mentioned in the introduction.
1. B   2. D   3. A   4. B

WEEK 5

DAY 1
Answers will vary but should include a logical explanation that relates to the information cited.
1. B   2. D   3. C   4. A

DAY 2
Sample answer: The list of materials is important for setup. The directions focus on what to do once you have the materials ready.
1. B   2. A   3. B   4. D

DAY 3
Sample answer: The intro explains that earthquakes can be measured and tells what the magnitudes in the chart mean.
1. C   2. A   3. A   4. C

DAY 4
Sample answer: It would be useful if someone was considering crab fishing as a career.
1. B   2. C   3. A   4. D

DAY 5
Sample answer: The headline catches the reader's attention; the bullets list fun activities; the testimonials show how much fun people have had there.
1. B   2. C   3. A   4. D

WEEK 6

DAY 1
Questions will vary but should refer to information from the passage.
1. D   2. B   3. A   4. C

DAY 2
Questions will vary but should refer to information from the passage.
1. D   2. D   3. C   4. B

DAY 3
Sample answer: The questions gave me something to look for as I read.
1. A   2. A   3. C   4. D

DAY 4
Questions will vary but should refer to information from the passage.
1. A   2. C   3. D   4. A

DAY 5
Questions will vary but should refer to information from the passage.
1. C   2. A   3. B   4. B

WEEK 7

DAY 1
1. B   2. D   3. D   4. C
Answers will vary but should include underlined statements that are challenging to understand.

DAY 2
1. D   2. B   3. A   4. B
Answers will vary but should include a sketch of a submarine with ballast tanks.

DAY 3
1. C   2. D   3. B   4. C
Chart should indicate the following schedule:
Tuesday: science club, swim practice
Wednesday: yearbook, tennis, guitar lesson
Thursday: dance class, volunteer at the library

DAY 4
1. C   2. A   3. A   4. D
Details will vary but should refer to descriptive information from the passage.

DAY 5
1. D   2. B   3. C   4. A

Answers will vary but should refer to directions from the passage.

WEEK 8

DAY 1
1. D   2. A   3. A   4. B

Sample answer: A hungry crocodile grabs the calf's back leg.

DAY 2
1. C   2. B   3. B   4. A

Questions will vary but should refer to information from the passage.

DAY 3
1. B   2. D   3. A   4. C

Students should reference any of the bullets and provide an explanation that relates to the information cited.

DAY 4
1. C   2. A   3. D   4. C

Questions will vary but should refer to information from the passage.

DAY 5
1. C   2. D   3. A   4. B

1st paragraph, last sentence; 2nd paragraph, sentence(s) about brain activity; 3rd paragraph, sentence(s) about paralysis during sleep; 4th paragraph, 1st sentence.

WEEK 9

DAY 1
1. C   2. D   3. B   4. A

Responses will vary.

DAY 2
1. D   2. A   3. D   4. C

Sample answer: It describes European dragons first, then Chinese dragons, then what they have in common.

DAY 3
1. B   2. A   3. D   4. B

Responses will vary.

DAY 4
1. B   2. A   3. C   4. B

Sample answer: The story is told in order and includes each action the police took. The reader follows the theft investigation the same way it happened.

DAY 5
1. B   2. A   3. C   4. D

Responses will vary.

WEEK 10

DAY 1
1. D   2. A   3. C   4. B

Sample answer: Yes. Diana never wanted illness, age, weather, or anything else to keep her from her dreams.

DAY 2
1. C   2. D   3. A   4. B

Responses will vary.

DAY 3
1. B   2. A   3. D   4. C

Sample answer: Yes. Sometimes it takes a bad situation to realize when you've got a good thing.

DAY 4
1. C   2. A   3. C   4. D

Sample answer: There are four sharks around me. They are huge! They swim peacefully and smoothly.

DAY 5
1. A   2. C   3. B   4. A

Sample answer: He holds the all-time hitting streak and he was a modest guy.

WEEK 11

DAY 1
1. C   2. B   3. A   4. D

Questions will vary but should refer to information from the passage.

DAY 2
1. C   2. A   3. A   4. D

Sample answer: My Jewish and Islamic friends do not eat ham or pork because their religion says not to.

DAY 3
1. A   2. B   3. B   4. C

Questions will vary but should refer to information from the passage.

DAY 4
1. D   2. A   3. D   4. C

Sample answer: I'm afraid of bees, but I appreciate their role in nature. I'll just stay out of their way.

DAY 5
1. B   2. B   3. A   4. C

Questions will vary but should refer to information from the passage.

WEEK 12

DAY 1
1. D   2. C   3. A   4. B

Sample answer: It's important to know how difficult the route is.

DAY 2
1. C   2. B   3. C   4. B

Sample answer: The chart lets you easily compare different aspects of each practice.

DAY 3
1. A   2. C   3. B   4. D

Sample answer: The diagram shows the order and how logistics relates to all the links in the chain. The passage gives examples of each link.

DAY 4
1. D   2. A   3. A   4. B

Sample answer: Many people have never seen a lean-to, so it helps to know what it should look like.

DAY 5
1. D   2. C   3. D   4. B

Sample answer: It helped me keep track of the many layers as I read their descriptions.

WEEK 13

DAY 1
1. C   2. A   3. B   4. D

Responses will vary.

DAY 2
1. D   2. A   3. A   4. B

Answers will vary but should include descriptive language from the passage.

DAY 3
1. B   2. D   3. C   4. C

Answers will vary but should refer to the Scoville scale.

DAY 4
1. D   2. B   3. C   4. A

Responses will vary.

DAY 5
1. A   2. A   3. B   4. C

Sample answer: Rereading the part about Earth's axis helped me understand why Arctic winters will still be cold for a while.

WEEK 14

DAY 1
1. B   2. A   3. C   4. C

Sample answer: the efforts made by firefighters in the second paragraph, the 1983 study in the last paragraph

DAY 2
1. B   2. C   3. D   4. A

Questions will vary.

DAY 3
1. B   2. C   3. A   4. D

Sample answer: information about the effects of wind, humidity, and smog

DAY 4
1. B   2. A   3. A   4. D

Questions will vary.

DAY 5
1. A   2. B   3. C   4. D

Sample answer: the information about sick people on ships in the first paragraph, the information about bacteria in the second paragraph

WEEK 15

DAY 1
1. B   2. D   3. A   4. B

Responses will vary.

DAY 2
1. A   2. C   3. D   4. B

Sample response: I didn't understand how igneous rock could be changed to metamorphic by magma. Then I reread the part about igneous rock being different from magma.

DAY 3
1. C   2. D   3. B   4. A

Responses will vary.

DAY 4
1. C   2. D   3. A   4. B

Sample answer: the description of how bacteria and earthworms eat the compost and break it down

DAY 5
1. A   2. B   3. B   4. C

Responses will vary.

WEEK 16

DAY 1
1. B   2. B   3. D   4. C

Sample answer: Habitat for Humanity is an organization that builds houses for people who can't afford them. It is a worldwide nonprofit organization.

DAY 2
1. A   2. D   3. C   4. B

Sketches should show the family rowing happily under a rainbow.

DAY 3
1. B   2. A   3. A   4. C

Sample answer: After you know what the point is, rereading allows you to go back and see how the characters learned their lesson.

DAY 4
1. B   2. B   3. A   4. D

Responses will vary.

DAY 5
1. B   2. D   3. A   4. C

Sample answer: He had a bulging portfolio. He has never missed an issue. He proved the editors wrong by continuing to come up with creative ideas.

WEEK 17

DAY 1
1. C   2. C   3. D   4. A

Questions will vary.

DAY 2
1. B   2. A   3. C   4. A

Sample answer: Life would not be nearly as convenient and people wouldn't live as long. However, we wouldn't have full landfills or floating islands of trash, either.

DAY 3
1. B   2. A   3. D   4. B

Sample question: How do you get rid of the bacteria after they deliver the tiny robots?

DAY 4
1. D   2. C   3. B   4. A

Responses will vary.

DAY 5
1. B   2. A   3. B   4. D

Questions will vary.

WEEK 18

DAY 1
1. C   2. B   3. D   4. B

Sample answer: No. It seems to be more about how the body works when there is nothing wrong.

DAY 2
1. D   2. A   3. B   4. C

Sample answer: Each part is about a different unrelated aspect of Pan.

DAY 3
1. A   2. A   3. B   4. C

Sample answer: I learned how water from lakes and trees becomes vapor, then clouds, then rain, then goes back into lakes and trees.

DAY 4
1. A   2. D   3. C   4. A

Sample answer: Its organization is problem and solution. The globe shows the problem of all the time zones meeting, and the map shows the solution.

DAY 5
1. B   2. D   3. A   4. D

Sample answer: The numbered list, because it describes the types of foods and how they should look.

WEEK 19

DAY 1
1. C   2. D   3. B   4. A

Sample answer: I understood the author's main point because I thought about each paragraph carefully before I continued and reread anything I missed.

DAY 2
1. A   2. C   3. A   4. B

Sketches will vary.

DAY 3
1. B   2. D   3. A   4. D

The timeline should include: the trip to Switzerland, the discussion around the fire, the challenge to write a story, and the writing of the novel, all in correct order.

DAY 4
1. C   2. C   3. A   4. D

Responses will vary.

DAY 5
1. D   2. B   3. D   4. C

Sample answer: I read that there was almost no sunlight during an eclipse, so I figured out that an eclipse is when something is being blocked.

WEEK 20

DAY 1
1. B   2. A   3. D   4. C

Sample answer: Abigail Adams was a strong advocate for equal rights who influenced the writing of U.S. equality laws.

DAY 2
1. C   2. A   3. B   4. D

Questions will vary.

DAY 3
1. C   2. A   3. B   4. D

Sample answer: the data about the number of kids and groups

DAY 4
1. C   2. A   3. D   4. A

Questions will vary.

DAY 5
1. C   2. D   3. B   4. A

Sample answer: the clinical studies in the 1990s that showed probiotics do help with digestion and allergies

WEEK 21

DAY 1
1. B   2. A   3. C   4. D

Responses will vary.

DAY 2
1. B   2. A   3. C   4. C

Sample answer: Paragraph 1 compares Robin Hood and fictional King Richard. Paragraph 2 compares fictional King Richard and John. Paragraph 3 gives similarities between real and fictional King Richard, and paragraph 4 gives differences.

DAY 3
1. C   2. D   3. B   4. B

Responses will vary.

DAY 4
1. A   2. D   3. B   4. C

Sample answer: The story is told in chronological order, presenting a goal first, then how they worked toward the goal, then what happened afterwards.

DAY 5
1. A   2. C   3. B   4. D

Sketches will vary.

WEEK 22

DAY 1
1. A   2. D   3. B   4. D

Sketches will vary.

DAY 2
1. B   2. C   3. A   4. C

Timelines should include competing internationally at age 8, the win in New York, becoming a grandmaster, beating Boris Spassky, and the win in Hawaii.

DAY 3
1. D   2. B   3. A   4. C

Responses will vary.

DAY 4
1. B   2. C   3. B   4. A

Responses will vary.

DAY 5
1. D   2. D   3. C   4. B

Sample answer: She returned to Burma to care for her sick mother. She joined the NLD and began giving speeches.

WEEK 23

DAY 1
1. D   2. B   3. A   4. C

Questions will vary.

DAY 2
1. B   2. D   3. A   4. A

Sample answer: I like glass bottles with screw-top caps because drinks taste better in glass and I like to be able to close the bottle again.

DAY 3
1. B   2. A   3. C   4. D

Questions will vary.

DAY 4
1. B   2. A   3. D   4. A

Sample answer: It would hurt our strawberry harvest.